Time Stands Still

Time is a fixed measure derived from the revolutions of the sky. Time begins there; and of this is believed to have been born Kronos who is Chronos.

Macrobius

Time Stands Still

New Light on Megalithic Science

By Keith Critchlow

Photographs by Rod Bull

Floris Books

First published in 1979 by Gordon Fraser Gallery, London.
This revised edition published in 2007 by Floris Books.
© 1979, 2007 Keith Critchlow

Keith Critchlow has asserted his right under
the Copyright, Designs and Patents Act 1988
to be identified as the Author of this Work.

All photographs are by Rod Bull unless
otherwise stated in the Image Credits.
Colour photographs © Rod Bull, 1979, 2007

British Library CIP Data available

ISBN 978-086315-587-1

Produced in Poland by Polskabook

To Motherhood in gratitude — and to the anonymous masters of the Megalithic Monuments of Britain

And in particular to Wendy Stewart, Gail, and the helpful children Louise, Amanda, Mathew and Amelia

Acknowledgments

Special thanks and acknowledgments must go to the following people who for various reasons, either known or unknown to themselves, have contributed to the contents of this book:

John Allen, The Alvey family (Benbulbin), Marsha Andreola, The Astronomical Group of the Goetheanum (Dornach), Professor R.J.C. Atkinson, Derek Birdsall, Black Elk and the Holy Men of the Red Nations, Frederick Bligh Bond, Tom Bree, Titus Burkhardt, Jane Carroll, Parish Chakraborti, Graham Challifour, Chisholm House (Beshara), Professor C. Cornford, David M. Critchlow, M.B. Critchlow, Rozalind R. Critchlow, John Davey, Andrew Davidson, Mircea Eliade, Ulrike Fischer, James Fraser, John Glover, Sir Victor Goddard, J.I. Gurdjieff, Alan Hacker, Jacquetta Hawkes, Eric Heaf, Robin Heath, Heywood and Jenny Hill, Amanda Horning, Jonathan Horning, Mrs Janette Jackson OBE, Michele Jones, Warren Kenton, Elizabeth Leader, William (Bill) Lewis, Mrs E. Lloyd, The Directors of the London Planetarium, Anne Macaulay, Professor E. Mackay, Paul Marchant, John Martineau, John Michell, Christopher Moore, Chris Morris, Dr S.H. Nasr, Thomas Neurath, Michael and Sally Oldfield, Paul Oliver, Scott Olsen, J. Purce, Kathleen Raine, Boulent Rauf, Professor C. Renfrew, RILKO (Research Into Lost Knowledge) Trust council members, 'Rock' Abercrombie, The Royal College of Art Librarians, The Salisbury Centre (Edinburgh), Kurt Schafhauser, Frithjof Schuon, Dr Ida Seymour, Professor Philip Sherrard, The Editors of *The Shrine of Wisdom,* Rudolf Steiner, Robin and Jessica Sutcliffe, Ririko Suzuki, Mike Taylor, Thomas Taylor, Professor Alexander Thom, A.S. Thom, William E. Thompson, Sylvia Thorne, Mark Trowbridge, Llewelyn Vaughn-Lee, Mrs E. White, Rodney Wilson, Nicholas Woodward-Smith

Also to the many students of both architecture and art who have discussed these matters with us over the years.

Contents

Foreword   9

Preface   15

Introduction   17

1. The Enigma of the Megaliths   23

2. The Ground Rules   39

3. Significant Number   81

4. Squaring the Circle   101

5. Qualitative Number: Number as
   Rhythm, Cycle and Sequence   121

6. Templates, Breastplates and Cosmic Calculation   139

7. Platonic Spheres — A Millennium Before Plato   161

8. The Planets as Time Keepers:
   Patterns in Space and Time   183

Conclusions   207

Appendix   213

Afterword to the New Edition   223

References   229

Bibliography   232

Image Credits   236

Index   237

1.
Trethevy Quoit, a neolithic burial chamber, near St Cleer, Cornwall

Foreword

Timeless science

Plato quite clearly announced, through the voice of Socrates, that geometry was the 'art of the ever-true.' No one has seriously challenged this realization since. All science — even a modern Godless parody — cannot argue its case for what it deals with without maths, which means Number. Number is therefore ever present as a constituent of human consciousness, a measure of sanity, and evidence of objectivity.

That Plato, Aristotle, even Euclid, had no written numerals is realized by few today, seeing as their works have had so pervasive an influence for the past two thousand years plus. All of the great classical mathematicians used small stone spheres or pebbles by which to do their maths. For Pythagoras or Plato they were called *khalix* which became *calcis* (or stone) in Latin which is where we get our word *calc*ulation from. That is, the manipulation of morphic numbers (spherical pebbles) allowed such as Pythagoras and Plato to see Arithmetic and Geometry as integral. Four pebbles were simultaneously a fourness as well as being the first 'solid' figure — the pyramid of four stones (or the tetrahedron).[*] Plato spoke much of oneness, twoness, threeness and so on, so that the *quality* of a numerical value was considered over and above its merely arithmetical quantity. Calculating with stone spheres simultaneously gave access to a complete integrality between number in space as stereometry (or geometry) and quantities *per se* as arithmetic.

After arithmetic and geometry, the remainder of the four areas of 'always true' sciences were the principles of harmonics or *musike* and, finally, the movements of the spheres of the heavens as astronomy. These *four* subjects have held a universal value for

2.
Pebble arithmetic, squaring of numbers:
$2^2 = 4$, $2 \times 2 = 4$
$3^2 = 9$, $3 \times 3 = 9$

---

[*] The concept of morphic number or experimental mathematics was given a new impulse by Richard Buckminster Fuller, who was my mentor and encouraged me to publish my findings as *Order in Space,* 1967.

all cultures throughout all time. Everyone who has ever awakened to the possibility that there is one single overriding mind (or logos) have found that $1+1=2$, and the most direct distance between two points (say fingers) is a straight line. And all humanity responds to one of the numerically based musical scales, be it pentatonic, diatonic, chromatic or even the sruti scale from India.[*] We all see the same objective lights in the sky: one circular Sun during the day and many many lights at night; most notably the Moon which passes through the same number of nights per phase before repeating. These time determiners, Sun and Moon, and to a lesser extent the planetary rhythms, have always marked the same intervals for all observers.

Thus we can appreciate the effect on the human mind of the value of not only knowing the importance of seasonal changes over a year but also the year's length itself. Not only this but together with the learning of the accuracy of the human eye to see in extremely straight lines, and with the numerical records of the cosmic rhythms, humankind should soon exhibit its difference from the rest of the animal kingdom (as it is called) by building monuments that could assess and *read* these rhythms, in short, the stone circles or temples.[†] Further, they could by observation and calculation make cosmic sense of them. These so-called megalithic achievements only go to demonstrate that to *be* human is to have intelligible access to timeless scientific values. This was understood by all civilizations in their higher reaches to mean the human mind *could* participate with the Divine mind given that it attended to the principles of the timeless sciences of the 'four universal truths.' There is one level of scientific accuracy measuring the manifest world; there is quite another, traditionally, which is measuring accuracy on a 'soul' level, that is timeless truth.

---

[*] The observant will note the closeness to the 'golden' series of these scales: 5, 8, 13, 22, sometimes known as the Fibonacci sequence.

[†] 'Temple' comes from the same root as time in *tempus* and space in *templum.*

Evolution, devolution and unchanging consciousness

Evolution of our animal bodies reached a point at which it was capable of hosting what we can call the 'human' consciousness.

We are all aware how vastly different our human consciousness is from the rest of the animal domain (kingdom). Even a cursory glance at our manipulation of the vehicles and structures we currently have devised is sufficient to guarantee this — even if we have reached the point of virtually consuming the ground we stand on!

However, physical evolution is only one way of viewing the scales of consciousness available in the world. To make materiality the *cause* of intelligibility is quite contrary to our immediate daily experience. All of us to one degree or another *consider* before we act on the manifest world. Or put simply, we all think before we do. Even if this is reduced to the level of a conditioned reflex, a neural impulse comes before a physical action.

Thus why should the greater evolvement of the creatures of our world differ from — or, in some people's views, *reverse* — this principle of consideration before action? As for the reductionist view of citing the 'genes' as the source of evolution, maybe these — whatever their ultimate physical structure — are only our 'memory bank,' like seeds guaranteeing that we avoid reversing the 'states' we have risen to.

The wise Plato writes about the three kinds of Soul within us (*Timaeus* 89e), each having its functional domain: each he stressed required exercise and that the different parts of the Soul should be in due proportion. Plato then uses a metaphor that implies that the highest part of our Souls is 'rooted in heaven' or is of a heavenly ('divine') origin and 'flowers' below in the body. There is only one way of taking care of things, Plato argues, and this is to give each the food and exercise which are natural to it. A person with only mortal desires and ambitions will remain in his mortal nature; however if a person is a lover of knowledge and of the true wisdom, then this person will have thoughts that are 'immortal and divine.' (*Timaeus* 90b) 'If they attain truth,' Plato argues, 'they will become altogether "immortal" and will have the divinity within them in perfect order. ... Each should follow ... the harmonies and revolutions (turnings) of the universe' which will correct the courses in our heads, which have been polluted by having to think on mundane matters alone.

Plato then moves into an immensely imaginative piece of metaphor. Here we have an extraordinary explanation of *de*volution — a concept completely the reverse of our contemporary mechanical materialistic (Darwinian) theory of evolution.

Having explained as carefully as possible how the 'higher' descended and continues to descend into the lower, or, put another way, how the more subtle and intelligible descends bringing 'form' into the human species as well as due proportion of 'divine' considerations over mundane ones, Plato proceeds to describe the generation of animals as being *de*-volved *from* the ideal human archetype. His gender ideas in this metaphor would not be fashionable, today but if taken as 'masculine' and 'feminine' they might become acceptable as aspects of consciousness 'donating' and 'receiving' as the ancient Chinese described them.

Plato continues to suggest those who led an innocent and light-minded life 'devolved' in the 'race of Birds.' Next the race of wild 'footed' animals 'devolved' from those people who had no philosophy in any of their thoughts — never considering the nature of the heavens — having ceased to use the courses in their heads, but followed the bodily needs. The more earthy the considerations, the more likely those people were to evolve into quadrupeds and even polypeds. 'God gave the more senseless of them the greater support that they might be more attracted to the earth.' The most foolish of them are those who *de*volved into crawling creatures without feet at all. The most outlandishly ignorant '*de*volved' into the race of fish and oysters that inhabit muddy waters and do not even breathe air. 'These are the laws by which all animals pass into one another, now, as in the beginning, changing as they lose or gain wisdom and folly.' (*Timaeus* 92c)

Plato summarized his cosmogony, the *Timaeus,* with the final words of integrality: 'The world has received animals, mortal and immortal, and is fulfilled with them, and has become a visible animal [living Gaia] containing the visible — the sensible god who is the image *(eikon)* of the intellectual (god), the greatest, best, fairest, most perfect — the one only-begotten heaven.'

Earlier, at the beginning of this extraordinarily influential dialogue, Timaeus, who is virtually the only speaker and a pythagorean by tradition, gives a lengthy speech (*Timaeus* 29e, 30) explaining the 'good' nature of this world. He also gives a warning against 'final explanations' reminding the small gathering that both he,

Timaeus, and they are all mortal and can only arrive at the most likely story, as there is an obvious limit to human understanding. We should 'do our utmost,' however, as he stresses, to get to this most likely story.

Timaeus completes this earlier speech by saying. 'On this wise, using the language of probability, we may say that the world came into being — a living creature truly endowed with Soul and intelligence by the providence of God.'

This latter point of view reminding us as human beings of our natural limitations as to understanding the whole of creation reminds us of the frailty of *both* viewpoints with regard to *ev*olution or *dev*olution, let alone creation from nothing, Big Bang *or* Divine Will (or creation by intelligent ordering, or the intelligible penetrating the sensible to create order.)

As to our attitude toward a so-called 'primitive' humanity being capable of sophisticated mathematics and spatial order *before* written languages of either words or numbers, this raises questions that our mechanical solutions are quite inadequate to answer if one is an 'evolutionist' of the materialist persuasion.

If the body 'invents,' 'gives rise to' or 'manufactures' consciousness, then these timeless mathematical symmetries in two and three dimensions must be the 'invention' of the primitive inhabitants of our British Isles. If, however, one takes the traditional view of wisdom — whether of ancient China, or ancient India, or ancient Egypt, even prior to the monotheistic faiths — then it is rather that the more subtle affects the more gross, or the intelligible informs the sensible, or spirit informs matter.

The present author finds the evident 'science' of early British communities of many thousands of years BC as challenging as any as to the source — and even goal — of humanity. If the human mind was capable around five thousand years ago of distilling the essential geometries of orientation and astronomical calculation — as well as being able to carve the Platonic figures out of stone — then we need to review what we mean by 'evolution.'

What can we learn from the Neolithic remains? That the society which made these artifacts, from stone circle 'temples' to Platonic stone spheres, placed their highest value on the objectivity of geometry. Their recognition or appreciation of the primary value of geometry indicates that 'humanness' seeks truth through objectivity. As noted above, there are four objective art/sciences: arithmetic, geometry, music and astronomy. Objectivity here means facts or truths that transcend estimation or opinion, to become 'wisdom' or, as Socrates chose to call it, 'the ever-true.'

There is no traditional or primary society known to us on mother Earth that does not reveal (a) a complex verbal language; (b) a use of arithmetic or pure number; (c) a practice of geometry either by sighting the star patterns or laying out their buildings; and finally (d) a full commitment to a spiritual reality which is invisible to the material or sensorial world.

These elements can be summarized as the Great Triad of the Heavenly or transcendental, from which we come and to which we return spiritually; the Earthly, or material and bodily, with which we integrate whilst in living form; and the Human, the intelligibility in which we participate and the ethical values that guide a peaceful life.

Keith Critchlow
March 2007

Preface

Professor R.J.C. Atkinson, the renowned authority on the archaeology of Stonehenge on which he has been working at intervals since 1950, says of the discipline he represents:

> We thus have the paradoxical situation that archaeology, the only method of investigating man's past in the absence of written records, becomes increasingly less effective as a means of inquiry the more nearly it approaches those aspects of human life which are more specifically *human*. (R.J.C. Atkinson, *Stonehenge,* note p.169)

If archaeology cannot by its nature deal effectively with the specifically, or might we say essentially, human aspect of its subject then we take it that this does not mean that 'archaeology' wishes the 'human' to be neglected — rather that it cannot in its own terms deal adequately with it. We also take it that the essentially human aspect of such an important matter as our 'origins,' or rather the origins of the making of 'permanent' structures, is too significant to be neglected. Therefore we offer our findings as complementary to archaeology, and have approached the subject from an architectural discipline with a philosophical perspective based to the best of our understanding on traditional values.

3.
Rollright, Oxfordshire

Introduction

Εν ἀρχῇ ἦν ὁ λόγος

In the beginning was the Word (Logos)

John 1:1

Our unquenchable thirst for knowledge of our origins lies in the intuition that we feel the clue to our destiny lies hidden in our origins. A birthday celebration expresses this as much as Darwin's elaborate 'Origins of the Species' theory. The great creation myths of humanity epitomize our need to transmit our roots and give original meaning to existence.* The value of creation myths lies in their effectiveness, not in their logicality. Myth is an inspired way of transmitting and maintaining those essential values and truths which each society deems vital. Only through myth can the expressive, poetic, intellectual and inspirational levels of the mind be united in the symbolic. Our fascination for the dignity and mystery of the megaliths stems from the recognition of our own mute 'creation myths' in stone. Their very presence seems to pose the perennial question: 'What does it *really* mean to be human?'

Those of us who are part and product of Western technological culture — significantly the minority of the current human family — despite our inordinate greed for energy and materialism, find ourselves in an exceptional phase of the life of humanity. We are unwittingly taking part in the anomaly of attempting to conduct society without the metaphysical or spiritual dimension. It is that very dimension which addresses itself to origins and destiny and humanity's overall relationships with our universe or the 'whole.' Because of the distractions of technological 'magic' and its obvious material advantages, we have failed to achieve a wholeness in

---

* We uphold the traditional sense of the term myth, which is a relating *in time* matters which are essentially timeless; matters which are central and psychological and spiritually accurate, yet not by their nature expressible in literal (a=a) terms, as they deal with the essential meaning of being human. Needless to say, Darwin's theory of the Origin of Species is a myth in the *modern* sense of a partial and plausible thesis in time only.

industrial or post-industrialized society. The paradoxes of increased material wealth and energy greed, natural resource destruction and the increase of mental illness all point to the fact that never before in human history has a culture been attempted without a spiritual dimension; in fact one could go further and suggest that a society is not correctly definable as 'human' without such a dimension.

The sad modern prejudice against 'religion' is due to the lack of differentiation between an individual's 'experience of religion' and 'religious experience.' Tradition is *certainty* orientated whereas modern 'replacement' theories support the doctrine of uncertainty, thereby giving uncertainty itself an absolute value; which is a simple contradiction of meaning. There can be no such thing as *un*certainty (as it is the 'lack of') if certainty doesn't exist first. We are not, in modern times, usually made aware of the significance of the choice between believing in certainty or uncertainty. For instance, Heisenberg doesn't ask us to be uncertain that there is a phenomenon which we call an electron; he tells us only that we can be sure that *its exact whereabouts* is *uncertain* at any given moment. His 'uncertainty principle' is naïvely cited by some as if it were a *philosophical* truth. In fact it only points to the impossibility of an empirical absolute — which accords with the metaphysical tradition.

The consensus traditions of humankind all indicate metaphysical dimensions, which we could call our spiritual heritage and without which life on Earth is meaningless.

In *Science and Civilization of Islam*, S.H. Nasr speaks eloquently of the traditional meaning of knowledge from the Islamic perspective (gnosis), which was to be considered either as 'worldly' (empirical), concerned with the realm of becoming and change (uncertainty) or as 'heavenly,' permanent, archetypal and immutable (certainty). The former was the basis of *scientia* and the separate sciences, and the latter of *sapientia,* an essential level of knowledge of being. Nasr describes *sapientia* as: 'A knowledge that illumines the whole of the being of the knower.' One can see how confusion has penetrated so-called 'modern philosophy' in that it allows equal status to relative opinions in the search for certainty. This competitive marshland of relative opinions has resulted in truth itself being questioned as a value. Leaving a residue of relative falsehood?

The Sun and the Moon are the two primary pacemakers of all biological existence, whilst at the same time they are the prime symbols of permanence and cyclicity. Therefore it is not surprising to find these two immediately attendant as foci of orientation both physically and metaphysically in the establishment of the human sanctuary — the temple. There is no reason whatsoever to consider the stone circles of Britain other than temples in the true meaning of the term.

Similarly the word origin is grounded in the early word *oriri,* to rise as the Sun, hence the link with east, or orient, and orientation: the direction of the new-born light. Lucid (clear, accurate), luminous and lunar come from the same source.

Professor Thom's findings have implicitly indicated the employment of Pythagorean triangles by megalithic temple-building man quite a millennium before Pythagoras lived. There is a remarkable parallel between these findings and the recent decipherment of certain Babylonian clay tablets which, coincidentally, are of about the same date as the stone circles. There is a particular tablet in the Plimpton Library of Columbia University, New York, which until recently was lumped together with many others under the loose title 'Commercial Tablets.' Yet this tablet, when analysed by a mathematical authority, revealed quite startling and totally unexpected results. These results have a direct relation to Professor Thom's findings, as the tablet contained sets of pairs of Pythagorean triplets: this means two of the sets of three side lengths of Pythagorean triangles. A Pythagorean triangle is a three-sided figure with one angle a right angle of 90° and with side lengths which are whole numbers; the third number can be ascertained if the other two are given. The startling fact of these number sets is that they would seem to indicate a quite different approach to and understanding of the nature of number and geometry from our own. We, for instance, would immediately resort to algebra, trigonometry or our pocket calculator to manipulate numbers like 12,709 and 18,541 to find the Pythagorean triplet of 13,500, as their squares, which are necessary to know, run into millions[*]; yet there can be little doubt that algebra was unknown in pre-Christian times.

From the power over 'number-theory' that the fifteen Pythagorean triplets implies the Mesopotamians possessed, certain questions must arise. As they are handling a general rule which is well known

---

[*] $12,709^2 = 161,518,681$ and $18,541^2 = 343,768,681$, with $13,500^2 = 182,250,000$. So that $343,768,681 - 161,518,681 = 182,250,000$; as $a^2 + b^2 = c^2$ or $c^2 - a^2 = b^2$.

to them, we cannot deny them the ability to express the generalization that $a^2 + b^2 = c^2$ yet they never do so. There must be a good reason for this.

Two obvious reasons come to mind: (a) that the mathematicians did not wish others to know of the generalizations, or: (b) that there was *no need* to express them in abstract form. The latter solution would imply that, for the people of that era, actual numbers conveyed some sort of immediate perception of the general relationships existing between these numbers.

Whatever we choose to believe, their ability to handle Pythagorean triplets cannot be doubted, as the evidence is concrete; the implications are, however, that such ability indicates a familiarity with:

— the number theory (principle) of Pythagorean triplets;
— the geometry of right triangles;
— the arithmetic of squares and roots of large squares;
— the elements of trigonometry; and
— the number theory of sexagesimal expansion.

And all this without algebra.

Measure and Number are the two keystones of logical or quantitive reasoning. Number, we can say, was the main concern of these Mesopotamians, whilst measure was that of the Egyptian civilization; our current knowledge of the Megalithic Briton is that he was concerned with both. Of the Egyptians and Babylonians, Professor John Kreitner has said:

> for the foremost achievements of their time, we have
> no record of method; we only know that they knew it,
> and that they lacked the *formal* tools of mathematics.
> Hence their very achievements imply a greater depth
> of intuition than the modern mind is capable of, and
> hence willing to concede.

It is because intuition represents just this antithesis to analysis that it is so suspect to our own times. We hope to demonstrate during the course of the book that it is just this remarkable balance between the intuitive and the logical that is to be found in the British megalithic artefacts and monuments that have come down through time to us today.

We also hope to take a new look at the techniques used by primordial societies — as distinct from sophisticated ones — called by the too general term Shamanism. Perhaps our studies will show them to be techniques that enable not only the intuitive mind to be brought into play, but into greater depths of consciousness than, to use Professor Kreitner's phrase: 'the modern mind is capable of, hence willing to concede.' Maybe we should say 'willing easily to concede,' as there is increasing evidence of an interest by modern Western psychologists in the realms of traditional psychology as represented by the Hindu Yogic tradition, the Buddhist meditative tradition, the Islamic Sufi tradition as well as the Christian contemplative tradition, and the archaic techniques of 'gnosis,' or knowledge of the self, upon which traditional societies base their view of the world.

Starting from the unity of existence considered as the prime characteristic of a traditional society, the indications are that the distinction *between* a temple and an observatory is unnecessary when considering the stone circles. Since it is not in doubt that the builders were what is ordinarily meant by a traditional society, it is more fruitful to attempt to put the conceptual evidence together with the evidence from stone circles themselves and to see what results emerge.

But at this point it is necessary to pay tribute to the heroic feats of surveying of Professor Alexander Thom, who made it possible to relate my own work as a geometer and architectural proportionalist directly to the arrangements of the megalithic structures.

It is not so surprising that the members of the archaeological community were so reluctant to listen to, let alone accept, the findings of Professor Alexander Thom with regard to the *geometric* structure underlying the stone circles of Britain. Even though he presented these findings in the most scientifically accurate way, this only served to make the effect one of 'delayed action,' as the community was not able to test all the mathematics and professional surveying immediately. On top of this there were inbuilt prejudices against the possibility of a pre-literate and therefore presumed pre-numerate society being capable of such mathematical activity. Another curious prejudice seemed to rest on the grounds that astronomical alignments meant 'observatory' and therefore not 'temple,' and implied loss of the religious motivation in the megalithic society. Such either/or logic is significantly a 'modern' division, as we hope to show during the course of the book, and therefore not likely to arise in the mind of the builders.

On the other hand, the long-held view was that these 'rude' stone structures were clumsy erections of primitive 'wild' peoples and therefore not worthy of further consideration, apart from the energy they expanded on humping them about. The exception was Stonehenge, which was constantly 'excused' on the grounds that the Romans or the Myceneans or the people of some other Mediterranean civilization were responsible. This attitude served to block our perception of the beauty and subtlety of these arrangements and of the stones in themselves.

This book was the result of being invited to join forces with Rod Bull, whose exceptionally intuitive and inspired images of the British stone circles were shown to us, and to present the accumulated research work of my own years of studying the same structures.

The sensitive work of Rod Bull, who succeeds in bringing out the essential and particular qualities of each stone and each setting, is evidence of a changing awareness of the beauty embodied in the arrangement and form of these massive stones. It is an awareness educated during the last century by our European contact with the great religions of the Orient, and quite specifically the 'timeless' sand and rock gardens of the Japanese Buddhist monasteries. Bull's images are not only evidence of the years dedicated to travelling the length and breadth of the British Isles to record the mysterious beauty of these monuments; they open up to all of us the majestic power and individuality of the stones that were so obviously chosen and placed with such care and particularity. These photographs are works of insight which capture some of the intuitive imagination and understanding of the original builders, and serve as a magnificent complement to our tendency to over-intellectualize such creative achievements.

Finally, on the occasion of this new edition, we welcome the appearance of the late Anne Macaulay's research work into proportion and geometry of the British stone circles, published in 2006 as *Megalithic Measures and Rhythms* (Floris Books, Edinburgh), which is to be recommended to any serious student of the megalithic builders.

1. The Enigma of the Megaliths

A man who has lost his sense of wonder is as a man dead.

Logic can take you from A to B, but imagination encircles the world.

    Albert Einstein

What a true symbol teaches is not subject to the limitations of verbal expression.

    Frithjof Schuon[1]

When traditional man looked at the stars he saw in the heaven of the fixed stars the limits of the universe. Beyond that heaven was not 'space' but only Divine Presence. This finite cosmos, however, was far from being a prison without an opening. On the contrary, by the very fact of its finite form it served as an icon to be contemplated and transcended. Thanks to its symbolism, the concentric spheres acting as a most powerful and efficient symbol for the states of being which man must traverse to reach Being Itself, the content of this cosmos was infinite and its finite forms like the forms of religion led to an inner content which is limitless.

    S.H. Nasr[2]

What is here is there, what is not here is nowhere.

    Vishwasara Tantra[3]

Origins

The challenge of the great standing stone monuments of Britain increases with each new study. This is due to both the greater accuracy of new scientific instrumentation and the change in modern ideas about what it means to be human.

There is a revolution in prehistory, as it has been called, affecting the current attitudes towards it. In other words, there is a 'turning round' and broadening of today's use of the terms 'history,' 'human nature,' 'scientific,' and even 'philosophy.' These terms are less watertight and strictly compartmentalized than they were even ten years ago, let alone in the floodtide of 'Darwinism' and 'positivism' of the 1920s and 30s.

This turning around of modern thinking is not due solely to the facts of the past as they have emerged, but it is influenced to a greater or lesser degree by the scale of events in which our science-dependent society has found itself. Atomic and nuclear weapons are one aspect, ecological disasters and the relationship between population expansion and natural resources are another; the 'energy crisis,' so-called, is a third. These problems have penetrated the most buried of scholarly fields as our collective sense of 'progress' and 'rightness' is challenged. Who can responsibly *define* a post-industrialized society?* The emergence in the contemporary scientific community of groups concerned with the social responsibility of science is a clear indication of this change in mood.

It is significant that more and more scientists and scholars are realizing that it is they themselves who are the ultimate instruments by which all their data, however processed, must be evaluated. This implies that the personal psychology, upbringing, circumstances and state of being of the observer colours the observed — even when the 'observer' is a team. Facts alone, however logical, are apparently not enough; their context, their application in society and a value system to monitor both are simultaneously vital and necessary. And all this hinges on what it really means to be human.

It is not only the balance of nature that has suffered from our 'modern' industrialized culture with its mechanistic and materialistic criteria but, possibly most important of all, we have suffered the loss of dignity and self-confidence by this same mechanistic attitude toward human nature.

However well-meaning aid to traditional societies may have been, it inevitably brought with it a dependency — political, economic and ideological — on the incoming new techniques, thereby disastrously affecting the traditional 'wisdom-structure' of those communities.

---

* The writings of William E. Thompson of the USA are a bold attempt, and the philosophy of E.F. Schumacher a wholesome directive.

4.
Carnac, Brittany

Potential global nuclear war and non-renewable fossil-fuel consumption are in constant attendance, yet it may soon be realized that the greatest threat our modern industrial culture poses for mankind is the denial of its spiritual heritage or the value system to control these negative elements. What we will call traditional or perennial wisdom is the foundation of all human communities throughout recorded and non-recorded time. It not only sets out to relate the individual to the cosmic scheme of things, but predicates a relationship of health or 'wholeness' between the natural environment and fellow beings. It is only in this realm that the full dimensions of our dignity and humanity are to be found, as it is the very principle of unity.

We believe it is in just this dimension of unity that we have most to gain from our study of the megalithic monuments, as their origins in this sense are our origins.

We have a scientific technique, never infallible, but currently acceptable, telling us through its analyses that many of the architectural feats of the stone temples, burial tombs and stone circles of Western Europe *predate* the urban civilizations of the Middle East. It is therefore no longer viable to ascribe the influence or inspiration of Stonehenge or Silbury Hill to Asian cultures. Academic archaeology can no longer rely on the axiom that such feats of construction as the great stone temples of Malta, the magnificent corbelled domes of New Grange and Maes Howe, the great pyramidical cone of Silbury Hill and the immense structure of Stonehenge are the informed work of a 'literate' urban society. The manpower alone required to raise these monuments is astounding.* Yet there is no direct evidence of a slave-pressured society for their accomplishment.

Colin Renfrew, as one representative of contemporary archaeological thinking, freely admits that neither the independent evolutionary theory nor the diffusionist theory are sufficient explanations in themselves for the new facts.[4] Neither position explains the motivating impetus that gave rise to these monumental innovations. The current position seems to indicate that both phenomena occurred: the independent discovery of new techniques and practices *and* the diffusion and exchange of these through exploration, trading and the resultant interchange of ideas. What is most dramatically changed is the certainty, held until recently, that the inspiration and directives could only have come from the Levant to account for these great megalithic feats of pre-recorded history in Europe. What is significantly missing from either view is the will or spiritual perspective for such massive feats of construction, to which we will return.

There are certain human monuments that bear the quality of timelessness. We believe the stone circle temples of Britain are fine examples. Standing before or within any of these profoundly simple, yet striking arrangements, one is without the normal clues as to their significance. Why is one so affected? There is nothing written by the builders which could explain the presence of the structures. They become deeply challenging to our sense of both the practical

---

* One calculation estimated that the whole of the known population of the British Isles would have had to be at work for seven years to raise the sarsen circle and great central trilithons.

and purposeful. To spend some time nearly two thousand feet up in the Welsh hills, shin-deep in snow, with a breathtaking panorama of constantly changing skyscape and light brings one very sharply up against one's own 'foreign-ness.' Yet one is standing in the habitat that was normal to the original builders. At this height the landscape is virtually the same, the weather, the nuances of the breeze, humidity, aromas, trees, birds and even animals to a certain extent, yet so few of us as urban town dwellers can 'read' these natural surroundings. One is faced with an overwhelming question: what is the intrinsic value of literacy and does *word* reading reduce our ability to read our natural surroundings? Is human wisdom only to be found in libraries, universities and technological wizardry? So many questions arise when one is put back into a natural perspective, humbled before a snow-covered hillside and overwhelmed by magnificent snow-laden clouds. One's humanity can be experienced as a natural *ingredient* of a whole phenomenon. No longer need it become a matter of intellectual effort, one is *part* of an experience. The questions of existence — existence both of oneself and of the nature of the whole of which one is a part — become far more important than speculations as to who did what, when and why. If these recorded experiences are becoming dangerously romantic for the 'factualists,' then we recommend that they too visit the more isolated of our great British megalithic monuments. Having done so they might ask themselves how 'literate' they find themselves in relation to the essential facts and forces, that is the *language* of the natural order.

In the hope that some of our findings will help to stimulate a better and fuller perspective for the study of the monuments, we must turn from the general to the particular. There is a series of perennial human issues which if considered in the context of our present study will help our aim.

First there is humanity's inherent need for locating itself in space, time and culture. Colin Renfrew puts this into a particularly significant frame when he says: 'Dating is crucial to archaeology, without a reliable chronology the past is chaotic.'[5] It is to this perennial and archaic human need to cope with and combat the chaotic that we shall turn in our later material, as it would also seem to be a fundamental motive for the circle builders too.

Another 'innovation' that has recently been introduced to the conventional field of archaeology is the important technique of cross-cultural comparisons.

> Ethnographic comparisons can be misleading if
> too much is made of similarities and differences in
> point of detail; and indeed, to make too close an
> equation between prehistoric Orkney or Arran and
> modern communities in Borneo or New Guinea
> would be rather foolish. Yet the comparison helps
> us to see how small family communities, living
> not far above the level of minimum subsistence
> and with very limited technologies, can co-operate
> in impressive enterprises. In the same way small
> Neolithic communities could well, in the right social
> framework, create monuments which at first sight
> seem more appropriate to a great civilized state such
> as Egypt.[6]

We find in this observation, as in other summaries of the conditions and social structure of the megalithic builders, that, important as they are, there is a neglect of the study of inspiration or *motivation:* what can only be called the spiritual dimension which is obviously primary, as it has been for the greatest history of all human societies. Nevertheless the monumental achievements are appreciated as an awe-inspiring fact.

Taking up the technique of cross-cultural comparisons, Renfrew reminds us briefly, but significantly: 'They (the great statues of the Easter Islands) were regarded by the Easter Islanders as Vessels which the spirits entered when invited by priests,' thereby putting into context what the builders and makers themselves intended for them.[7] Unfortunately Renfrew uses the term 'cult' when referring to the Easter Islanders' religious attitudes, which has the great disadvantage of being both unspecific and belittling, and placing negative overtones on what was obviously the central driving force of the whole community, namely its religion. Not only were the Polynesians capable of performing minor 'miracles' in recorded history through their religion, i.e. the walking on fire and passing metal through their bodies without bloodshed, but the whole issue of the bringing of 'Western technical culture' and its inevitable judgments to these beautiful Pacific Island communities is very much in question in many quarters today.

5.
Five Wells, Buxton,
a 'chambered tomb'

The interest in generalization is perhaps the most
important single feature of the new outlook in
prehistory. It has made us realize how much the
pre-historian still has to learn from the study of non-
industrial societies.[8]

This quotation characterizes our own position, as we believe that
it can be shown that the fundamental inspiration for a pre-industrial
society is its tradition* which is rooted in the psychological and
spiritual realms — without forgetting Renfrew's parting remark:
'For obviously the task of reconstruction begins with the artefacts:
they are the basic material.'[9]

An appropriate way to integrate the apparent differences between
what could be called the 'domestic' or 'pragmatic' and the 'sacred'
or 'transcendental' dimensions in any traditional community's
affairs is to discuss the nature of *symbols* as contrasted to *signs* and
indications. The artefacts we are going to investigate, including the
stone circles, would appear to embody both these aspects.

At risk of over-simplification we might say the fact that the
stones are standing is a sign, an indication, that people in the past
erected them and the shape, placing and significance of those same
stones were no doubt also symbols to those builders. By a true
symbol we mean a truth that permeates the spiritual, intellectual,
emotive and perceptive responses, both indicating and being part of
the instrument that carries it — be it stone, metal or timber.

It is the recognition of the multivalent nature of a symbol as
opposed to the simplicity or conventionality of a sign, that introduces
the subject of comparative philosophy and comparative religion.
Humankind's concern and need for symbols is an essential part of
his humanity. This realm has been called the sphere of human depth
psychology. Symbols have also been described as archetypal patterns
emerging in both instinctive and inspirational lives of people, due to
their common genetic ancestry. Others take the view that cultural
patterns are a matter of environmental inheritance; certain collective
behaviour patterns they believe to be the result of a cultural ethos,
subconsciously and consciously conditioned into a psychology of
each member during development. A third position is represented

---

* By tradition we mean the consensus wisdom that is the animating norm,
  inspiration and social cohesive force of that society.

from within the religious dimension itself, one which complements and includes the previous two and is described by the term 'revelation.' This last perspective accepts the emergence into consciousness of those archetypal ideas that are of an order beyond the 'closed' individual system. In order to understand the ancient monuments we believe it is to this latter area that modern mind must turn.

The intellectual challenge that these megalithic monuments present to us is very much bound up with our own sense of what we take to be self-explanatory. The tendency is to make the stones fit neatly into either an 'irrational' religious or 'cultic' category, or a wholly rational 'observatory' category. The fact that there are such obvious contradictions to either of these extremes, if one or other is taken as providing the 'correct' answer, should warn us to be wary of our modern mental habits.

Direct experience of the stone circles arouses an immediate sense of drama, power, and concrete reality: we recognize a tremendous driving force. Because there are none of the normal associations of ego-aggrandizement the idea of the sacred inevitably arises. On the other hand the precise studies and hypotheses of Alexander Thom and others demonstrate what we can only call a 'scientific' motivation.[10] For our modern Western categorizing mentalities, this tends to force a choice between the 'irrational' and 'rational' interpretations, when in fact there is every good reason to accept both. It is by reviewing the meaning and nature of *temple,* that we believe a solution emerges.

In an effort to regain or recollect the primordial sense of those ingredients which traditionally serve to make a place sacred, we have communities with pre-industrialized economies to turn to, particularly those who use megaliths as an essential part of their living tradition.

Maintaining our awareness of the dangers of apparent similarities between cultures which are by definition different, we proceed on the assumption that there are intrinsic human qualities that allow us to use collective terms.* On this basis we will look at three

---

* There are moderns who even object to the use of the collective term 'Man' as they say there are only 'people' — yet this argument would lead us to a *reductio ad absurdum,* whereby we have to say there are no people but groups of organs and no organs but groups of cells and so on. This is just the reductionism that Mircea Eliade warns leads to the banalization of the world — and takes away from a person his or her humanity.

6.
New Grange, a passage tomb in County Meath, Ireland

7.
Cross-section of the Atreus tomb build around 1250 BC at Mycenae

8.
Maes Howe, a neolithic chambered cairn and passage grave, situated on mainland Orkney

representative pre-industrial societies to seek their essential *motivation* for raising large stones, so far as records allow.

The first is the Minoan civilization, the second the Gadaba community of India and the third the Easter Islanders of the South Pacific.

At the turn of the century the great British archaeologist-scholar, Sir Arthur Evans, made discoveries in Crete which were to change current thinking completely regarding the early Mediterranean civilizations. The power and extent of the Minoan civilization were revealed after thousands of years of semi-legendary darkness. Current dating techniques have pushed the assumed dates further back than Evans would have dreamed and the height of Minoan civilization is now believed to have been contemporary with much of our British stone circle building.

It is thought that there was a relationship between the Minoans and the Mycenaeans of the Greek mainland. Both produced large and small stone buildings of an outstanding quality. There are remarkable similarities between the famous conical dome of Atreus at Mycenae, Scotland's Maes Howe and Ireland's New Grange, but it is Evans's conclusions about the Minoan proto-religion, which he studied in relation to the later classical Greek civilization, that are relevant here. He compared this religion of 'stocks and stones,' as he called it, with other early religions, and he pointed out that survivals of the early ritual techniques are to be found in the stones which evolved into the sculptured images of the inhabiting divinity. Instances of this are Apollo with his laurel wreath (a symbol

of vegetative life) and the sacred stone in Delphi, the Omphalos or world's navel. The most important theme is Evans's observation that: 'The Baetylic stone was always at hand as a material home for the spiritual being, brought down into it by due ritual.'[11] He stressed how transitory was 'possession' of the stone. The otherwise inert object was only 'charged' (Evans's own choice of word) with the presence of the divinity through the innovations of the appropriate ceremony, and only when it was so charged did it become a true Beth-el (house of the Lord).

Evans also felt there was a connection between the presence and withdrawal of the charge of the divinity in the stones with the sap rising in the apparently inert wood, causing the trees (stocks) to flower and bear fruit: part of the natural mystery of the yearly cycle. The religious theme of trees and stones appeared side by side right through the classical period to the backgrounds of the Pompeian wall paintings.

The second pre-industrial society we shall turn to is reported by Karl Isikowitz, whose studies took him to the Orissa region of India in 1952.[12] There he was fortunate enough to witness the Gotr ceremony of the Gadaba. The Gadaba live on the Koraput plateau and are responsible farmers and herdsmen, using a complex and multiple-year rotational crop system. Their villages are characterized by a central space in which stand 'rooted'* (and lie) the ancestral megaliths of the tribe. Isikowitz considered himself exceptionally fortunate as he happened on the ceremony during which these great stones were placed. It was unexpected, as he had been led to believe that the practice had died out, the only records being those of C. von Furer-Haimendorf.[13]

'If one is rich and does not hold a Gotr, the cattle will die and the harvest will be poor,' Isikowitz was told. This was the Gadaba's way of explaining their intimate connection with the spirits of their ancestors and the motivation behind the whole act of erecting or 'rooting' their megaliths. Thus the Gotr ceremony is considered the greatest and most significant of all ceremonies for the Gadaba. A generation after the death of a particular descendant of the village founder, the central area in which stands a 'bo' tree (*Ficus religiosa*) and the arrangement of stones (sodor) are ceremonially prepared

---

* I am grateful to Dr M. Yorke for the translation of the term for 'standing' stone as *rooted*.

9.
The Omphalos marked out Delphi as the navel of the world

10.
Pompeian wallpainting showing the religious theme of trees, c. 10 BC.

for the new chieftainship. Isikowitz tells us there are three important people in the village management and leadership: the chieftain
himself assisted by a barrik (herald) and the dissari (shaman).

The ceremony Isikowitz witnessed on 10 January, 1952, had
been fixed precisely by astronomical calculations by a shaman from
a neighbouring village. The whole ceremony was conducted within
the rhythm of the Moon's cycle and the high point of the feast was
reached at the following full Moon. He describes the performance
of this special ceremony:

> Around two o'clock after the first day, they took two
> stones and placed them where the shaman had decided
> ... one of the stones was laid flat on the ground and the
> other placed upright behind it. The shaman then placed
> an egg on the flat stone and mumbled something.
> Simultaneously with this act he decided when the
> actual final ceremonies would be held. At the same
> time two big poles or branches of a similli or red silk
> cotton tree (*salmalia malabarica*) were taken into the
> village and driven into the ground on each side and
> just behind the upright stone. This was followed by the
> beating of drums all through the night.[14]

Isikowitz faithfully reports the details of behaviour, music,
dance and ceremony, unfortunately too long for our purpose, but he
did summarize the following:

> The Gotr ceremony is a kind of *rite de passage* ...
> These rites are a transition from one to another of life's
> phases ... a kind of 'social transformer' which mark
> the transition ... from a magic or religious action to
> one of a productive technical character, or the reverse
> ... a social transformation ... of a number of different
> elements of which the physical change is one.

And he further observes:

> the stones and the two poles ... which were erected
> at the beginning of the ceremony are very important.
> Apparently, this is a kind of isolation of what is holy,
> just as one sets up an entrance or gateway to an altar.

And, in relation to the idea of the stones being inhabited, we could use Evans's term 'charged.' He says:

> The Gadaba say that by seating themselves on the sodor ... the stones ... the council members are in some way influenced by these ancestors so that their deliberations will benefit the people. The life power of their forefathers would thus supposedly be bound by these stones and influence those who came after.[15]

Isikowitz tells us of the blessings that are conferred on the descendants of the ancestor who 'inhabits' the stones when they stand on them. He goes on to remark:

> This is no unusual phenomenon; the Koya, the neighbouring tribe, erect a stone for a certain person before he leaves for the tea plantations in Assam ... so that the traveller's life power will be bound to the village and can return home if he should die.[16]

Before leaving this perceptive first-hand experience of a contemporary megalithic ceremony in India, two more very interesting points are made by analogy, each concerned with the energy transformations of this group of peoples. First, on the action of the stone's 'charge':

> The life power of the ancestors cannot be seen, but it influences the harvest and health and it appears again in the production rhythm and closes the circle exactly as in the grounding of an electrical circuit.

Secondly, on the unbroken interdependency between the seen and unseen energies of the tribe:

> The life cycle absorbs the accumulation from the production cycle. The production cycle brings in a material result and gives out a religious result. This influences in its turn the goodwill of the powers, and this again has its effect on the production cycle.[17]

Here the psychological and physical forces complement each other and are self-reinforcing, on condition that the correct rituals are observed.

This interdependency between physical and spiritual factors is explicit in the Hindu manuscript called the *Mānasāra Shilpa Shāstra,* an ancient manuscript which is concerned with the preparation of sacred ground for temple building and which will be used as part of the analyses of the British circles in the ensuing chapters. According to this authority, before the actual geometrical ceremony an annual cycle had to be completed to clear away evil spirits. A crop was planted in the chosen ground, oxen led over to graze and fertilize the site and, after the corn had sprouted, grown and ripened, the people prepared food which they then ate in order to close the ecological cycle ritually. Certain of the meal cakes produced from the harvest were sacrificed in the founding ceremony.

For the third and last example, we move on to the so-called Easter Islanders, mentioned earlier, to investigate what might be known about their huge megalithic images which stare so enigmatically out to sea from the hillsides of their Pacific island.

Easter Island and Malta have been made into a 'splendid analogy' as 'both islands are remote ... and bear the enigmatic signs of activities on a gargantuan scale by a vanished population,' which naturally directs us once again to the question of motivation.

Renfrew quotes Mrs Scoresby's evidence of a burial at Easter Island which he believes, by comparison, 'may embody many of the features of megalithic burial at Orkney or Arran' (the Scottish islands).[18]

A massive physical effort was obviously involved: not only erecting the huge images, but carving them first. To discover the motivation we must ask: what did the Easter Islanders themselves believe the statues' function to be? Metraux gives us evidence on this point: the massive megalithic images were 'vessels which the spirits entered when invited by priests,' and some of them apparently *embodied* the spirits of certain ancestral figures who had become deities of the tribe,[19] obviously implying a function as vital to the community as the *sodor* of the Gadaba.

Each of our three examples clearly indicates that the body of the stone was as much a repository for a certain kind of 'life' as our human bodies 'carry' the mysterious span we call our own life.

It is too easy to put the ancient or traditional viewpoint into a 'naive' or 'superstitious' category but modern science is no nearer

11.
Callanish, Isle of Lewis

to being able to explain the meaning of our own lives, however much molecular biology demonstrates the wonderful intricacies of the mechanisms. It may be a form of *naïveté* on our behalf to dismiss a tradition as inconsequential when we may be ignorant of the values that gave rise to it. What seems evident is that the great megaliths would not have been achieved without this dimension of inhabitory spirits.

It is a particular 'modern' view that treats the metaphysical factors of human existence as hermetically sealed from the physical, and is part of the contemporary habit of compartmentalizing or atomizing human experience and activity. It is as 'unwise' as sealing off 'mind' from 'brain' or function from structure. For traditional societies based on the continuity of an integrative wisdom transmission, the metaphysical not only permeates the physical but is the 'cause' and 'maintainer' of the physical. A similarity by analogy would be a universal law of nature which a modern scientist would take as permeating and maintaining physical form — like, for example, the form of a hydrogen atom or the cohesive law of gravity.

For those hard-line rationalists who would like to do without the metaphysical altogether and reduce their world to the physical behaviour patterns of energy, it is salutary to look up this word 'energy' in the dictionary. It merely means 'the ability to do work.' Reductionism can lead us as certainly to poverty as it can to essence. However our aim is to attempt an understanding of the megalithic builder in his own terms, that is, according to all reasonableness, in *traditional* terms.

2. The Ground Rules

We know that its centre is Your dwelling place. Upon this circle the generations will walk.

Black Elk[1]

But there is nothing either natural or necessary in the use of huge unwieldy blocks of stone where much smaller ones would have sufficed.

T. Eric Peet[2]

I have never valued or studied the mere sophistry of word-knowledge set down in books in conventionalized form of questions and answers to be committed to memory (and fired off at one's opponents); these lead but to mental confusion and not to such practice as bringeth actual realization of Truth. Of such word-knowledge I am ignorant; and if ever I did know it I have forgotten it long ago.

Milarepa[3]

By all the Greeks the honours due to the images of the gods were paid to unwrought stones.

Pausanius on the early Greeks, ix. 38.1[4]

The giving of grounds

The most comprehensive yet simple form for defining a sacred area is the circle. This 'opening to the transcendental' is achieved either as the result of setting out the parts of the temple as a whole or is literally symbolized by a physical feature such as a central pole or the smoke hole above the altar fire. The vertical pointer represents the ontological axis, which has its symbolic equivalent as much in the Buddhist pagoda and Tibetan chorten as in the spire of Salisbury Cathedral. (Despite being finished considerably later than the main body of the building, the central tower of

12.
Salisbury Cathedral, view of the central
spire and the two western towers

Salisbury Cathedral is symbolically appropriate here as the two towers of the west end represent a duality, so the spire over the central crossing, the heart of Salisbury, stands for reconciliation and unity.)

Any human endeavour, on whatever scale, needs sufficient reason and motivation for its beginning. The larger and longer the project, the more will-power, intellectual conviction and sense of purpose is required for its completion. Nowhere is this more evident than when technical resources are minimal and manpower needs high, as was obviously the case with the placing of the lithic circles. As the psychological motivation invariably precedes the physical project it is to the former we need to look.

Kerenyi and Jung discovered the 'giving of grounds or reason for being' is one of the oldest and most basic of recorded myth structures, since it is fundamental to the fabric of each community's and individual's psychology.[5] The giving of grounds (sound siting) as the 'giving of substance to' is closely related to 'stance' and 'under-standing' (foundations), as the basis of both psychological and physical security. Psychologically it is the rebuilding of the world, a rebuilding from and about that central point where one's origins or one's 'grounds for being,' are. 'Origin,' according to Kerenyi, has a derivation linking it to the Latin *oriri,* to rise, an awakening relating to the rising Sun at the *origin* of each day.

If we turn to the traditional psychological viewpoint[*] on the theme of grounds for being, it is not the world (the physical environment) that gives grounds or a basis for constructing a cosmological image (the true framework of a temple) but the macrocosmic image itself, the archetype. This archetypal image is ultimately based on the same divine ground as the world and so it becomes the dwelling place of the gods and thereby regenerates the world. In other words, the archetypal pattern is prior to and contains the

---

[*] A traditional psychology is one, as defined by F. Schuon, which locates humankind's consciousness in a spectrum of consciousness, taking into account expressions more subtle and dense than those studied by other psychologies. It incorporates the most inclusive possibilities as well as limitations and accidents, and its aim is unitary consciousness, the fullest realization of potential. This latter has been given many names such as pure being, or enlightenment.

regenerative properties that are necessary for the sustained 'becoming' of the world. Humankind both affirm their own grounds for *being* by their capability of conceiving this archetypal pattern, and sustain their world by re-creating it in that world.*

S.H. Nasr, in discussing traditional theosophical doctrines of Islam, states that the underlying metaphysical principle is that knowledge and being are ultimately one and that through intellection the cosmos has gained its existence.[7]

The contemplation of the divine, therefore, takes on not only an important but vital role in the sustenance and preservation of the cosmos. To 'do this in remembrance' as Christ requested at the Last Supper, also reflects this role of *re*-membering or re-collecting, putting the members back together through the contemplation of the divine.

One manifestation of this principle of sanctifying or reconnecting with the transcendental is in the Vedic ritual for taking possession of a territory as cited by Mircea Eliade:

> One says that one is installed when one has built a
> fire altar *(garhapatya)* and all those who build the
> fire altar are legally established. By assembling the
> fire altar the presence of Agni and the transcendental
> world is established. This is re-enacting creation,
> in effect making a cosmos, reflected in detail by
> the number of bricks and their displacement, each
> standing for a cosmic period or pattern as formulated
> by the sages who devised the ritual.[8]

In the light of these traditional patterns and the research of Jung, Kerenyi and Eliade, it seems very likely that the stone circles have many of the characteristics of temples. All societies

---

* The image as model is best understood by taking the proposal of Henri Corbin that we use the word imaginal for the realm of archetypal images.[6] This is a level of reality accessible intelligibly but not sensibly: in other words, interior 'visions' or the emergence of an archetype into the individual consciousness indicates that this imaginal realm is a psychological reality and is in no way dependent on the physical realm. In fact the traditional view is the reverse of the empirical, holding that the physical is dependent for its form and significance on the intelligible or archetypal world.

in recorded history, prior to the modern occurrence of pragmatic materialism, have lived within a transcendental framework; it is therefore unreasonable to consider the stone circle builders in any other context.

The word 'temple' has its roots in the Ancient Greek *temnos,* to cut off a sacred area, as well as in the Latin *templum* (space), which has survived in the modern 'template,' and *tempus* (time). Thus the word implies a paradigm for both time and space and hence a sacred basis for these conditions of existence. The temple was a centre expressing the controlling archetype, a timeless source of time and a spaceless source of space, a centre of the world from which one could find the centre of oneself, the central reality of one's own being. Sacred space is an area set aside from worldly concerns for specifically religious reasons and for the contemplation of existence and ultimate causes. It has an opening upward to the transcendent worlds and, according to Eliade, another below to the underworld and the world of the ancestors.

The opening to the transcendental can be taken both as a centrality and as a vertical axis. Eliade, and before him Guénon, have interpreted its presence in the core of the sacred space, seen variously as the world mountain (Meru), the Ziggurat, the universal column, Jacob's ladder, the maypole and the shaman's pole.[9] In the human body the opening for this axis has also been related to the fontanel in a newborn child. When the core is only a point or intersection at ground level it becomes an 'omphalos,' or the symbolic navel of the world. For other symbolic expressions it will be made into a sacred hearth or an altar, and if the axis is located by a hole in the ceiling or apex of a dome it becomes the smoke hole or the 'eye of heaven.' The 'unmoving' Pole Star as a rotational axis of the heavens is also associated with the transcendental axis of the cosmos.

Although sacredness is One and representative of the principle of unity, to understand the traditional position of mankind in the establishment of sacredness we can look to the Far Eastern Triad which represents the separation of unity into three primary realms. Lao Tsu characterizes this process thus:

> Tao generates one. One generates two. Two generates three. Three generates all things.[10]

Ho Shang Kung, the earliest recorded commentator on Lao Tsu, develops this as follows:

> Tao generates one: what Tao generates in the
> beginning is one. One generates two: it generates
> Yin and Yang. Two generates three: Yin and Yang
> generate the harmonious, the clear and the turbid,
> the three atmospheres which are divided into
> heaven, earth and man. Three generates all beings:
> heaven, earth and man together generate everything.
> Heaven expands, earth changes, man educates and
> nourishes.[11]

This commentary is traditionally believed to be over two thousand years old. It is characteristic of the consistency of Chinese civilization that one thousand years later Chu Hsi taught in his compiled wisdom:

> Therefore it is said that 'Yin and Yang are established
> as the way of Heaven; the weak and the strong as the
> way of Earth; and humanity and righteousness as the
> way of man.' It is also said that 'If we investigate the
> cycle of things we shall understand the concepts of
> life and death.'[12]

As if to reinforce the essential nature of the centre of things Chu Hsi places the sage* at the centre of both his own being and the world:

> Therefore the sage abides by the mean, correctness,
> humanity and righteousness. His activity and
> tranquillity are pervasive but in his activity
> tranquillity is always fundamental. This is why he
> can occupy the central position and neither Heaven,
> Earth, Sun and Moon, the four seasons nor the
> spiritual beings oppose him.[13]

---

* The word 'sage' here is not to be confused with the modern usage. It refers to an individual who has reached psychological integration or enlightenment, the fulfilment of disciplined spiritual practices.

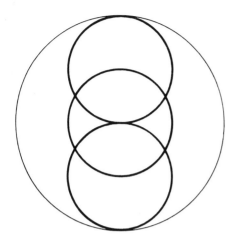

13.
Three reflections of unity

14.
Avebury

One method to visualize the interrelationship between the three primordial realms is by drawing a diagram. A geometrical diagram holds a special value as it partakes of the principles of symmetry and order on which creation is structured and therefore is both symbolic and descriptive simultaneously. It is in this intrinsic qualitative nature of geometry that the primordiality and primacy of the megalithic circles lie. This diagram can be visualized in two dimensions as three interlocking circles and in three dimensions as three interpenetrating spheres. Each circle, or sphere, represents the spheres of heaven, earth and man. In this scheme the uppermost sphere is heaven, the lowest is earth and the central linking sphere is mankind. These three primordial reflections of unity have been described variously as: the gods, the ancestors and society; or as the upper world, the underworld and 'our' world; or the upper as the sphere of ideas and pure being, the symbolic, next the lower, the diabolic, world where order is continually dissolved into less integrated states (an entropic world of increasing disorder) and centrally the balancing sphere of human

consciousness. In the religions of many societies, and markedly in the shamanism of Siberia, there is a symmetry of divisions above and below the sphere of mankind, that is, there are as many heavens as underworlds.

One ancient Chinese tradition states that in the capital of the Perfect Sovereign the sundial must give no shadow at midday of the summer solstice. The heavenly archetype is described as existing at the centre of the universe near the miraculous tree 'standing wood' *(Kien Mon),* and here the three cosmic spheres, heaven, earth and hell, intersect. There is a parallel symbolism in the Vedic Indian tradition of the three *gunas:* Rajas, Sattva and Tamas. Sattva is light and corresponds to the enlightening power of heaven; Rajas is movement and corresponds to the horizontal axis in the human plane; while Tamas is inertia or darkness and can be related to the entropy of the underworld.

The triads of Barddas, a traditional oral teaching, outline in Christian terminology the way in which it is believed the Druids, the last priests and teachers to use the stone circles before the coming of Christianity, may have used the symbolism of the three archetypal spheres:

> There are three circles of existence: the Circle of Ceugant where there is nothing but the God, of living or dead, and none but God can traverse it; the Circle of Abred, where all things are by nature derived from death, and man traverses it; and the Circle of Gwynvyd, where all things spring from life, and man shall traverse it in heaven.
>
> The Circle of Abred in which are all corporeal and inanimate existences.
>
> The Circle of Gwynvyd in which are all animated and immortal beings.
>
> The Circle of Ceugant where there is only God, the perfect rim that bounds the immensity of existence.

There is also a semitic tradition reflecting the three primordial spheres which states that the Rock of Jerusalem is held in the mouth of the serpent Tahom, being the point of intersection of the underworld and the upper world. This point marks the opening to the watery chaos that precedes creation and symbolizes the reintegration into the physical formlessness that follows death.

15.
Man's relationship to heaven and earth

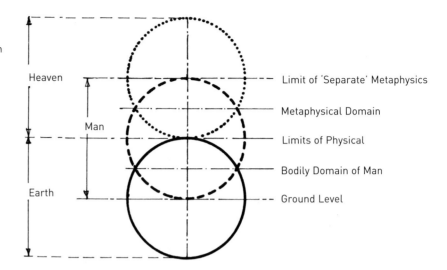

Heaven — Limit of 'Separate' Metaphysics

Metaphysical Domain

Man — Limits of Physical

Bodily Domain of Man

Earth — Ground Level

If we take the three interpenetrating spheres and consider them as a vertical axis, we can place ground level at the base of the human sphere where mankind touches the ground, a plane midway through the material, earthly sphere. This is the ground on which we stand and raise ourselves. The third sphere is the heavenly or archetypal sphere 'above' the human plane yet interpenetrating it. The primary demarcation of sacred space establishes the boundaries inside which the temple proper reflects the structures of the cosmos, a model of the 'untroubled circulations' of the heavenly bodies. This contrasts with the 'troubled' unpredictables of the domestic life of communities making their way in the natural world. These can be conceived as increasing in potential chaos as they extend from the hub of the community. The wilderness and realm of aliens is just as real for any human group whether it extends merely to the next village or to so-called outer space. It is the realm of increasing unpredictability, the indefinite not the infinite.

A village properly comes into being as another aspect of this conjunction between gods, ancestors and people. The central meeting place, or village green, is for ceremonials and is 'common ground,' both in the sense of ownership and rights, and, at another level, as the common ground of being of that society, making it vital to the maintenance of correct relationships within the three spheres.

Having changed the axis of the symbolism we can see that the underworld and the lateral unknown territories outside our own region can be compared. The thresholds of habitation, seen as affording increasing sanctuary, conform to concentric circles, the centre being the most protected from surrounding chaos. So it may be possible to identify the stone circles as protected areas, both in the psychological sense of sanctuary and in the practical sense of the knowledge they embody as information necessary for the community to orientate itself to the rhythms of the solar system.

Plutarch's description of the foundation ceremony for the city of Rome is a good example of the way a rite as psychological grounding is related to the physical layout procedure for sacred geometry. In his biography of Romulus, Plutarch relates that a central pit called *mundus* was taken as the centre of a ploughed circle, and *mundus* was considered to be an actual or potential opening both to the underworld and the ancestral spirits. Another Roman author, Varro, confirms Plutarch's description when he says that the Roman *coloniae* on their foundation were called *urbes* from *orbis* meaning round and/or *urvo* meaning to plough round.

One parallel between this ceremony, apparently inherited from the Etruscans, and the laying out of a stone circle is in practical geometry. The circles are most likely to have been staked out with sharpened wooden poles and rope or cord of some kind. The large trammel (compass) that must have been used to obtain the curves for the ground rules would probably have had a sharpened stake at each end: one controlling the centre of the arc, the taut cord taking

ploughed circle

16.
A proposed method for the geometrical construction of the stone circles with stretched cords and stakes

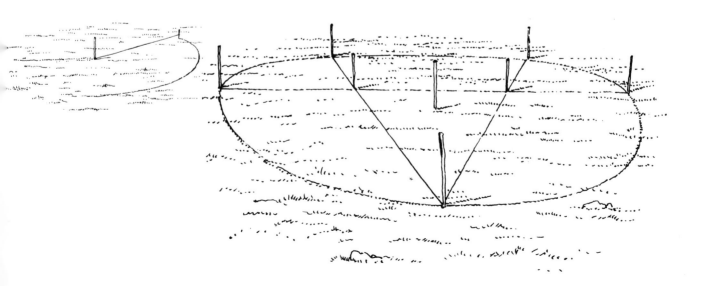

up the radius; the other, the scribing end, cutting or lightly plough-
ing the desired areas. The same method could have been used on a
larger scale when founding the site of, say, Avebury.

Perception and the ground rules

As our perceptions are inevitably influenced by what 'experts' tell
us, an unavoidable conditioning, if we wish to see freshly a special
effort is required to keep our minds open to alternative frames of
reference. When viewing examples of great architecture so much of
our appreciation depends upon our cultural background and therefore
our frame of mind. If we were shown one of the Japanese Buddhist
temple gardens with their stones magnificently placed in sand, as
Westerners, we would have been conditioned to respond aestheti-
cally.[*] If, however, we were conducted around the Jantar Mantar at
Jaipur, where the Moghul Maharaja Jai Singh II built a series of enor-
mous astronomical instruments, similar in size to the sarsen circle at
Stonehenge, we would be influenced to approach them as technological instruments.[†] Yet both of these examples contain symbolic values
on the one hand and precise cosmological values on the other.

   If we are to ascribe to the builders of the British stone circles
an astronomical understanding of the sophistication that modern
research implies, then we must be equally generous toward all of
their sensibilities. We need to make a very real effort to banish any
idea of crude and insensitive people when considering these megalithic builders. As one becomes aware of the Far Eastern masterly
stone placings one finds a new level of understanding and appreciation through these sublime relationships.

   In the British arrangements there is an amazing balance between
the geometric order and asymmetry of the placings of the stones in

17.
Large solar clock at Jantar Mantar,
Jaipur, Rajasthan, India

---

[*] Ananda Coomeraswamy comments aptly on current Western taste: 'Our
"aesthetic" appreciation is essentially sentimental because it is just what
the word "aesthetic" means, a kind of feeling rather than an understanding,
and has little or nothing to do with their *raison d'être.*'

[†] The megaliths in Buddhist temple gardens are placed according to certain
constellations. The Jantar Mantar is an instrument for direct astronomical
readings.

size and closeness. There seems no doubt that here is a sensitivity to individual stones that we have tended to miss by paying too much attention to the rather more uniform Stonehenge. Due to the precision of the ground rules we have to take a new attitude to the form and placings of the stones.

It is a brave person who dismisses the professional surveying of Professor Thom, even if he cares to differ over his metrological and astronomical conclusions.[14] From an architectural standpoint we find the geometrical thesis of his important findings not only acceptable but a milestone in the appreciation of the subtleties of the Neolithic mind. The intelligence implied by these subtleties is the major concern of this book.

With the geometry behind the appearance established by statistical method, it now becomes important to appreciate the other

18.
Avebury consists of a large henge and several stone circles near the village of Avebury in Wiltshire. The site is about 5,000 years old, predating Stonehenge.

deliberate effects that the circles embody. With very few exceptions
the centres of the stones are not evenly placed around the 'circles';
this is an important factor as it would not only be more obvious but
also much easier in terms of 'pacing out' to have made them so.

With no exceptions the stones differ in size and shape from
each other. Notwithstanding the reluctance to work the stones this
we must accept as a deliberate intention by the builders and not a
contradiction to the idea of creating the geometrical order of the
circle. To reinforce this viewpoint there are usually stones available within the working area that are nearer to a consistent size.
Not only this, but should we seek to rearrange the existing stones
in any circle in a more 'orderly' manner we would have plenty of
room for manoeuvre. We are forced to recognize a paradox; here
is the sophisticated accomplishment of symmetry — asymmetry or
what we might call 'random-order' where precise placement and a
recognition of the unique quality of each stone are in equilibrium.

In addition to the pure circle it is the almost circular structures,
such as the ellipse with two centres and the egg shape with four
centres, that seem to have held particular significance for the henge
builders. This fact alone prompts us to examine the other shapes
more closely as they are far more sophisticated and difficult to create geometrically than the primary circle.

Another important aspect in the choice and placing is the physical properties and quality of stones used. We can no longer ignore
these physical properties for they might be an essential reason for
the apparent randomness of placing and difference in size. As to
the quality of the stones, there may be subtleties and conditions
known to the builders of which we have yet to become aware.
Those of us who have been brought up in an urban, industrialized
society find sensitivity to stone difficult, even in differentiating it
from concrete or composite stone. In much the same way we experience difficulty with many types of sensitivity; for instance a full
sense of landscape — grass, bush, tree and animal life, no less than
wind, plant aromas, firmness or softness of ground and all natural
signs which indicate the quality of a day or place: to summarize,
we have sacrificed our subtle sense of balance between the primary elements of our experience through urbanization. Our minds
having been directed toward the overriding importance of wages,
prices and incomes, are left no time to ponder the underlying reality of each man's relationship to natural resources, particularly
the quality of the produce of the soil — our daily bread. Equally

we have been diverted from the sense of permanence symbolized in the standing stones. Only a transcendent reality can satisfy the human intellect — even if it is temporarily diverted into believing in the absurdity of according relativity an absolute value.

The 'concrete' reality for traditional societies was metaphysical and grounded in the gods, whereas in our contemporary Western society it is literal and grounded in mechanisms. Hence our contemporary repetitive concrete 'boxes' — the tower blocks, flats and offices — proclaim an equality of identity to such a degree that they become mechanically identical and therefore anonymous, thereby denying the first law of the natural order of manifestation — variety and multiplicity in Unity, or uniqueness in unicity.

It would appear that there were simultaneously intellectual, artistic and technical inspirations behind the building of the stone circles. This implies the most interesting integration between day-to-day human affairs on the one hand and the idea of space and time 'in eternity' on the other to the community for whom they were built. The abstract concepts of calculation, the calendar, time and space all related to their immediate present. What could have been the one overriding motive power for this? If we turn to the great sagas and creation myths we find the recurrent theme of the gift of knowledge coming from the gods. We can expect therefore not only that the 'ground rules' emanate from the gods but that the prime purpose of the temple circle would have been to maintain this contact with the transcendental spheres.

The primordial fact of a standing stone is that it is no longer lying down — or 'dead.' It contradicts its material nature and is 'raised.' This change from a horizontal to a vertical position denotes a change in metaphysical being and points heavenward to the realm of the gods, one 'world' becoming another. The link between these worlds was clearly indicated by Plato when he suggested that it was in contemplation of the 'untroubled paths' of the planets that we should seek to solve our own troubled souls.[15]

We find in the great majority of pre-industrial communities the conviction that the positions of the heavenly bodies affect human affairs. This has the traditionally respectable title of astrology and yet 'contemporary' materialistic science has firmly placed it in the realm of a folk art and not the logical science that its name implies, astro-*logy* (star logic). However, the extensive and painstaking work of Professor Michel Gauquelin has found new respectability in the thesis of traditional astrology, that is, birth, time and planetary position linked to adult livelihood. If there is truth in the phenomena then we would expect the idea and establishment of such correlations to have originated out of acute observation in earlier periods — as would have been the connection between the weather, the seasons and the interrelated phases of the Sun and Moon over a year's cycle. When one pauses to consider, one soon realizes how reliant non-industrialized peoples are on the phases of the Moon and the moods of the weather. No planned night expedition would be conceivable without taking into account the phase or light of the Moon. Harvest Moons are also matters of importance for gathering the winter's sustenance for many communities. Human sensitivities, survival strategies and the movements of the heavenly orbs having been traditionally linked, the logical outcome of these observations would be to establish techniques of anticipation. By these methods people might plan for the effects of the phases of Sun, Moon and planets. Some form of observatory would enable the community to be forewarned of both positive and negative values associated with these relationships between Sun, Moon, planets and the Earth. How important these predictions may have been can be imagined in the case of the pile-village dwellers of estuary tidal waters at spring and neap tides.

A simple upright gnomon would be sufficient to make the measurement of the length of the midday shadow from which it would be possible to fix midsummer day. Another method would be to use the Pole Star as a permanent fix in the heavens.

How early observations and sightings were accomplished can only be a matter of speculation, but Professor Thom's precise surveys of Neolithic edifices have led him to propose adequately feasible techniques. His great inspiration was the accurate measurement of the stones as they stand, rather than digging for remnants and refuse around them in order to assemble a theory.

Though Professor Thom has raised the study of stone circles to a completely new level there is no substitute for visiting the sites oneself. The experiences to be gained are manifold and bring alive a synthesis between intelligent study and direct perception. The multidimensional nature of the whole setting is never less than awe-inspiring.

Documentary evidence for the ground rules

Our speculations as to how stone circles were laid out in a pre-documented period are based on evidence of the earliest written temple orientation procedures. These, to the best of our knowledge, are found in an ancient Hindu manuscript, the *Mānasāra Shilpa Shāstra,* and the details of technique bear most closely on our interpretation of the geometry used in British circles.

According to this document the initial act, establishing the ontological axis, is to erect an upright pillar, which tapers toward the top, in the ground at the centre of the chosen site. This recalls the world tree and echoes in Hindu symbolism the sushumna which is described as a 'ray joining every being to the spiritual Sun.'

Next a circle is traced around the pillar with a radius twice the height of the column using the pillar as the central stake of a rope trammel (compass), which effects the enclosing of a 'cosmos'

19.
Borneo tribesmen using the gnomon to establish the length of the midday shadow, over the year

within from the relative chaos without. At sunrise the shadow of this gnomon-pillar is longer than the radius of the circle. During the morning the shadow of the tip of the column strikes the outline of the circle and the point of intersection is marked. The shadow lengthens during the afternoon and the second point is marked when the shadow of the tip cuts the circle again. These marks made in the morning and evening are joined to give an accurate east-west axis. This is the first cosmic axis on the horizontal plane: that of the daily path of the Sun, thereby aligning the site to the solar system, pointing to the origin and termination of the day. To establish this east-west axis on the centre line of the circle a small circle is set out from the pillar to tangent the cord stretched between **a** and **b**. This small circle is struck at **a** and **b** and a new cord tangent between them stretched — this is a true east-west axis from the major circle's centre.

Using a rope trammel the western point is staked as centre and a radius taken across to the eastern point. An arc is then cut which is not less than one-sixth of a full circle on either side of the eastern point. The same procedure is then followed from the eastern point as centre and the second arc made to cut the first above and below the east-west line. The 'fish' form produced by these two arcs is known as the *vesica pisces* in the Christian tradition as it is also a version of the yoni, the feminine principle in Hindu symbolism. In this sense with due ritual the site is 'opened' and the connection with the transcendental is made possible.

When arcs are produced from the points N and S in turn, a second fish-form results. When the four intersections made by the fish-forms themselves are joined, the circle is divided into eight equal segments. The axial division of this circle into four equal parts, the

20.
Hindu temple-founding geometry according to the *Mānasāra Shilpa Shāstra:*

a. The first circle or sacred area with central pillar

b. The dawn and dusk shadow lines establish the east-west axis

c/d. The establishment of the east-west axis as a diameter of the circle

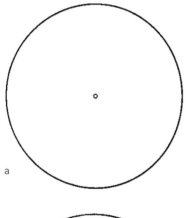

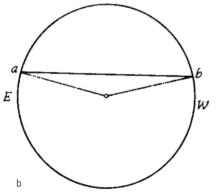

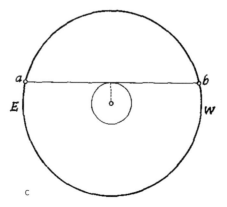

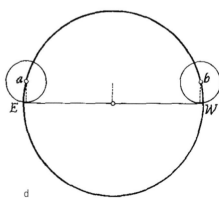

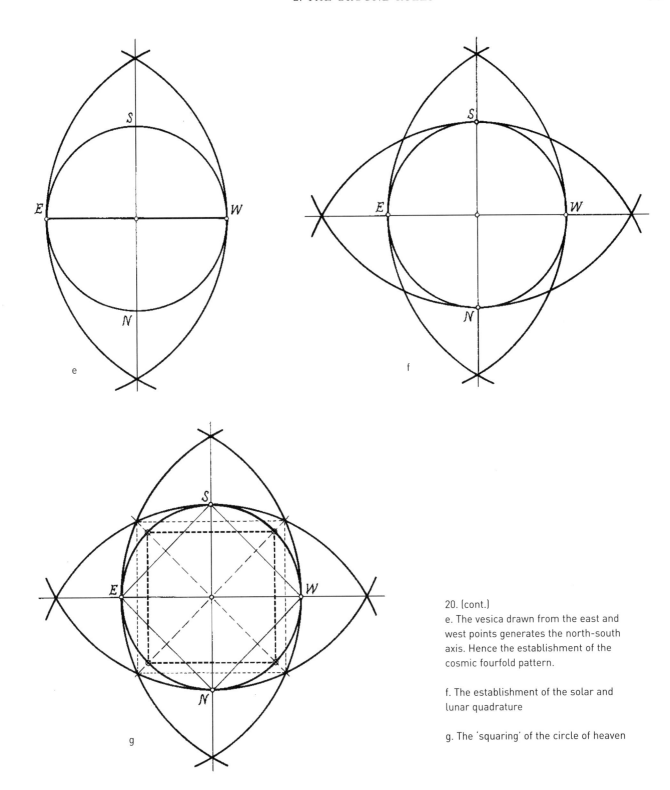

20. (cont.)
e. The vesica drawn from the east and west points generates the north-south axis. Hence the establishment of the cosmic fourfold pattern.

f. The establishment of the solar and lunar quadrature

g. The 'squaring' of the circle of heaven

'quadrature,' relates to both the solar cycle, solstices and equinoxes, and the four obviously recognizable phases of each lunar cycle and has also been called the squaring of the circle of heaven.* The elaboration of the plans of Hindu temples from this basic 'squaring' is a ritual expressive of Creation from its source, multiplicity reflecting Unity.

This procedure is a rite in the full meaning of the word, linking the form of the sanctuary as a microcosm to the solar system as the macrocosm. Orientation gives direction and is the vital factor in ensuring the effectiveness of a holy place. A clock face on which we measure the recurrent twelve-hour cycle orients us temporally in the day by remaining static relative to the hands which circulate as pointers. In a similar way the static primary circle of a temple is an unmoving presence (an eternity) against which we can measure our worldly eccentricity as we traverse the years and the circuits of our lives. As we shall see later, in the North American Indian tradition the 'circle of the year' represents the 'world,' an instantaneous image of the passing of time over the basic cosmic cycle: one complete planetary journey around the Sun.

Having cited two recorded traditions which involve sacred geometry we can test these principles on British stone circles. Before doing so, however, we must draw attention to the significant geometric fact that emerged from Professor Thom's surveys of many sites: more than one in three of the enclosures he has surveyed is geometrically more complex than the circle and many have a double centre. From his surveys Professor Thom discovered four basic

---

* By tradition the principle of duality or complementarity is considered to be expressed in the macrocosm by the primordial divergence of the axes of rotation of the Sun and Earth creating longest and shortest days in the year. This difference establishes in human experience the quadrature of the year. In other words, because of the differences in rotational axis we get a shortening of days in winter, a lengthening in summer, and the exact equation of nights and days in the spring and autumn.

   Titus Burkhardt, in commenting on the cosmology of Ibn Arabi, says: 'If the two great circles, that of the celestial equator and that of the solar cycle coincided, there would be no manifestation of the seasons. The divergence of the two great celestial cycles evidently expresses therefore the rupture of the equilibrium which engenders a certain order of manifestation, that is to say that of contrasts and of complementaries.'[16]

types of layout based on the circle, the ellipse, two types of 'flat-tened' circle (designated type A and type B by Professor Thom) and egg shapes developed from right-angled triangles.*

21.
Castle Rigg stone circle, Cumberland

---

* In a later publication, a fifth type has been added which is an egg-shaped circle with a semi-elliptical end, designated type III of the egg-shapes. See A. and A.S Thom, *Megalithic Remains in Britain and Brittany* (Oxford, 1978) p.18.

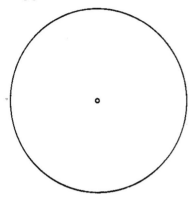

a.
The circle

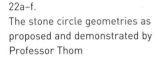

22a–f.
The stone circle geometries as proposed and demonstrated by Professor Thom

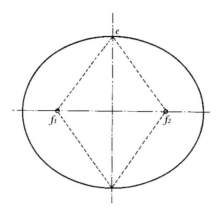

b.
The ellipse. This can be 'drawn' with a rope length equal to **f₁ef₂**. With a rope tied to fixed stakes **f₁** and **f₂** looped round a stake at **e** the stake at **e** when moved round keeping the rope **f₁ef₂** always tight scribes an ellipse on the ground. Professor Thom points out that not until Menaechmus, mid-fourth century BC, do we have documentation of the ellipse. Whereas in Britain it is certain that our forefathers were laying them out in the second millennium before Christ!

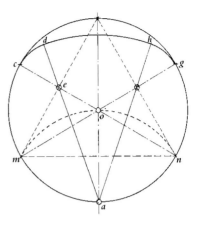

c.
Type A 'flattened' circle. To set this out one starts with a circular arc of 240° from centre **o** starting at **c** through **man** to **g**. The 120° angle **coa** is easily set up by making the two equilateral triangles **com** and **moa**. Next bisect **oc** at **e**. Then **e** is the centre of the arc **cd** (also by symmetry we can construct the arc **hg**). The remaining flattened arc **dh** is centred on **a** at the bottom.

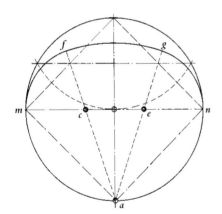

d.
Type B 'flattened' circle. To construct this ring is easier: first divide the diameter **mn** into three equal parts at **c** and **e**. These are then the centres for the smaller arcs **mf** and **gn**. As with type A the closing arc **fg** is struck with centre **a**.

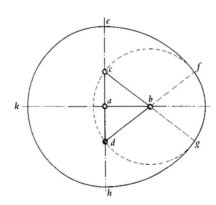

e.
Type I egg-shaped ring. This is based on constructing two right-angled triangles placed base to base (**abc** and **adb** along base **ab**). A semi-circle **ekh** is drawn with centre **a**. Next **d** is taken as centre and the arc **ef** drawn and with centre **c** the similar arc **gh** is drawn. The 'sharper' end of the egg is drawn from **f** to **g** with centre **b**.

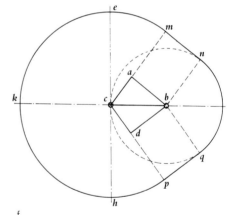

f.
Type II egg-shaped ring. This type has two straight lines joining its two arcs and therefore is not a continuous curved boundary. The right-angled triangles mirroring each other: **acb** and **cbd** are joined along the hypotenuse. A semi-circle **ekh** is drawn as before and then each end of the hypotenuse of the right-angled triangle is the centre of the larger and smaller arcs respectively: with centre **c** arcs **em** and **hp** are drawn and with centre **b** arc **nq**. The arcs are joined by straight lines **mn** and **pq** which are drawn parallel to the sides of the triangle **ab** and **cd** respectively.

The first circle we have chosen to examine is the beautifully sited Castle Rigg near Keswick in Cumberland. Professor Thom's accurate survey will be used as a starting point and, in the light of the remarkable number of coincidences between the geometry of the circle's layout and the astronomical requirements of a temple just described, Thom's proposals will be examined.

By using a statistical method Thom obtained (from his Castle Rigg survey) the curves of the flattened circle type A. When he examined in detail the positions of the stones they gave him seven solar and lunar readings; that is, major extremities in the cycles of the risings and settings of both Sun and Moon. Four of the azimuths giving these declinations are defined by the geometry of the type

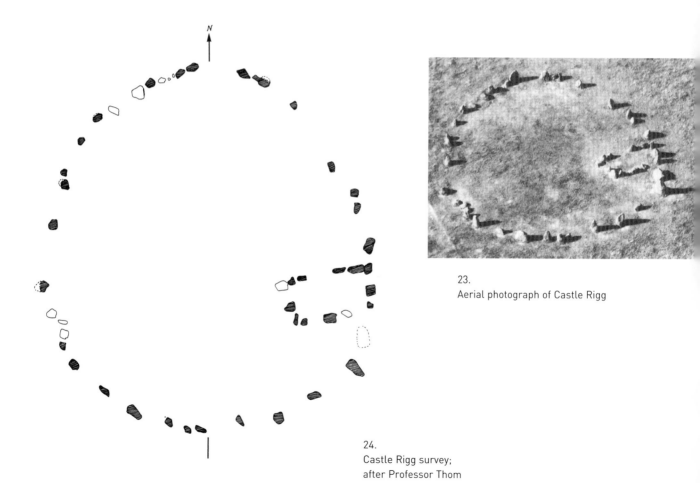

23.
Aerial photograph of Castle Rigg

24.
Castle Rigg survey;
after Professor Thom

25.
Stonehenge

A system.* Thom placed this proposed construction on the survey of the circle and found the axis of symmetry of the flattened circle (the line **bc** in Fig. 26) lay at an azimuth of 67° east of due north which he believes to be within a few fractions of a degree of the original orientation at the time of construction. He has remarked on the feat in siting that this represents, comparing it with the difficulty

---

* The azimuth of a star or terrestrial object defines the direction in the horizontal plane in which we have to look to see the star or object. Azimuth is measured in degrees clockwise from geographical north, not magnetic north which varies from year to year.

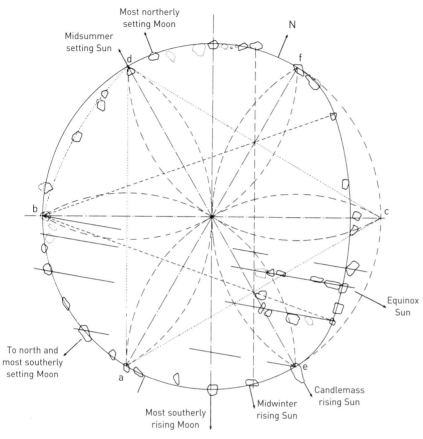

Most northerly
setting Moon

N

Midsummer
setting Sun

d

f

b

c

Equinox
Sun

To north and
most southerly
setting Moon

a

e

Candlemass
rising Sun

Midwinter
rising Sun

Most southerly
rising Moon

26.
Geometrical analysis of Castle Rigg based
on Professor Thom's type A system

a whole team of modern engineers would have and the time they would need to find a site with the right kind of horizon for viewing the rising and setting of the 'heavenly lights,' besides finding a conveniently flat part of a field on which to place the construction in relation to its horizon.

The degree of accuracy put forward by Thom for the Castle Rigg orientations means that more precise techniques than the ancient Hindu vertical pole shadow method must have been used: for a discussion of this point see Thom.[17] However, the significance of the first two arcs in the Hindu procedure may have held a similar symbolic value in relation to the actual Sun and Moon orientations as Castle Rigg. Lama Govinda, the German scholar and Buddhist who has become one of the most explicit interpreters

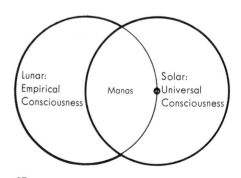

Lunar:
Empirical
Consciousness

Manas

Solar:
Universal
Consciousness

27.
Solar and lunar symbolism;
after Lama Govinda

of Buddhist psychology to the modern Western world, comments on the symbolic meaning behind the two overlapping circles. This interpretation ascribes universal consciousness (the realm of archetypes) to the first circle, and empirical consciousness to the second circle (that which 'sorts out and judges the results of the five kinds of sense consciousness') and finally *manas* to the area of overlap. *Manas* is described as the balancing consciousness that 'either binds us to the world of the senses or which liberates us from it.'[18] *Manas* has been etymologically linked via the archaic Indo-European language with the word 'man' — the conscious animal.

Govinda has this to say about *manas,* the overlapping region:

> the double character of *manas* which, though being without characteristics of its own, becomes a source of error if it is directed from the universal towards the individual, or in the opposite direction, from the individual towards the universal, it becomes a source of highest knowledge. The difference in the effect of these two directions may be compared to the vision of a man, who observes the manifold forms and colours of a landscape and feels himself different from it (as 'I' and 'there') — and the vision of another one who gazes into the depth of the firmament, which frees him of all object-perception and thus from the awareness of his own self as well, because he is only conscious of the infinity of space or of 'emptiness.' His 'I' here loses its position through lack of contrast or opposition, finding neither anything to grasp nor from which to differentiate itself.[19]

Thus the individual becomes integrated with the whole. These directions along the ontological axis are featured in the archaic shaman religion which we shall turn to later.

If we now transpose the symbols for universal consciousness, empirical consciousness and manas (balancing consciousness) into Sun, Moon and human consciousness, we have a basis upon which to suggest how the geometrical procedure might relate to Castle Rigg. In doing so we must keep in mind two of Professor Thom's major ideas. The first is that the flattening of the circle enabled a whole or rational number to replace the 'irrational'* circumference of a pure circle. Thom believes the builders of the circles abhorred 'incommensurable' lengths. The second is his calculation of the megalithic unit of measurement used in the construction of the circles.

If Socrates found it so difficult to circumscribe justice in the perfect state, why should we believe the great intellectuals of stone-building ancient Britain found it any easier? The establishment of justice in the administration of human affairs is facilitated by the standardization of conventions for number, weight and measure. It is for this reason as well as the knowledge of man's need to understand the rhythms of the cosmos, (rhythms which pacemake all biological events) that we are led to accept Professor Thom's findings on the existence and size of the megalithic yard (abbreviated to MY). The megalithic yard integrates the function of a number of conventions and astronomical measurement through the alignment of the stars. The dimension he arrived at by a statistical method was: one megalithic yard equals 2.72 feet. Without going into the process, we can summarize that he distilled this figure from 383 surveyed sites to an accuracy ± 0.003 of a foot. 'It is fortunate for us,' writes Professor Thom, 'that megalithic man liked, for some reason or another, to get as many as possible of the dimensions of his constructions to be multiples of his basic unit.' This was written in 1955, and all his subsequent work appears to confirm his calculation. He later introduces an interesting set of variations on an Iberian offshoot or related megalithic yard called the *vara* which is believed to have survived through the Spanish invasion and settlement of South America. Values, in feet, for the *vara* published by Professor Thom are as follows: 2.766, Burgos; 2.7425, Madrid; 2.749, Mexico; 2.778, Texas, California; 2.75, Peru. Like the yard and the French *verge,* the Spanish *vara* has an etymological root in the sense of 'a rod' which is much the same as the recently abandoned 'yardstick' of Britain and America. As for the medieval cathedral builders, the carrying of the measuring rod and compasses was the sign of authority and mastery and there is no reason to believe that peoples who could fashion such precise stone-tools and work decorative bone-ware were not capable of fashioning equally precise measuring rods.

---

* From the above comments of Lama Govinda, it can be seen why the circle and its *pi* characteristic can be either 'irrational' or 'transcendental' according to 'direction' viewed.

There were two 'prehistoric' measuring rods found, one in a Early Bronze Age burial mound at Borum Eshoj in East Jutland, Denmark, which was described by P.V. Glob in 1875 when it was uncovered, as being 30.9 (Danish) inches in length. Glob believed it was used to lay out the circular burial mound and thrown into the grave on interment. E. Mackie calculated that 30.9 Danish inches is 32.01 British inches or 0.813 metres, and so the length of the rod on discovery was 0.63 inches shorter than a megalithic yard — this difference may well have been shrinkage over the three thousand years within the grave.[21] The date has been estimated at the second millennium BC. Further interest is added by the fact that the rod is notched as follows: $^1/_5$, $^1/_5$, $^2/_5$, $^1/_5$. Mackie remarks that this could be a connection with the Sumerian *shusi* as each $^1/_5$ would be equivalent to 10 such *shusi*.

The second wooden rod is of the Iron Age and excavated at Borre Fen, a fort in Himmerland. This rod of oak was 53.15 inches with a button at one end and pointed at the other, and in this case divided into eight equal parts. Each division is given as 6.5 inches a pair making up 13.0 inches or a large foot. Yet if the total is equally divided the figure should be 6.64 inches. In this case five eighths of the rod would total 32.5 inches (or possibly 33.2 inches), as Mackie says, 'very close to the megalithic yard.'

Testing the ground rules

Taking the clues offered by the Hindu manuscripts in conjunction with Professor Thom's survey we will try the implication of these findings on Castle Rigg.

The builders of Castle Rigg found a site with a convenient horizon for measuring the exact sun-setting axis on midsummer day. This is the key axis of the year for it marks the turning point of the light of the Sun. The winter solstice is of equal cosmic importance but at the summer solstice the Sun is at the height of its power, clearing the skies for uninterrupted measurement. From this axis (**df** in Fig. 28a) a precise calendar can be constructed.

A full circle is drawn from centre **o** which we will propose symbolizes the solar circle (Fig. 28a). Although this $53^1/_2$ foot radius circle produces an irrational diameter (in terms of megalithic yards) this appears to allow the lunar orientations to be determined by the second circle which, according to our proposed symbolism, would be traditionally the Moon circle. This is constructed by placing its centre on the periphery of the solar circle at point **b**. The reason for the original radius becomes clear as our second circle establishes the Moon sighting (most southerly rising Moon) in this particular location from the direction **ofx**. Having chosen the centre, there would be only one radius that could produce this most southerly moon-rising axis and be part of the geometrically rational scheme uncovered by Thom.

In our illustration we have drawn the 'solar' circle (the main geometry of the stone circle), diameter **ab**, in heavier line and the secondary 'lunar' circle, radius **ob**, in the lighter line. Also shown is the next stage in the construction (with a dashed line): the drawing of a semi-circle of similar radius centred at **g** which indicates points **x** and **e**. This latter arc, by cutting the 'lunar' circle at **x**, gives the most southerly moon-rising axis **ofx**. Not only does it perform this function but it also sets up the 67 degree azimuth axis of the whole construction by cutting the solar circle at **e**. The line **eoc** is the central axis of the final flattened circle, and is 67° from the true north.

If the arc-making device (Fig. 28b) is now placed on point **e** and the second arc drawn from **g** to **a**, without changing the radius this re-affirms the midsummer solar setting axis (**boa**) on the opposite side of the 'solar' circle from the centre of the 'lunar' circle. Joining directly points **a, c** and **g** we obtain a perfect equilateral triangle pointing both in the direction of the symmetry of flattening toward **c** and the summer solstice sunset toward **a**. This also gives our *third* centre for obtaining the flattening, point **h**, which is the exact middle of the intersection of the solar and lunar circles — the original

28a–b.
The setting out of Castle Rigg

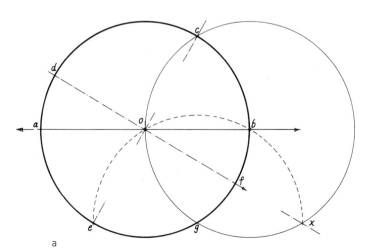

a

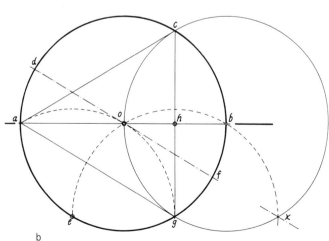

b

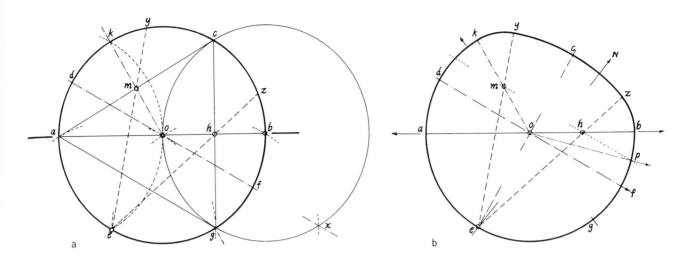

a

b

29a–b.
Geometrical analysis of Castle Rigg based
on Professor Thom's type A system

post position in the Hindu ritual. (The second centre for the flattening was at **e**.) These centres are required to construct the continuous
outline used for placing the stones in their final 'flattened' form.

The next arc in our procedure (Fig. 29a) is inscribed from **e** with
centre **a** through to **k**. If we now join **ok** both **ac** and **ok** are bisected
at **m**. Point **m** is our fourth and final centre for the construction of
the complete flattened circle outline.

We now have four positions and the appropriate radii to construct the shape which Thom calculated statistically most fitting
for the existing pattern of stones. In terms of reconstructing the
original ritual, the final shape can now be inscribed or ploughed
more heavily into the ground. Starting with our original circle, only
a proportion of the perimeter is used which is represented by an arc
that travels from **b** (the centre of the 'lunar' circle) clockwise round
to position **k**, the whole centred on point **o**. With point **m** (Fig. 29b)
becoming the next centre (radius **mk**, that is half the first circle
radius) an arc is drawn to point **y**, whose position is determined
by a line from **e** passing through **m**. At **y** the continuity of the
shape is taken up by moving the trammel to centre **e** and engraving an arc from **y** through direction point **c** to point **z**. Position **z**
is obtained in the same way as was position **y**: from **e** through **h**.
At **z** another small arc with radius one half of **ob** and centre at **h** is
drawn through to our starting-point at **b**. It is on this flattened circle
that Thom proposed the positions of the enclosure of stones were

set. Of the 31 stones still standing, 25 are either intersected by this construction or are tangent to it. Allowing for frost movements and deliberate deviations (the reasons for which are yet to be discovered) we find this degree of conformity statistically satisfactory to verify Thom's hypothesis.

There is a clue to what may have been further alignments in an arrangement or 'cove' within the circle on the eastern side (see Fig. 24, p.59). Thom demonstrated (Fig. 29b) that, should a line be drawn through points **m** and **h** and extended to the outer circle at **p**, we find a stone conveniently placed to sight over from the centre of the construction **o**. This line not only establishes the innermost limits of the cove but, in addition, the direction **op** gives a reading for the midwinter rising Sun, the day of rebirth of the year. The equinoctial rising Sun can be read over a stone at point **b** on which we established our construction and this axis (**ob**) also passes through three stones of the cove.

A neighbouring circle to Castle Rigg is Long Meg and her Daughters. Compared to some of the circles such as Allan Water and Moel Ty Uchaf, it is very large and is dominated by the huge presence of Long Meg herself, standing clear of the enclosure of her daughters.

30.
Aerial photograph of Long Meg

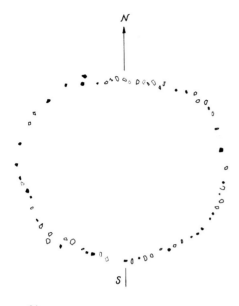

31.
Long Meg and her Daughters; survey
after Professor Thom

Long Meg's daughters (Fig. 31) conform to Thom's type B flattened circle and can be constructed with a fair degree of accuracy according to the procedure of the *Mānasāra Shilpa Shāstra* (Fig. 32a). The Hindu document prescribes that a circle would have been drawn around a gnomon pillar at the centre **z**, following which full circles are drawn centred at **a** and **b** (the east-west axis points) on the centre circle corresponding to those proposed by Thom. These two are not *precisely* east-west as the Indian document would have them, but when the north-south axis, which falls somewhere between true and magnetic north, is put in, using the upper and lower intersections of the fish-shape (**c** and **d**). We have drawn in the east-west arcs also to conform to the Indian practice, though the early British builders were obviously not concerned with making a square enclosure. There is however a possible function for position **t** as a centre to which we will return.

From here the procedure takes on a characteristically Hyperborean tone (Fig. 32b) and we see how the flattened circle is developed. Returning to the centre **z** and taking the most westerly and easterly points of our first two circles, **g** and **f** respectively, we have a new diameter set for us. We now follow the procedure,

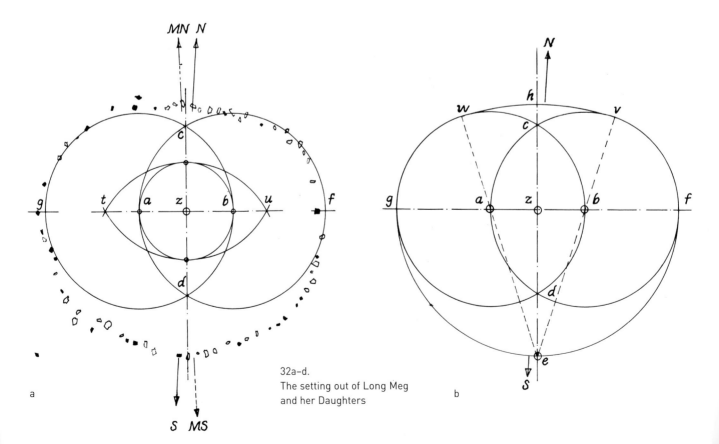

32a–d.
The setting out of Long Meg
and her Daughters

according to Thom, and cut a large semi-circle to the south from **g** to **f** with centre **z** and complete the Thom type B construction by linking the northerly points **w** and **v** with an arc centred at **e**: **w** and **v** are located exactly by respective axes from **e** through **a** and **b**.

We have still to locate the most dramatic member of this community, Long Meg herself, in the scheme of things (Fig. 32c, below). By exploring the natural divisions of the *full* circle diameter **gzf** and taking point **g** as the centre for a full circle of the same radius it marginally encloses Long Meg at its most southerly point. Now, by observing true north and taking the south direction from the centre **z**, we cut the large circle at stone **o**. By placing the compass on this south point of the circle we find that our arc of the same radius cuts right through Long Meg. If we do the same from point **p** to establish point **k** at the northerly extreme of the dashed circle, this north point sets up a true north tangent to a point due west of the centre **z** (just north of point **g**) sighting just inside the three deviant stones outside the circle to the west. Meg is thereby due south from point **g**. So we can say Long Meg is aligned in the sense that she is due true south from the westernmost point of her daughters' circle.

33.
Long Meg, near Penrith, Cumbria

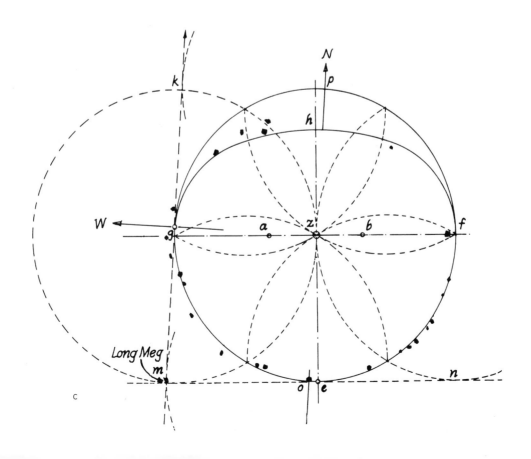

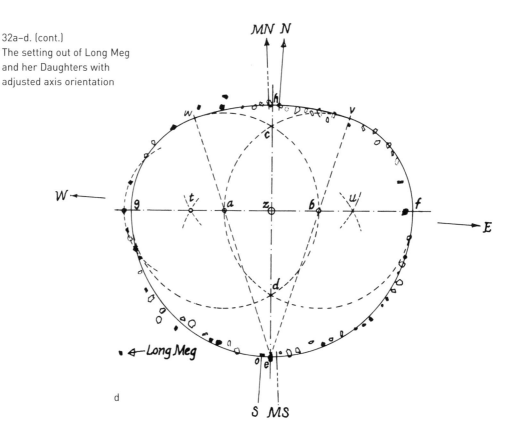

32a–d. (cont.)
The setting out of Long Meg
and her Daughters with
adjusted axis orientation

d

Finally we have the complete construction (Fig. 32d) with the suggestion for a possible function for point **t**. We find if we draw a circle centred at **t** with an approximate 85-foot (31¼ MY) radius, it intersects the three stones outside **g**. Strangely, the eastern axial stone (inside **f**) does not conform to this circle geometry, yet it does fall on the axis. Maybe this was deliberately done to establish the distance between the outer extremities of these two stones which curiously measures 365 feet. Unfortunately this idea causes more problems than it solves as we have no particular evidence of the use of the British foot at so early a date. The dimension's reflection of a solar figure for the days of the year, however, puts it well within the bounds of possibility. After all, the foot is reputedly a *human* measure whatever other claims may have been made for it, and we can be certain that the megalithic builders also paced across these sacred areas on their feet!

Also, because **zb** is one-sixth of **fg**, the diameter of the 'solar' circle, this represents a division into twelve equal parts of the whole circle, which could be interpreted as the twelvefold division that is traditionally called the fixed stars. These are the background of 'static' constellations against which astronomers measure the transits or movements of the Sun, Moon and planets of our system. Thus with amazing adroitness, no doubt the result of long deliberation, two intersecting circles and a third linking arc, all of the same dimension, simultaneously establish a fundamental orientational pattern and become the basis of a totally integrated symbolic and physical system.

Now we turn to the Midlothian circle known as Borrowstone Rig (Fig. 34a–b). Although there are only ten stones remaining upright in this unusually large enclosure they all accord well with Professor Thom's proposed geometry for a type II egg-shaped ring. Taking the survey of Professor Thom as our starting-point we accept the hypothesis in principle of the two circles which are found by straight lines as the determining geometry of the 'circle.'

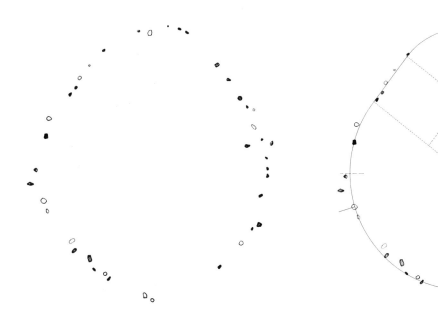

34a.
Borrowstone Rig; survey after Professor Thom

34b.
Professor Thom's proposed geometry

Firstly we explore the possibility of a method for 'founding' this geometry (Fig. 35) which would be similar in principle to the ancient Vedic method as recorded in the *Mānasāra Shilpa Shāstra*. This means that the diameter of the primary circle of the Vedic method (**aob**) is the same as the radius of the smaller circle as suggested by Professor Thom in the establishing of this circle as a type II egg-shaped ring, that is, $15^1/_2$ MY.

If we follow the procedure for orientation — the cardinal directions as described in the ancient Vedic manuscript — we would expect a shadow pole to be set at **o**, next a circle described around it with diameter **ab** (in this case $15^1/_2$ MY), followed by the establishment of the east-west axis by the tip of the shadow of the central pole cutting the circle in the morning and evening respectively. Having transferred this axis through the centre of the circle at **o** two circles of $15^1/_2$ MY radius are now inscribed, one with a centre at **a** and the other with its centre at **b**. The **a** centred circle is identical to the small arc Professor Thom proposes for the overall 'egg' form of the structure. Next the change in orientation of the overall 'egg' form needs establishing as its central axis is not due east-west but rotated some 12 degrees south of due east and north of due west. The following proposal is suggested for this shift in orientation: the two circles with radii of $15^1/_2$ MY with centres **a** and **b** intersect at **c** due north from **o** and at **d** due south from **o**. If one then connects these four points **a**, **c**, **c**, **d**, a 'diamond' form is described which is made up of two equilateral triangles **abc**, **abd**. Next the centre line of this 'diamond' form is drawn from **c** to **d** followed by the two further axes of symmetry of each of the two equilateral triangles: from point **b** to point **e** and from point **a** to point **f** in the triangle **abc**, and similarly points **g** and **h** connect to **b** and **a** respectively in triangle **abd**. This establishes two new centres for smaller circles, **m** and **n** respectively. The sizes of the circles are obtained by a radius equal to **mo** and **no**, respectively. When inscribed these circles cut the original circle (diameter **ab**) at the very points **e**, **f**, **g**, and **h**. Now the point of this procedure is to inscribe this smallest circle at centre **b**. Because when we do so it cuts the largest circle with centre **a** at the point **k**. Now a line which passes through **a** and **k** becomes the central axis of the overall 'egg' geometry of the stone 'circle' and point **k** becomes the centre of the larger of Professor Thom's proposed arcs for the larger arc of the 'egg' construction, that is a circle with a radius of 25 MY. The north-south axis can now be transferred to point **k**.

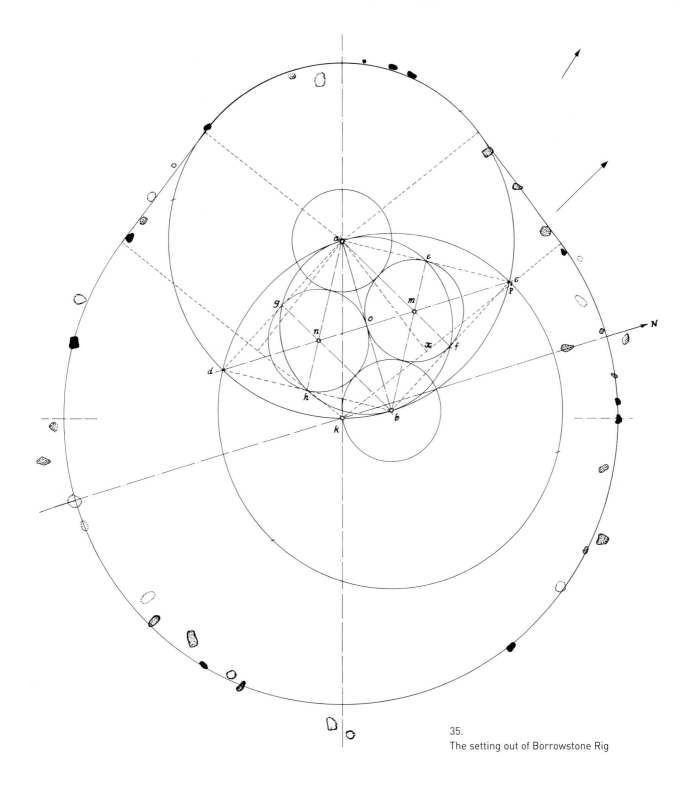

35.
The setting out of Borrowstone Rig

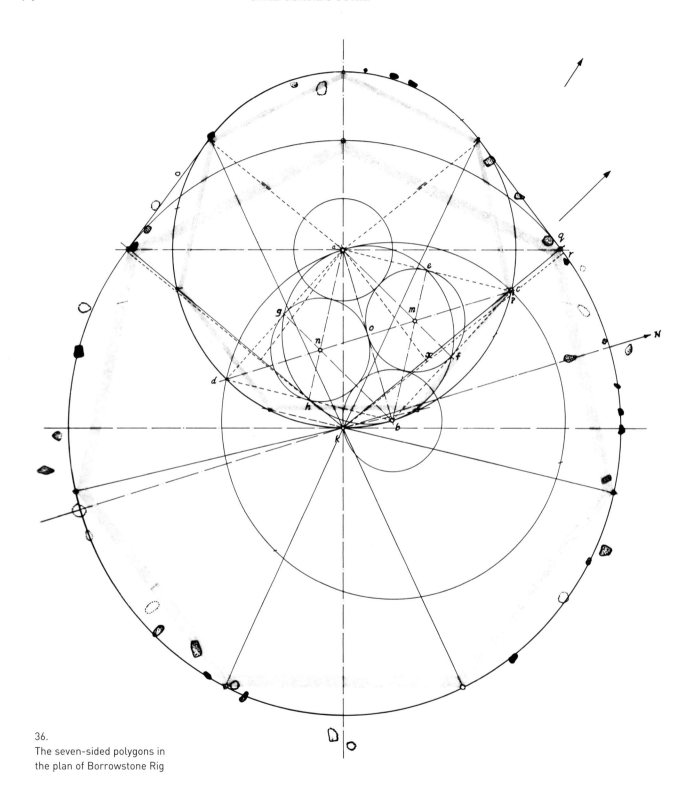

36.
The seven-sided polygons in
the plan of Borrowstone Rig

Professor Thom has remarked how unusual this particular construction is and the very small, hardly perceptible, discrepancy in the Pythagorean triangle **akx** whose sides are $15^1/_2$ MY, $12^1/_4$ MY and $9^1/_2$ MY (see Fig. 34b). If one squares $15^1/_2$ it equals 240.25 and if one squares $9^1/_2$ it equals 90.25 which when added to $12^1/_4$ squared (150.0625) totals 240.3125 giving a Pythagorean discrepancy of 0.0625 or 2 inches! Nevertheless this discrepancy could be taken as a hint that other values, both geometric and numerical, were being incorporated into the layout; there would be no obvious reason why any discrepancy need be built into such a construction as 'perfect' Pythagorean triangles were normally used at this time.

A critical comparison between the Vedic procedure described above and the geometrical construction proposed by Professor Thom reveals that point **c** (the northern intersection) is about $^1/_4$ MY west of Thom's northerly limits of the radius of the greater arc of the egg construction (from a point marked **p**), that is one degree from centre **k**. Moving less than half a degree further to the west from centre **k** gives another remarkable coincidence: the close coincidence of the geometry proposed by Professor Thom to two-sevenths of a circle in the smaller arc and five-sevenths in the larger. The closeness of the three 'processes' led us to believe that they were deliberate ingredients: that is the Vedic orientational procedure, the Pythagorean triangulation and the sevenfold division of the circles, each contributing to the 'cosmological' significance of reconciling 'rationals' and 'transcendental' values through geometry and number.

Figure 36 demonstrates the sevenfold interpretation of the completed circles proposed by Thom for the arcs of the 'egg' form. The precise sevenfold geometry moves away from the Pythagorean triangle but fits the overall profile quite as accurately. Interestingly the centre axis of the smaller western circle, set at right angles to the main axis of the egg form, more nearly coincides with the sevenfold division point **q** than the Pythagorean tangent point **r**. From the development of the thesis of this book the appearance of the heptagonal pattern integrated within the temple shape should not be surprising due to the traditional cosmological significance this number holds. However, the subtlety of meaning this particular shape held for the builders — the way one sevenfold symmetry 'grows out of' the other — is still far from understood but our diagram shows certain linear symmetrical coincidents between the two sevenfold divisions of both smaller and greater circles which add to our admiration for the 'mathematics' of the builders.

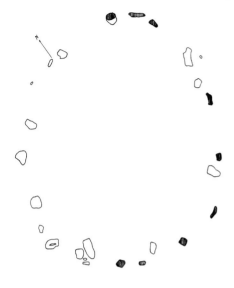

37.
Allan Water; survey after Professor Thom

38.
Allan Water stone circle, Hawick area,
Scotland, looking north-northeast from
within the circle

From Borrowstone Rig we travel across Midlothian to another, smaller but beautifully egg-shaped enclosure known as Allan Water (Fig. 37), high up on a hill above the lake that lends its name to the site. Allan Water has nine stones still standing in their original positions and at least twelve stones of a similar size lying recumbent around the perimeter.

Although this is the fourth site we are analysing it was in fact the first to be discovered to have a star polygon in its construction. Llewelyn Vaughn-Lee, whilst a student and co-researcher of the author, had the insight to see the nine-sided star polygon within this particular circle. From this insight our analyses have developed. It is of interest to note that our three examples have minor discrepancies as far as the strictly megalithic yard interpretation of Professor Thom is concerned, as he readily points out in his own book. We believe, however, that these serve to reinforce the general thesis of megalithic man's mathematical ability, as they are seen to be an adjustment to achieve an even subtler embodiment of form in the circle temples.

A close look at this circle of Allan Water (Fig. 40) reveals the subtlety of its reconciliation between geometry and arithmetic. Thom points out that a different unit of measure, in this case $^1/_2$ MY, was taken for this form, in itself an interesting fact, and this produced an imperceptible discrepancy of 1 in 580 which we could consider an adjustment to allow the smaller arc to achieve its nine-foldness. This gives a breathing space between the numerically 'irrational' (transcendental) geometric proportion and the 'rational' measurements of megalithic yards.

Figure 40 is a schematic representation of Thom's proposals for the controlling geometry parallel with the development of the main divisions of the enneagon (nine-pointed star). We propose to use the two overlapping circles with their symbolisms of Sun and Moon, but not in this case giving rise to the cardinal directions. As we proceed, however, the north direction does become established.

Thus with centre **o** and a radius of 8 MY we draw the primary circle. Taking the same radius and placing the new centre **y** on the upper periphery of the primary circle a new circle is drawn which intersects the primary circle at points **b** and **c** and creates our recurrent fish-shape. The central axis of the fish (**cb**) cuts the central vertical axis in the drawing at point **p** which is 4 MY above the primary centre **o**. Having established point **p**, the exact centre of the fish-shape, the next procedure is to establish a tangent to the lower circle at **o** at right-angles to the vertical axis. We suggest that the builders could have taken $2^1/_2$ MY up from the point **p** towards **y** to establish the centre **m**. It is at this point that the Pythagorean triangle suggested by Thom enables us to establish the right angle at **o**, by firstly, with centre **m**, cutting two arcs of $8^1/_2$ MY radius thus approximately fixing points **r** and **s** as falling somewhere on these arcs. Secondly, with the trammel centred at **o** and with a radius of $6^1/_2$ MY two further arcs are drawn and their intersection with the first two arcs precisely establishes **r** and **s**.

The four points **r**, **o**, **s** and **m** are those that Professor Thom proposes as the respective centres of the four arcs which constitutes the egg-shaped profile on whose perimeter the stones are placed. These points make up two mirror-image Pythagorean triangles (**mor** and **mos**) whose sides measure $8^1/_2$ MY, $6^1/_2$ MY and $5^1/_2$ MY. Based on $^1/_2$ MY units we have sides of 17, 13 and 11 units which, when put to the Pythagorean test, gives us $11^2 \times 13^2$ equals 290 and 17^2 equals 289. 'The discrepancy in the hypotenuse is only 1 in 580 and would hardly be appreciable' as Thom puts it.[22]

39.

The geometrical structure of Allan Water showing the two nine-sided star polygons within the circle

40.

Schema of controlling geometry. Basic Pythagorean triangles of 11, 13, and 17.

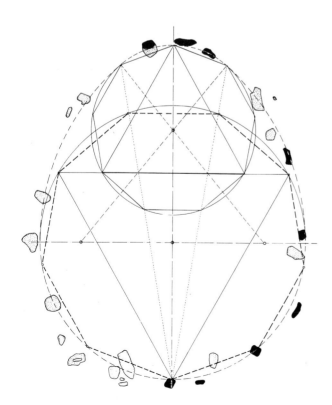

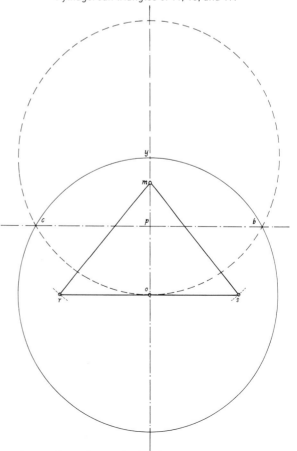

In order to draw the complete outline of the egg-shape (Fig. 41a), each centre determines a special segment of a circle to form a continuous outline. Firstly, the centre **o** and radius **ox** determines the bottom semi-circle. Secondly, the centres **r** and **s** and radius **re** and **sd** (13$^1/_2$ MY) determine the lateral curves from **x** to **e** and **z** to **d** respectively. Finally, with centre **m** and radius **me** an arc joins **d** to **e** to complete the outline.

We have already a completed circle from centre **o** (our primary circle) (Fig. 41b) and if we now complete the circle centred on **m** with radius **me,** the arc of which **de** provided the final section of the Allan Water layout, we find that although the relationship between the larger and smaller circles is not the same as became obvious in the Borrowstone Rig geometry, a new significance emerges whereby the proportion of nine is established. The points **c, b** and **f** when joined, describe an equilateral triangle in the larger circle the top edge of which cuts across the upper smaller circle at **g** and **h**. The line (**gh**) also establishes the base of an equilateral triangle contained in the smaller circle (**ghk**).

41a–b.
The setting out of Allan Water

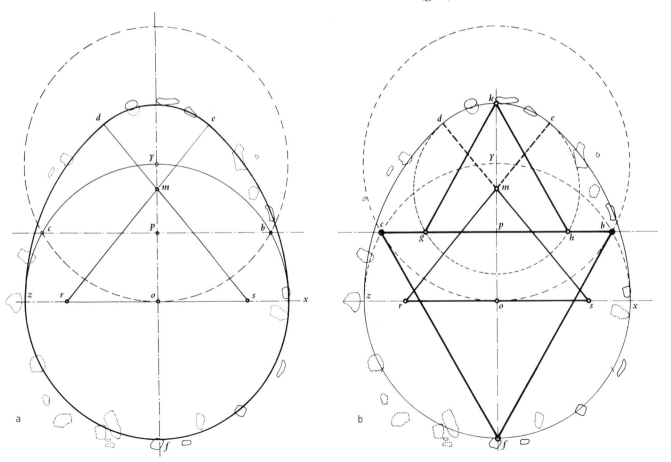

If we take the sides of the right- and left-hand Pythagorean triangles (Fig. 42a) and extend their hypotenuse — from **s** through **m** and from **r** through **m** — until they cut the perimeter of the egg form, we find that these divide the perimeter of the smaller circle into two-ninths, sector **dke**. This means that from either **d** or **e** on this smaller circle two other equilateral triangles can be constructed $dd_1 d_2$ and $ee_1 e_2$ within the circle and these exactly cross over the first triangle based on the **bc** axis so as to make up a regular nine-pointed star. In our next illustration (Fig. 42b) the two nine-sided polygons are drawn which bound the nine-pointed stars with their primary equilateral triangles.

Once again we have a remarkable set of reconciliations between the whole numbers, the 'earthly' and measurable, (qualities represented by the Pythagorean triangles) and the transcendental ratios represented in this case by the ninefold polygon with its root three properties. We have no doubt that there are more subtleties, not only within this 'circle' but probably the vast majority of stone circles. They were certainly put together with a totally different attitude and knowledge from that which motivates the construction of a large building today.

42a–b.
The ninefold nature of the setting out of Allan Water

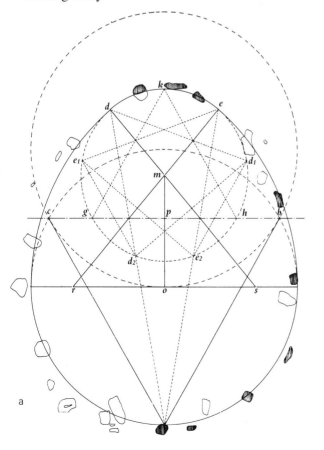

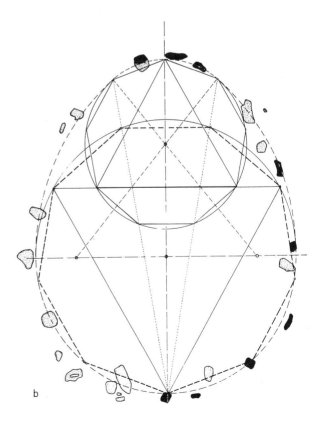

43.
Ring of Brodgar, mainland Orkney

3. Significant Number

*You see there is significance for everything, and these
(numbers) are the things that are good for men to know,
and to remember.*

    Black Elk[1]

*All that has by nature with systematic method been arranged
in the universe seems both in part and as a whole to have been
determined and ordered in accordance with number, by the
forethought and the mind of him that created all things.*

    Nichomachus of Gerasa[2]

*Every diagram, system of numbers, every scheme of harmony,
every law of the movement of the stars, ought to appear one to
him who studies rightly.*

    Plato[3]

Ancient shamanism and northern mythology

Shamanism has been described as a surviving form of an archaic
religion. It has been studied as far afield as Siberia, North and South
America, Indonesia and the Pacific Islands. Religious techniques,
common to shamanism, survive in Tibetan Buddhism, Tantrism and
certain aspects of Islam. Eliade's monumental work, *Shamanism:
Archaic Techniques of Ecstasy,* has placed shamanism among the
acceptable subjects of comparative religion. When Western scholars were first confronted by the ecstatic technique of shamans they
found it quite illogical and could therefore classify it only as a form
of 'primitive' madness. However difficult analysis and understanding of the techniques of shamanistic ecstasy are, and were, for
Western observers, what does stand out as strictly determined is
the fundamental structure of their cosmology: particularly in the
numbers of 'heavens' which are given as seven or nine according
to perspective and circumstance. In this chapter, our investigations will be focussed on these two particular numbers as both are

revealed in the mythological structure, not only of shamanism but of the sagas of the Celtic races, who latterly inhabited the areas of the stone circles.

Elémire Zolla, Professor of Philology at the University of Genoa, puts forward a personal conviction that language carries its own archaeology in its etymological roots. In a recent publication he suggests a common structural cosmogony for all Indo-European languages:

> by the use we make of Indo-European roots, we affirm implicitly the cosmological process which is described in the Vedic Scriptures. Every root that gives birth to words meaning 'Oneness' will also give birth to the *nine* following layers of meaning representing the nine stages of manifestation.[4]

It is important to remember that these 'stages' of manifestation are part of an 'ever present' structure of creation that both the shaman or mystic are concerned with attuning to — an integrative understanding of the physical world is the end result of the process.

The *worldly* nature of the shaman among the Papago Indians has been strongly commented on by Ruth M. Underhill who was working with them up to 1935. The shaman, she said, paid for his eminence with the constant threat to his life. At the risk of lynching he must know in advance the correct outcome of war and the local games as, if he failed, he had no equivocation ready. Only the bold, astute and exceptional could survive by the accuracy of their visions and the effectiveness of their information. Sorcery was absolutely forbidden and a shaman's family could be killed if it were proved that he was using this. His role was one of diviner and prophet.

The central anchor of shamanistic cosmology is the symbol of unity exemplified by the unmoving Pole Star, so vital, according to Thom, for the orientation of the northern British circles. This star established the unitary axis of the cosmos and has various denominations depending on region. The Konyak and the Chukchee call it the Nail Star, the Samoyed call it the Sky Nail, and similar imagery is found among the Lapps, Finns and Estonians. Further south and east the image of a pillar becomes connected with the star: the Golden Pillar of the Mongols; the Iron Pillar of the Kirgis, the Bashkir and the Siberian Tartars; the Solar Pillar of the Teleut, and so on. It seems certain that there is a direct symbolic reflection of the 'World Pillar' (to which all the other stars are 'tethered like a herd of horses') in the central stake used as a gnomon for geometric and astronomic orientation in the layout of the stone circles.

In the domestic dwellings (or yurt) of certain of these peoples the sacred pillar is replaced by the hole in the apex of the roof through which the smoke escapes. The Ostyak for example speak of the 'golden flues of the Sky House,' and the 'seven flues of the Sky God,' and it is through these 'flues' that the shaman in this case passes from one cosmic zone to another. Thus from here is obtained the significant number of heavenly divisions on the vertical axis. It is this transcendence up the vertical axis which links the cosmology of the shamans and the great Celtic sagas.

In the ancient Irish sagas the paradisic world on the ontological axis is variously called the 'land of the young' or 'the delightful plain.' It was visited occasionally by mortals whose trips were referred to as *echtrai* (adventures) or *baili* (vision ecstasies). Their destination was the 'land of promise' or the world of the source of supernatural knowledge. One significant saga is that of the God Midir of Bri Leith which links the gods of the Sid-Mounds (the barrows) with the gods of rebirth. It tells of the claims of Midir on Etain, his wife in a former existence, who was separated from him by the magic of a jealous rival. Etain then married Eochaid, King of Tara and Midir schemed to reclaim her. Eochaid accepted Midir's challenge to play two games of chess; Midir won the second game and came to claim Etain, his prize, at a feast at the court of King Eochaid. The entrances to the 'hall' were all barred, whereupon Midir miraculously appeared in their midst in great supernatural beauty and carried Etain off through the smoke hole in the roof.

The number of heavens, or transcendental planes, that the shamans experienced when their souls travelled up the vertical, ontological axis becomes particularly significant when one imagines what graphic symbols would be appropriate to signify these heavenly realms in 'our' world. As we have stated, the two most recurrent and significant numbers in shamanistic cosmology are seven and nine. In the language of geometry (geo-metry as earth-measure) these 'dimensions' of heaven may be represented in simultaneous form by a seven-sided shape or nine-sided shape within a circle; thereby the 'dimensions' of the transcendental world are expressed in concentric rather than serial form.

To explore this phenomenon of polygons within circles and the associated stars we can start with the pure circle and cut off nine

44a-e.

The four ways of symmetrically joining nine points equally distributed on a circle

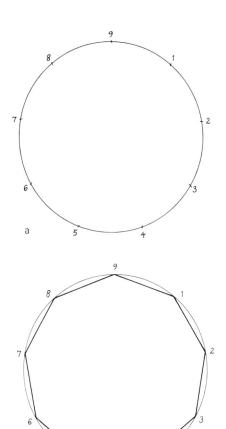

equal intervals — a construction we have already covered (see Figs. 44a–e). To make the polygon or nine-sided shape we simply connect up the points one by one or we can trace one of the following patterns. We can make a linear path around the nine points by missing every other point and travelling in the following sequence: 9, 2, 4, 6, 8, 1, 3, 5, 7 and back to 9. This results in a 'blunt' nine-pointed star. If we miss two points in the sequence we do not get a continuous flow, but rather three intersecting equilateral triangles. The fourth version becomes the most interesting because it contains all the other versions within itself. This star is created by following the sequence: 9, 4, 8, 3, 7, 2, 6, 1, 5, 9.

The development and application of the geometry of seven and nine in the breastplates of the Bush and Clandon Barrows in southern England will be demonstrated later (see Chapter 6). Here further examples of the numbers themselves will be discussed. Some of these examples are as far apart, both ethnically and seemingly culturally, as the Ngadju Dyak of South Borneo and the Ostyak and Lapp shamans of the far north. For instance Eliade believes that the semitic seven-branched Cosmic Tree can be identified with the seven planetary heavens and may be due to influences originating in Mesopotamia. But he does not think this in any way implies an oriental transfer of the ideas to the Siberian shamans, as the axial ascent up the world 'tree' or pillar is a universal and archetypal idea.

The Altaic shaman uses a post with seven or nine notches (tapty) to represent the celestial levels. There are obstacles (pudak) to be overcome at the entrances to the respective heavens. Similar symbolism is found amongst the Yakut and Sibo who journey ecstatically through seven or nine celestial regions. The Ostyak's Cosmic

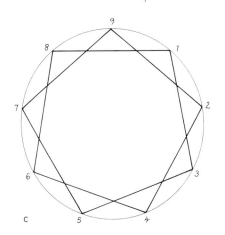

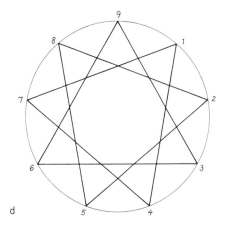

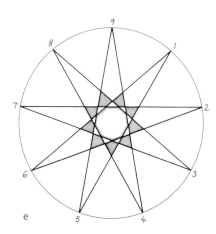

45.
The Menorah, or seven-branched
Hebrew candlestick, representing
the seven-branched Tree of Life

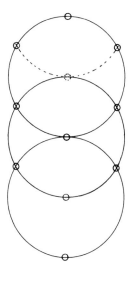

46.
Geometric construction of
the Tree of Life, see Shimon
Halevi's *Kabbalistic Universe*

Pillar has seven notches which we believe could reflect the archaic genesis of all notched measuring rods.[*]

It is also a common recurrence to find the reflection of the number of heavens above with the underworlds below in most north and central Asian peoples. For the Altaic shaman the problems of passing through the obstacles of the underworld were similar to those

---

[*] The seven-foot measuring rod of the medieval European builders has been a mystery to architectural historians, but it quite possibly has connections with both the ancient Egyptian rods on the one hand and the seven gifts of the holy spirit on the other. The extra foot above the head, it has been suggested, might be a spiritual rank amongst true master masons of this period of Christianity. It may also relate to the seven liberal arts and the Moon cycle.

of traversing the seven consecutive obstacles of the heavenly world.
Eliade also draws attention to the occurrence of these numbers in
Oceana for the celestial regions. Although he puts their dissemination
down to archaic shamanistic influence, he also believes that they cannot now be separated from Indian (Buddhist and Hindu) influences
that have since been superimposed. This connection with Buddhism
and Hinduism reminds us of their three primary realms: heaven, earth
and man. Eliade states his conviction that three times the primary
three is the basis of the nine realms.[5]

Returning to our graphic representation, if we draw a line from
the centre of the heavenly circle to the centre of the earthly circle,
we have represented the ontological axis or the pole of ascent. It
can be seen that the three becomes nine if each realm is described
in terms of its relation to each other: earth relates to itself, mankind
and heaven, its source; mankind takes the central role of linking
heaven, the source and archetypal world, to both itself and the earth;
heaven is self-sufficient but also relates to its two major creations,
mankind and the earth. Hence the three are essentially nine, by
reflection.

As another way of accounting further significance of nine, Rhys
has suggested it be related to the ancient Aryan eight-day week,
which was arrived at by the northern convention of counting nine
nights each side of the eight days.[6] A further expression of this in
mythological terms was the eight rings that dropped from Odin's

47.
The three primary realms,
a schema common to many
traditions

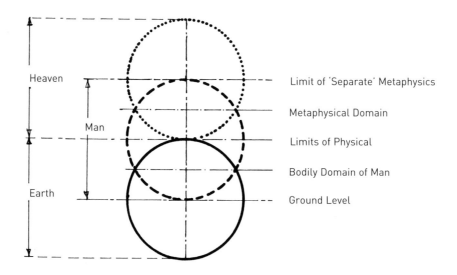

ring every ninth night, as also that Odin rode an eight-footed steed.[7] The battle between warmth and cold plays an understandably large part in the Eddic mythology; this also relates it to the universal fertility cycle which underlies all mythologies to a great extent — as it is the rhythm of life itself. In the *Thrymskvitha* legend one version has Niord, patron of the sea and consort of Skaldi, goddess of snow-skates, singing:

> I love not the mountains, I dwell not long in them.
>   Nine nights only;
> Sweeter to me is the song of the swan than the wild
>   wolf's howl.[8]

Skaldi replies to this song that she is disturbed by the screaming of the sea-birds.

Their marriage represented the relationship between the three summer months of the life of the flowing waters of the sea and nine winter months of gestation of the snow maiden Skaldi. Here the Nordic experience was a direct parallel between the gestation of vegetative and human life and gives a basis for the division of the year into threes.

Odin, Thor and Frey, chief of the Nordic gods, and related to the three roots of the Yggdrasil or sacred tree — the northern version of the ontological axis linking centrally the three cosmic regions — affirm the primordiality of three and its natural reflection in three times three or nine.[9] This is brought out in another context in the Eddic poem the *Havamal*. Here the God Odin is represented in a form of crucifixion — or spirit impaled in matter — one way of demonstrating, in a mythological structure, the ultimate 'imprisoning' of being in the last stages of the cosmogonic structure:

> I know that I hung
> On the wind-stirred tree
> Nine nights long
> Wounded by spear
> Consecrated to Odin
> Myself to myself;
> On the mighty tree
> Of which no man knows
> Of which no man knows
> Out of what root it sprang.[10]

48.
Devil's Den, Wiltshire

However in this story Odin also after great personal suffering managed to bring the knowledge of the runes back down to Earth. As if to further emphasize this cosmic structure, we also learn that the roots of the Yggdrasil are in the nine worlds or 'dark hell' of *Niflhel,* the home of the dead. There are also records of a festival or fertility feast recurring every nine years, believed to be on the equinox and lasting nine days in Uppsala, according to Adam of Bremen.[11] This curious interweaving of cosmic rhythms and ontological states is further emphasized by the enforced delay in the marriage of Frey to Gerda by nine nights, and the nine giantesses on the edge of the sea and land who mothered Heindall, watchman of the Norse Gods.[12] Another example is found in the rhythmic battle between Thor and the sea serpent, when he takes nine paces in his march against his foe only to be 'slain' himself at the approach of each winter.

Returning to the Celts: the Irish are on record as having denoted a length of time by the term *nomaid* (or *nomad*) which because of its root *noi,* (nine) meant some sort of division into nine.[13] Possibly there is a connection with the Nordic nine-month and nine-night system. In the great Cuchullin saga, Conchobar sent out nine men to seek a wife for Cuchullin, and his house had nine compartments, an echo possibly of the divisions at the centre of the Bush Barrow template, a subject of detailed examination in a later chapter.

The following examples demonstrate the significance of nine for the Celtic peoples. In the *Vita Merlini* Merlin had nine bards and there were nine dragons.[14] Nine witches are mentioned in *Peredur.*[15] Beowulf slew nine *nicors,* and the Fortunate Isles were ruled over by nine sisters.[16] Perhaps they were feminine relatives of Skaldi, the snow-skates consort of Odin? Could they also be related to the wonderful cauldron of the Head of Hades, kept boiling by the breath of nine maidens?[17] Uther Pendragon claims 'a ninth part in the prowess of Arthur' in the *Book of Taliesin.*[18] In the 'Kulhwch and Olwen' Kei could exist nine nights and nine days without sleep, and Bedwyr's spear made nine wounds as it was withdrawn.

Myths and sagas in the oral tradition embody a total cosmology — an integration of psychology, number and cosmic rhythms. The original form of transmission of these sagas was the spoken word, as in the great tales of Homer. The mistake that has been made for too long now is to necessarily equate an alphabet and a recorded numerical system with the ability for abstract thought. Maybe our own inability for the *Gestalt* experience is an inverse reflection of an earlier phase of mankind, who refused to break up the totality of experience by the replacement mechanism of an abstract sign language and preferred the oral and craft tradition for transmitting wisdom. We have the remarkable testament of Julius Caesar who described the threefold nature of the 'Gaulish' society: Plebs (the husbandmen), Equates (the warriors), and Druides (the philosopher-priests). Of the latter he elaborates:

> It is said that they commit to memory immense amounts of poetry and some of them continue their studies for twenty years. They consider it improper to commit their studies to writing, although they use the Greek alphabet for almost everything else. They have

also much knowledge of the stars and their motion, of the size of the world and of the earth, of natural philosophy, and of the powers and spheres of action of the immortal gods, which they discuss and hand down to their young students.[19]

Myles Dillon and Nora Chadwick, the contemporary Celtic authorities, like Professor Zolla of Genoa, say that they are overwhelmed by the evidence linking the Celtic and ancient Indian Vedic civilizations. Speaking of the ancient Irish philosophers, known as the *filid,* who maintained a similar oral tradition, they say that 'both the form and content of their learning shows astonishing similarity to brahmical society.'[20] They go on to assume a link between *filid,* druid and brahmin inherited from a common tradition, which serves to reinforce the theory that there may have been an extensive archaic Indo-European culture.

There is also evidence that the druid oral tradition was taught in triads, that is in short poems with a content of three elements. In the case of the ancient Welsh triads the letters of the alphabet were themselves composed of three basic elements. A similar parallel can be seen in ancient China: when Confucianism became the state philosophy a certain scholar, Wang Ying-Lin (1223–96), was reputed to have committed to writing a previously ancient oral tradition in the form of *The Three Character Classic* (San Tsu Ching).[21] Two relevant examples of these Chinese triads are numbers 13 and 14: 'Three mighty powers; Heaven, Earth and Man,' 'Three great lights; Sun, Moon and Stars'; the first of which has become known as the Far Eastern Triad.

Chadwick and Dillon believe that the same Celtic peoples inhabited the British islands up to two thousand years before the arrival of the Romans. What is certain is that Caesar records the Druides as having 'much knowledge of the stars and their motion.' Whether the Celts are the actual descendants of the circle builders is not so important as that they most probably inherited the astronomical and philosophical wisdom of their predecessors. To have 'much knowledge of the stars' one needs to have a technique for applying, measuring and checking such knowledge. Caesar's report would imply that they certainly inherited the knowledge of how to use the stone circles even if they were not the originators. He also tells us that the Gauls worshipped Mercury, Apollo, Mars, Jupiter and Minerva — five named deities which have upset scholars because

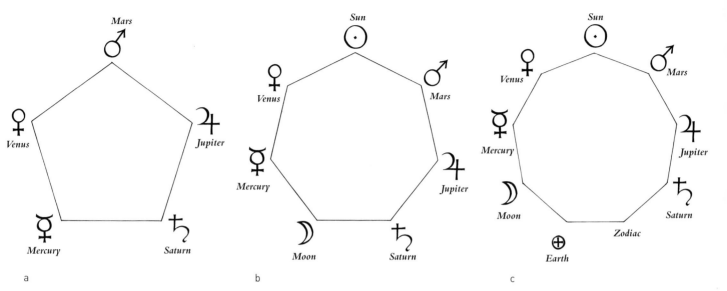

a

b

c

he gave no Gaulish names. Maybe Caesar felt it obvious that they referred to the planets as their embodiment and saw no need to elaborate further.

It is these five planets together with the Sun and Moon which make up the most primordial cosmic set of seven. There is a tradition that makes up the complement of nine by including the Earth (the sublunar sphere) at the centre surrounded by the Moon, Mercury, Venus, the Sun, Mars, Jupiter, Saturn and finally the sphere of the fixed stars or zodiacal belt.

49a.
The five planets

49b.
The seven 'wanderers'

49c.
The seven 'wanderers,' the central Earth and the background constellations, making nine

Number as pattern

Having demonstrated the importance of nine and seven in the mythological and cosmological structures of the northern peoples, both Celts and Norsemen, we will now turn to parallels in other traditions and examine the doctrine of archetypes implied.

Around the year 1000 in Basra, Iraq, a certain group of Islamic scholars, professionals, artisans and philosophers, formed themselves into brotherhood under the name of the *Ikhwãn al-Safã,* the Brotherhood of Purity. Their aim was to collate all relevant knowledge available to them and to publish it for all to read. In their own words:

> Our purpose embraces of necessity all that which
> permits man to ameliorate his life on Earth and to
> assure his happiness and salvation in the eternal world.

In their work, the *Rasā-il,* they demonstrate their belief in the archetypal and even supra-human content of astronomy, the science being revealed to the prophet Idris (Hermes Trismegistus) who, significantly, 'journeyed to Saturn' (Chronos) in order to be instructed and returned to Earth to relate the basis of the science of the heavens. This latter in its own way reflects the journey of Odin to obtain the knowledge of the runes.

In the Islamic perspective, after the seven spheres which are, when counted out from Earth as the centre, Moon, Mercury, Venus, Sun, Mars, Jupiter and Saturn, there is the 'heaven' of the fixed stars or zodiacal belt which is sometimes equated with the *kursi* (pedestal of God). The ninth 'heaven' is the *arsh* (throne) thus conforming to Quranic terminology. Thus the footstool and the throne of God make up the seven heavens of the Quran into the full nine. After describing the earth-centred scheme of natural perception, the *Ikhwān* gives an important clue to the double meaning hidden in traditional wisdom:

> God has placed the Sun at the centre of the universe
> just as the capital of a country is placed in its middle
> and ruler's palace at the centre of the city.

This means the solar sphere is the centre of the nine with four below and four above, also suggesting an esoteric knowledge of the heliocentric mechanics of the solar system.

Like the Pythagoreans, the Brotherhood of Purity held particular numbers to have cosmological significance both for their individual qualitative value and their cosmic structural aspect. These were, in particular, the numbers seven, nine, twelve and twenty-eight, all of which have the common value of being composites of the archetypes three and four. Professor Zolla points out that 'unity is always inherently threefold: itself, itself as identical to itself and itself as the standard of identity.'[22] Three has primacy after the fundamental principle of one (unity) in the *Ikhwān* system because it represents the essential tendencies inherent in the universal spirit (*al-Rūh*): this is expressed in triangular form as the descending movement away from the first principle, the horizontal expansion and finally the returning ascent back to the first principle. (We can recognize here a flowing version of the three realms of the Far Eastern triad: heaven as donating; the earth as receiving and expanding horizontally; man representing the re-unifying spiritual ascent.) Four was cardinal for it represented the polarization of universal nature into the active qualities of heat and cold and the passive qualities of moisture and dryness. These qualities were also associated with the fourness of the solar system in terms of the winter and summer solstices, the longest night and longest day respectively, and the equinoxes of spring and autumn when day and night are of equal length, as we have noted earlier.

Thus seven, nine, twelve and twenty-eight correspond archetypically and numerically with the planets, the spheres or heavens, the zodiacal constellations and the lunar mansions. We find a similarity to the Islamic tradition in the description by Black Elk of the Sun Dance Lodge:

> I should explain to you here that in setting up
> the Sun dance lodge, we are really making the
> Universe in a likeness; for, you see, each of the
> posts around the lodge represents some particular
> object of creation, so that the whole circle is the
> entire creation, and the one tree at the centre, upon
> which the twenty-eight poles rest, is *Wakan Tanka*,
> who is the centre of everything. Everything comes
> from Him, and sooner or later everything returns
> to Him. And I should tell you why it is that we use
> twenty-eight poles. I have already explained why the
> numbers four and seven are sacred; then if you add
> four sevens you get twenty-eight. Also the Moon
> lives twenty-eight days, and this is our month; each
> of these days of the month represents something
> sacred to us.[23]

The *Ikhwān* viewpoint is expressed as follows:

> The Pythagoreans who think that beings correspond
> to the nature and properties of numbers know also the
> perfection of Divine Wisdom which is its origin. In
> fact the numbers 7, 9, 12 and 28 are the first numbers
> which are called complete (*Kāmil*), odd, square,

exceeding and perfect respectively. Also the cause of the exclusivity of those numbers comes on the one hand from the fact that $7=3+4$; $12=3\times4$; $28=7\times4$ and on the other hand $7+12+9=28$. Thus noble beings correspond to noble numbers.[*]

The Islamic scholar Frithjof Schuon describes the intimate connection between qualitative number and geometrical figures as follows:

> This is, numbers in the Pythagorean sense, of which the universal rather than the quantitative import is already to be divined in geometrical figures; the triangle and the square are 'personalities' and not quantities, they are essentials and not accidentals. Whilst one obtains ordinary numbers by addition, qualitative number results, on the contrary, from an internal or intrinsic differentiation of principial unity; it is not added to anything and does not depart from unity. Geometrical figures are so many images of unity; they exclude one another or rather, they denote different principial quantities; the triangle is harmony, the square stability; these are 'concentric' not 'serial' numbers.[24]

To expand this theme we will take one such number which, by necessity, holds a special place in Babylonian, Egyptian, Hindu, as well as Christian, Muslim and Jewish cosmologies and religions: the number seven, already shown to be evident in the layouts of at least two of the British stone circles.

Taking a seven-sided polygon and the 'stars' within it, we can place one each of the traditional set of visible planets on each of the points. We propose to take the particular arrangement communicated to us privately by Marcel Hinze as a result of his studies into ancient Egyptian knowledge and practices. By this method (see Fig. 50), we place the Sun at the top followed on

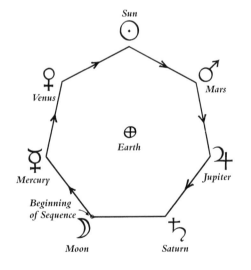

50.
The geocentric planetary sequence

[*] S.H. Nasr, *An Introduction to Islamic Cosmological Doctrines* (London, 1979), p.78. In addition to the $7+12+9=28$ another correspondence to the archetype of seven is that $28=1+2+3+4+5+6+7$.

its right by Mars, then Jupiter, Saturn, the Moon, Mercury and Venus. By following this sequence from the bottom and proceeding clockwise we have the planets as they relate in distance from Earth: the Moon is nearest followed by Mercury, Venus, the Sun, Mars, Jupiter and Saturn. This is the perceptual or observational pattern and is quite irrespective of whether we take the Sun to be moving around us, as it is seen to do, or whether we interpret the pattern using our knowledge of the Sun as the centre of the system. In our illustration the difference in 'knowledge' about the mechanics of the solar system is shown. By taking the planets at their greatest distance from Earth we show how the sequence is identical in principle from either the geocentric or heliocentric viewpoint.

Having placed our 'planets' (strictly speaking the Sun is a star, hence placed at the top) around the heptagon we now have a chance to read the significance this arrangement is believed to have had for the ancients. There are three ways in which one can travel sequentially around the set of seven points. We take the most 'energetic' and longest route (or sharpest pointed star) by missing two adjacent positions and moving to every third point until we return to our starting-point. We find that we have drawn a sequence which follows the days of the week (Fig. 51). If we start on Monday (Moonday; *lundi* in French, *lunedi* in Italian, following *luna*) we travel up to Tuesday (old English Tiw's day, an ancient Germanic deity identified as Mars; *martedi* to the Italians and *mardi* in French). Next we cross to Wednesday (Wotansday, Wotan corresponding to Mercury; *mercredi* in the French, *mercoledi* in Italy). We now move straight across to Thursday (Thor's day. Like the Roman god of thunder, Jupiter or Jove, Thor was the northern god of thunder; *jeudi* for the French and *jovedi* for the Italians). The star path now proceeds up to Friday (Freya's day, the Nordic goddess who corresponds to the Roman Venus; we have *vendredi* and *venerdi* and *freitag* in Europe). From here we follow the path down to Saturday (Saturn's day) and finally up to finish on Sunday, the day of the Sun and day of rest for Christendom.

Here we are on familiar ground and we have shown one kind of logic pattern behind the reason for allocating particular days to particular planets, a sequence which is not obvious from the order that the planets appear in the sky. Hinze also pointed out the ancient Egyptian custom of allocating a planet to each *hour*

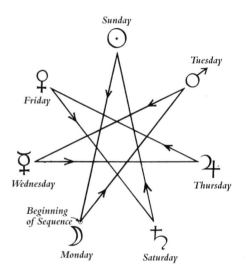

51.
The days of the week and their related heptagon. Following the star we find it gives the sequence for our current convention for naming the days.

Night hours / Day hours	☉		☽		♂		☿		♃		♀		♄		
	Day	Night	Day	Night	Day	Night	Day	Night	Day	Night	Day	Night	Day	Night	
First	☉	♃	☽	♀	♂	♄	☿	☉	♃	☽	♀	♂	♄	☿	1
Second	♀	♂	♄	☿	☉	♃	☽	♀	♂	♄	☿	☉	♃	☽	2
Third	☿	☉	♃	☽	♀	♂	♄	☿	☉	♃	☽	♀	♂	♄	3
Fourth	☽	♀	♂	♄	☿	☉	♃	☽	♀	♂	♄	☿	☉	♃	4
Fifth	♄	☿	☉	♃	☽	♀	♂	♄	♀	☉	♃	☽	♀	♂	5
Sixth	♃	☽	♀	♂	♄	☿	☉	♃	☽	♀	♂	♄	☿	☉	6
Seventh	♂	♄	☿	☉	♃	☽	♀	♂	♄	☿	☉	♃	☽	♀	7
Eighth	☉	♃	☽	☿	♂	♄	☿	☉	♃	☽	♀	♂	♄	☿	8
Ninth	♀	♂	♄	☿	☉	♃	☽	♀	♂	♄	☿	☉	♃	☽	9
Tenth	☿	☉	♃	☽	♀	♂	♄	☿	☉	♃	☽	♀	♂	♄	10
Eleventh	☽	♀	♂	♄	☿	☉	♃	☽	♀	♂	♄	☿	☉	♃	11
Twelfth	♄	☿	☉	♃	☽	♀	♂	♄	☿	☉	♃	☽	♀	♂	12

52.

The 'Solomonic' calendar of hours

of the day. In this case (see Fig. 52), the first hour of the day of, say, Saturday would be governed by Saturn, the second hour by Jupiter, then following, Mars, the Sun, Venus, Mercury and so on recurrently continuing until the twenty-fourth hour of Saturday is reached which we find is governed by Mars. Therefore the *first* hour of *Sunday* is dominated by the Sun. If we continue this process we arrive at a situation where the first hour of each day is dominated by the planet appropriate to that day. This pattern flows backwards, or anti-clockwise, around the perimeter of the heptagon.

Hinze, having discovered a pattern which demonstrated a logic to the planetary allocations for the days as well as the hours of each day, pointed out to us that the ancients divided the period between dawn and dusk into twelve hours irrespective of season. This meant the length and quality of an hour changed with the quality of the season and time of year. As there is no direct evidence of an earlier use of this sevenfold system, we suggest that there may well have been an earlier oral tradition based on observation which would give practical reasons for embodying the sevenfold patterns within the megalithic temples.

Although we have yet to touch on the later metal-working periods in British history, we find it relevant to extend our study of the sevenfold pattern to the ancient allocations of metals to the planets: this means in traditional terms that those archetypal principles which are represented in the planets macrocosmically are also represented in certain metals microcosmically. If we take the sequence that has arisen out of Hinze's studies and place the metals with their respective traditional planetary partners we get the following correspondences: silver — Moon; quicksilver — Mercury; copper — Venus; gold — Sun; iron — Mars; tin — Jupiter; and lead — Saturn (Fig. 53). Hinze, as a physicist, felt convinced there was more to this traditional allocation than fancy or mere colour correspondence. He investigated many possible aspects and properties that might reveal a pattern, until a remarkable correspondence arose from a totally unpredictable source of data: the periodic table of the elements. This modern convention of categorizing the naturally occurring substances according to their atomic number, which is equal to the number of protons in the nucleus, revealed an orderly sequence in the following way.

When the atomic numbers for the respective metals are placed on the heptagon, according to the planetary correspondence (Fig. 54) we get the following sequences: in ascending order of atomic number we start with iron (Fe) which has an atomic number of 26, followed by copper (Cu) with 29, silver (Ag) with 49, tin (Sn) with 50, gold (Au) with 79, mercury (Hg) with 80 and finally lead (Pb) whose atomic number is 82. The rather startling result is that our path has constructed a further, different, seven-pointed star — on this occasion created by missing one interval per move.

Hinze was so delighted with this pattern he had chanced upon that he took it to his physics professor. The professor's reaction was to calculate the statistical number of chances of the pattern

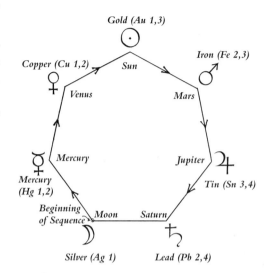

53.
The traditional allocation of metals to planets and the atomic valency sequence. There is a semi-anomaly between tin and lead.

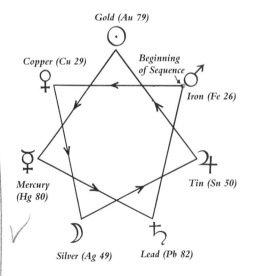

54.
The atomic number sequence of the metals associated with the seven wanderers

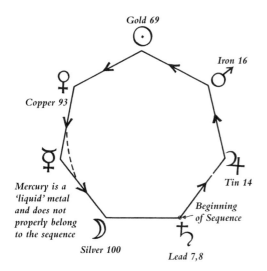

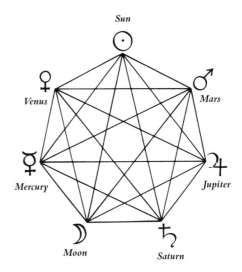

55.

The electric conductivity sequence
and its related heptagon

56.

The combination of all possible
symmetrical moves around the heptagon

having registered in this way — the result is 5,040-to-1 against
the occurrence! It is difficult to know what to conclude from such
a discovery. We should bear in mind however that the ancients
had a different approach as well as different attitudes toward
the attainment of knowledge from that of ourselves. Their techniques are far more likely to have been in tune with the tradition
embodied in the Vedas, where knowledge is acquired through
inner experience under the psychological discipline of one of the
forms of Yoga.

Before leaving the strange symmetry of the heptagon and the
patterns there is another sequence of interest which emerges from
atomic valency-characteristics of the metals; that is, their propen-
sity to link with other atoms. Starting with silver, which is univalent
and placing the elements in order of increasing 'jointing' potential,
we have quicksilver (mercury) and copper, both of which are uni-
and bi-valent, followed by gold which is uni- and tri-valent, iron
which is bi- and tri-valent, tin which is tri- and quarto-valent and
finally lead which is bi- and quarto-valent. Here again we have only
one 'semi-anomaly' among the seven, that is the relation between

tin and lead. Otherwise the correspondence follows exactly as the 'planetary' sequence which we laid out to begin with.

One more observation on the metal patterns is the electrical conductivity of each. This produces a pattern (see Fig. 55) which moves around the heptagon in the reverse way starting with lead, at 7.8, to tin, 14, to iron 16, to gold 69, to copper 93, (mercury as a 'liquid' metal cannot correctly be included) and we finish at silver with a conductivity value of 100. We are grateful to Wilhelm Pelikan for the data of these last two patterns.[25]

If there have been certain recurrent patterns found to be 'useful' to mankind in quite diverse circumstances, the patterns observed outside 'in the world' were conceived as having their 'reality' within, in the psychological and spiritual dimension. This reflection inextricably related human nature to all other natures and was the basis of the sense of unity, in other words, the traditional principle of correspondence; this means that there are archetypal bases to which all the different manifestations owe their particular characteristics, and all realities were to be found in mankind.

To summarize: we are proposing that the megalithic temple-builders were naturally disposed, like so many other ancient peoples and civilizations, to lay out a pattern of their cosmos within which and from which they could gain greater understanding of their own position and role in the scheme of things. Such patterns incorporating significant numbers were the basis of their temples. And their temples in turn by embodying the archetypes help 'stabilize the world.'

> *If the measurement of the Temple is in every way perfect, there will be perfection in the Universe as well.*
>
> Mayamata, xxii, 92.

57.
Sunset over Kintyre as the unity of light
and *one* source of life

4. Squaring the Circle

[The Onikare (sweat-lodge) of the Oglala Indians] ... utilizes all the powers of the Universe; earth and the things which grow from the earth, water, fire and air. The willows which make the frame of the sweat-lodge are set in such a way that they mark the four quarters of the universe; thus the whole lodge is the universe in image. The round fire place in the centre of the sweat-lodge is the centre of the universe: 'the ritual leader' makes an altar of the centre hole by placing tobacco at the four corners which are the cardinal directions.

 J.E. Brown[1]

In the solstitial rite of the 'sun-dance' the Arapaho Indians build a great lodge, in the middle of which stands the sacred tree, representing the axis of the world. The lodge is constructed of twenty-eight pillars in a circle, and sustaining the rafters of the roof which meet the tree in the centre ... the form of the Sanctuary is related to ... the lunar cycle ... the 28 pillars of the enclosure correspond to the 28 lunar mansions.

 Titus Burkhardt[2]

No progress in ethnology will be achieved until scholars rid themselves once and for all of the curious notion that everything possesses history, until they realize that certain ideas and concepts are ultimate for man.

 Paul Radin[3]

The reconciliation of heaven and earth

During the execution of a plan to re-direct a road through the archaic earthworks of Durrington Walls in Shropshire, the excavations revealed foundation holes of a large archaic wooden structure. This structure has been likened to certain of the great timber lodges constructed by particular tribes of the indigenous peoples of North America, for so long misnamed American Indians.

We have accepted the technique of cross-cultural comparisons, having compared Asiatic shamanistic cosmologies with the numerical structure of certain British stone circles, thereby implying a possible connection with Neolithic British cosmology. Following our general thesis of archetypes we believe it is also permissible to compare another shamanistic cosmology, that of the original North Americans, due to their common ground in the importance attached to the cosmic cycles and the number of the planets.

The word planet, derived from the Greek, means wanderer and traditionally this group of seven moving lights are representative of 'heavenly' archetypes. These are the Moon, Mercury, Venus, the Sun, Mars, Jupiter and Saturn. From humanity's point of view on Earth, the Sun also moves across the background of the stars in the sky.

Because of the number of 'wanderers' in the heavens and the natural four-phase division of the twenty-eight day lunar cycle, we believe the number seven may have had for archaic Britons a similar traditional value to that of the Indian shamans of North America. We are not the first to make this comparison of archetypes. Titus Burkhardt, describing the ritual of the Arapaho Indians, says that these people:

> ... build a great Lodge, in the middle of which stands the sacred tree, representing the axis of the world. The lodge is constructed of twenty-eight pillars erected in a circle, and sustaining the rafters of the roof which meet the tree in the centre. On the other hand the lodge of the Crow Indians is open above, while the space surrounding the central tree is divided into twelve sections in which the dancers take their places. In both cases the form of the sanctuary is related to two cycles, that of the Sun and that of the Moon. In the first case the lunar cycle is represented by the twenty-eight pillars of the enclosure, corresponding to the twenty-eight lunar mansions; in the second case it is represented by the twelve months. The rites accompanying the erection of the tree for the 'sun-dance' show striking analogies with the Hindu rites connected with the erection of the sacrificial post, which is also the axis of the world and the cosmic tree.[4]

The twenty-eight mansions of the Moon relate to the quarters of seven-day weekly periods while the twelve relates to the zodiacal mansions and the double sixfold division of a circle. These fundamental numbers also reflect the primary triad of realms: the circle (hence the hexagon) symbolizes the realm of heaven, the triangle symbolizes mankind as the harmonizing human consciousness, and the square symbolizes the stability of earth or physical experience.

The geometry of the stone 'circles' uncovered by Professor Thom embodies these three archetypal shapes. In all but the purely circular layouts the axes are long and short and establish a central 'squaring' whether or not this is related to the cardinal directions. The triangle is always present, either as a Pythagorean whole number triangle (as the three, four, five triangle) or as the rope needed to triangulate the drawing out of the ellipse. Finally, none of the enclosures move far away from the circle, as their perimeters are invariably some kind of closed curve, hence the definition of 'stone circle.'

If we move on to the more complex polygons as aspects of the numbers seven and nine it is as well to examine more closely the universal meaning of the unity of a 'sacred' space representing that which is situated outside time and outside space in a primordial state, 'prior' to space and temporally 'in the beginning.' Titus Burkhardt in his book, *Sacred Art East and West,* says that, 'spiritually speaking, a sanctuary is always situated at the centre of the world, and it is this that makes it a *sacratum* in the true sense of the word: in such a place man is protected from the indefinity of space and time, since it is "here" and "now" that god is present to man.' Later he gives a most interesting insight into the deeper motivation as to the concern megalithic builders apparently showed for making rational whole numbers around the perimeters of their enclosures: 'whereas the spherical form of the sky is indefinite and is not accessible to any kind of measurement, the rectangular or cubical form of a sacred edifice expresses a positive and immutable law.'[5] Squaring the circle therefore represents the achieved equilibrium between heaven and earth.

Constantly recurring throughout the great majority of cultures of the world is reference to the relationship between mankind, as anthropos, and the cosmos. The reciprocal archetypes that are found to be animating or motivating natural phenomena are also found to be the inner motivations of humanity — hence the realization of the idea of correspondences and recognition in the Platonic doctrine of recollection. This complementary relationship of archetypal man

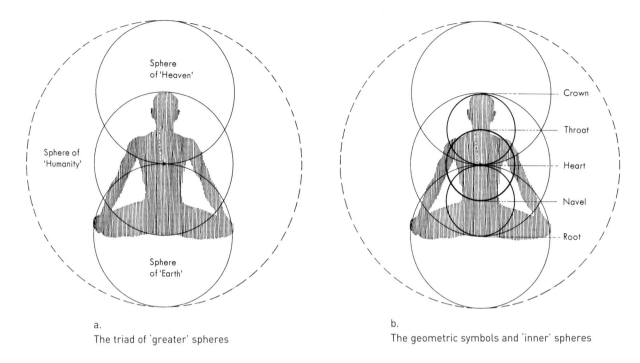

a.
The triad of 'greater' spheres

b.
The geometric symbols and 'inner' spheres

58a–b.
The schema of the archetypal
relationship between man
and the cosmos (After Keith
Critchlow)

and the cosmos is manifest in schematic form as the determinant of the proportions of the altar or altar and whole temple.

It is therefore a predominant feature of primary and traditional societies to hold an image of the Anthropos or archetypal symbol of humanity. This can be in the form of an ancestor figure or, as the Vitruvian man, as a paradigm for architectural proportions, or an Adam figure, or as in the Hindu tradition as Purusha.[*] In our illustration we have chosen the meditative sitting position to demonstrate the geometric symbolism of the three circles (see Figs. 58a–b).

The three larger circles are centred on the root, symbolizing the earth, the heart, symbolizing mankind, and the crown of the head, symbolizing heaven.

In the 'inner' or smaller circles of the body the same symbolism is reflected within the subtle body. In the Vedic system the centres

---

[*] To reduce this image to a universal language we have chosen a geometric schema: one which is divided naturally into three, as the three reflecting domains, 'heavenly,' 'earthly' and 'humanly.'

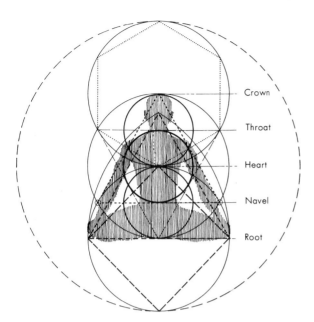

a.
The inner geometry of the 'greater' spheres. They symbolize the square for earth, the triangle for humanity and the hexagon for 'heaven.'

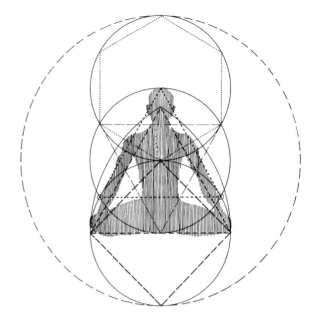

b.
Full sequence of heaven, earth and man relationships

59a–b.
Schematic developments of man/cosmos relationships (After Keith Critchlow)

of the circles now lie on what are called the navel, heart and throat centres with the base of the lower circle representing the root centre and the top of the upper circle the crown centre.

These same circles can be transposed into symbolic shapes which figure in the temple-building symbolism of Buddhist temples. The earthly is represented as a square (the four elements), the realm or circle of mankind is represented as a triangle (the three properties of consciousness — knower, known and knowing) and the upper circle of heaven is represented by the hexagon (the 'perfect' number 6). It can be seen that the equilateral triangle can take up two positions in the diagram which relates symbolically to 'shift' in the centre of consciousness in the heavenward direction.

We find this law reflected in diverse cultures where a schematic human form is drawn in the proportions of either the altar or altar and temple. There are the continual hauntings of Leonardo da Vinci's Vitruvian man, even with us, standing in a square and circle — uniting our two primary polar forms. In the Vedic tradition this figure is Purusha, who is the Divine Essence behind Man the builder, the altar and the fire of the altar. The

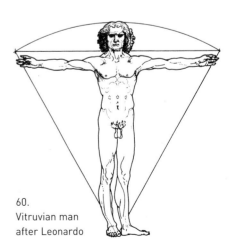

60.
Vitruvian man after Leonardo

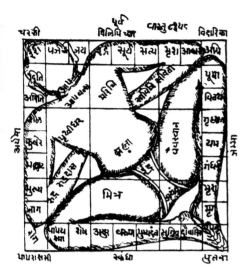

61.
Purusha: the Vāstu-Purusha-Mandala.
Fundamental schema of the universe as
guide to the layout of Hindu Temples.
Purusha is the Anthropocosm.

concept of proportions deriving from this figure is enshrined for the Hindu temple build in the Vāstu-Purusha-Mandala, a geometric formalization of Purusha as the immanent spirit of existence. This Mandala 'is an image of the laws governing the cosmos, to which mankind is just as subject as is the earth on which they build. In their activities as builders men order their environment in the same way as once in the past Brahma forced the undefined Purusha into a geometric form.'[6]

As we are dealing with Neolithic or basically 'settled' peoples, who could sacrifice so much of their economy to the building of these manifested stone structures, we may consider them proto-temples in the pure meaning of that term. Here we have 'concrete' expression of the nomadic circular form in transition to the sedentary square. It is in these great prototypes that we would expect to find the enshrinement of important archetypal patterns underlying the changing world, the permanent within the apparent.

In applying some basic principles of orientation and geometry described in the *Mānasāra Shilpa Shāstra* to the constructions of Castle Rigg and Long Meg's Daughters we found valid correspondence, even in the assumed procedure. We have seen how the division of six is inherent and fundamental to the circle (its own radius will always mark out six equal parts of its perimeter) and how this gives rise to the hexagon when these points are connected by straight lines. The most primary polygon, the triangle, arose from the intersection of the first two arcs in the east-west orientation procedure and was completed by connecting this intersection of the two circle centres with straight lines. Next, the square stabilized and fixed the site within the solar system by giving exact north, south, east and west positions, the four cardinal directions.

The constructions arrived at by Professor Thom for Castle Rigg and Long Meg were typical of those which numerically rationalize the perimeter of the primary circle. This balance between 'irrational' geometry and rational numbering is a fundamental reconciliation lying at the roots of sacred geometry. It is important to remember at this point that we are speaking horizontally, in terms of harmonizing the 'irrational' geometry with a whole number system in the plane of the earth. If we were talking in vertical symbolism, it would be necessary to take into account the existence of the irrational (chaotic and laval) underworld to complete the three realms — the other two being the rational world of mankind and the supra-rational world of archetypes.* The squaring of the circle is a perennial philosophical symbol: it is the establishing of heaven on earth and an act which informs as well as enforms that aspect of the cosmos which is furthest or most obscured from its archetypal source.

It is so commonplace for us today to experience the way in which even the most elementary pair of compasses will draw a circle that it is difficult to imagine the feelings of awe, mystery and power that this feat would have given our ancestors. Couple this with those sets of experiences which taught them that without changing the radius of their compass (or forked stick) they could complete a cycle in *seven* controlled moves and divide the original circle into exactly six. The seventh circle would complete the six-petalled flower pattern within the first. This hexagonal flower is culturally universal as it is precise, and we may speculate that the creation of this pattern established the perfection of the number six, which is also said to be 'perfect' because of its divisors totalling six: 1+2+3.

As there seems to be such an extreme difference between the circle, with its elusive numerically transcendental *pi* characteristic, and the square (the easiest area to measure), we would like to re-emphasize the fact that all regular polygons are embraced exactly by the circle. This makes it pre-eminently both a philosophic and geometric symbol of unity. The simple regular polygons are a profound study in themselves as they have been used by all philosophic and religious systems to represent facets of unity.

The squaring of the circle is sometimes presented as a geometric problem demanding that a square of equal perimeter or area should be found in relation to a given circle. At other times it is used to symbolize the virtually impossible task of making one order of things conform to another. Its real importance is that it works on many levels of both practical and psychological significance. In its most direct form the symbolism can be interpreted as the square of earth representing the sensorial order of the four elements, that which is measurable, whilst the circle, which has neither beginning nor end, symbolizes the perfection and timelessness of the archetypal realm, heaven. Squaring the circle can

62.
The six-petalled flower pattern. The perennial symbol of the six days of creation and the central seventh day of rest.

---

* This is a constant issue in the use of terms. From the viewpoint of one realm the other is 'irrational' but from the viewpoint of the other realm this irrationality is supra-rational or transcendental. In a similar way that intuition is supra-logical in the correct usage of terms.

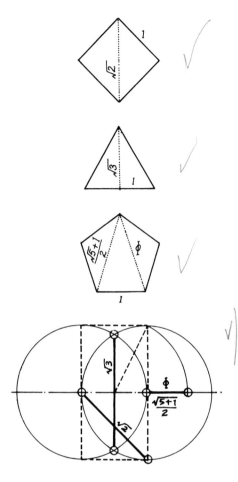

63.

The proportional ratios: √2, √3 and the 'Golden Mean.' √2 is the diagonal of the square. √3 is the height of the equilateral triangle. The 'Golden Mean' is the diagonals of the regular pentagon. All shapes with side = 1.

be taken to mean the establishment or maintenance of heaven on earth. In one sense this is a contradiction in terms; in another sense it recapitulates the essential truth that time depends on the timeless and that manifestation depends on its motivating principle. Principle formulates matter and matter expresses principle. Traditional societies see their task as regenerating and sustaining the world by the constant re-establishment of first principles through their rites, ceremonies and sacred structures: to live as the world lives by constant renewal.

The subject of incommensurables as transcendentals in mathematics has engaged many people over thousands of years and is vast in its ramifications. Whole numbers belong to one order of mathematics and because they have a precise quantity, are associated traditionally with the earthly order; by contradistinction transcendentals or incommensurables and related to proportional ratios, regular polygons, and the length of the perimeter of a circle — the inevitable *pi*. As incommensurables are strictly speaking *rational* it is therefore misleading to call them 'irrationals'; on the contrary they would be better described as supra-rational or transcendental because they are qualitative in nature like their associated polygons.

Special examples of the geometrical or proportional ratios which are incommensurable are the set of 'root' ratios, $\sqrt{2}:1$, $\sqrt{3}:1$, and $(\sqrt{5}+1) \div 2:1$, the Golden Mean ratio. These three special ratios are directly related in the above order to the triangle, square and pentagon. They recur consistently throughout the proportioning of the great sacred buildings of humankind. They can be taken to be of the same symbolic order as that of squaring the circle — rationalizing the irrational — unifying the paradox.

This symbolism of squaring the circle, or constructing an enclosure that partakes of both the incommensurability of *pi* in the circle and the whole number measurability of the square, is clearly found in the British stone circles. This fact emerged through the findings of Professor Thom who showed that the flattening of the circles enabled the builders to achieve whole number perimeters. This flattening clearly indicated a heavenly form, the circle, moving toward an earthly form, the square.

The circle on the Hill of the Highest House —
Moel Ty Uchaf

To take this point of symbolism in relation to the British stone circles, we will investigate in depth one of the particularly subtle and well-preserved examples: Moel Ty Uchaf.

In the remote mountainous foothills of the Bala region of North Wales, one of the most perfect settings in the British Isles, lies perhaps the most geometrically sophisticated of all the Neolithic structures. The overall setting of stones would fit within the great maze on the floor of Chartres cathedral, but the resonances from the cathedral-sized plateau on which this small circle sits echo all around the huge encompassing bowl of hills. These magnificent silent masses stretching back and away from the circle, to the southeast, form a huge horseshoe with a perimeter of five miles and rise to their highest point almost due south-east of the circle, the 2,572 foot high Bwrrd Arthur (seat of Arthur). Moel Ty Uchaf, which can

64.
Moel Ty Uchaf

65.
Moel Ty Uchaf: survey
to Professor Thom with
geometrical principles

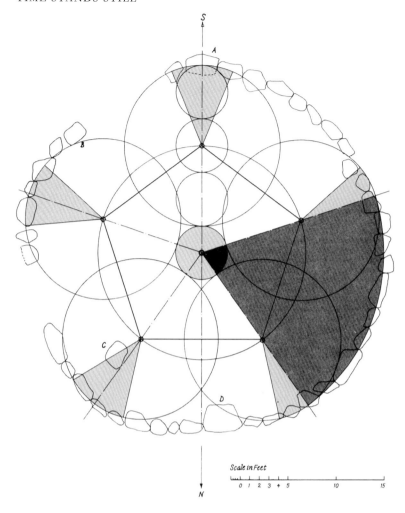

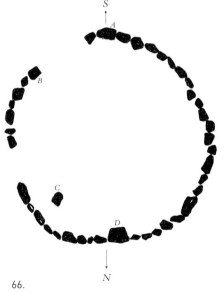

66.
Moel Ty Uchaf: survey after Professor Thom

be translated into the Hill of the Highest House, is described by Thom as one of the compound rings and represents a far more difficult achievement than those rings formed on the Pythagorean triangles. In the conclusion to his important volume *Megalithic Sites in Britain* he is drawn to remark how 'strange that the beauty of design achieved at Moel Ty Uchaf or Easter Delfour is not and cannot ever have been apparent on the site' and that he believes the 'designs with these properties probably took years of many men's time.' 'Perhaps' he adds, 'the proportions were worked out on the sands of the seashore, only to be expounded to the chosen few.'[7]

Moel Ty Uchaf in Merionethshire is under 40 feet at its greatest outer dimension, the girth of its three largest stones a mere four feet at their widest. The whole is an arrangement of 42 stones, one of which lies well within the enclosure. This does not include a centre stone which Thom believes to have been added at a later period. There are two gaps or entrances in the continuous encirclement which are symmetrical to the axis. The entrance to the east is four and a half feet smaller than the other which faces south-east. Thom's admiration for the accomplishment of the builders of this small but subtle temple layout is mainly based on his analysis of the manipulations of the megalithic measure. This he believes is founded on a 14 MY circle which would give an approximate 44 MY (43.9823) circumference, and by flattening four of the sides a $42^1/_2$ MY circumference is arrived at. The reason for this subtlety, according to Thom, is that the builders required a circumference with rational increments of $2^1/_2$ MY. He discovered that the symmetry chosen to accomplish this was a perfect pentagon of five centres on the circumference of the inside determining circle which has a diameter of 8 MY.

To account for this preference for the pentagonal division he cites the azimuth of the rising star Deneb — which is actually 17.3° whereas the orientation of the circle is 18° (the pentagonal angle is one-fifth of 90°). Despite this small discrepancy Thom considers the siting a great achievement. Having established this relationship he thus found a beautiful fivefold symmetry for constructing the flattening of four of the sides, the flattening which gave the necessary outer perimeter of $42^1/_2$ MY.

It is fascinating that when we come to look closely at the final pattern we see that the nearest overall symmetry to the whole construction is 90° to the Deneb azimuth. This is because it is to the west-north-west that the pentagonal outline has a full segment of a circle. Not only this but the 'apex' of the pentagon opposite has seven stones almost symmetrically placed either side of the axis. It is through this larger opening we would expect any sightings of the most southerly rising Moon and midwinter rising Sun to have been made, possibly with calibrated stakes across the openings, but these observations are without verification at present.

We now propose to repeat orientational procedures according to the Vedic tradition, bearing in mind Thom's warning that an upright gnomon was unlikely to have been used due to the mountainous horizon. It is within the bounds of possibility that the architects of the circle might have used a small 'table' of slate (an abundant local resource here) to perform a miniature orientational ceremony at the solstice. In this case a table could have been arranged and corrected with a water level so that sightings could be made in miniature to compensate for the irregularities of the actual horizon.

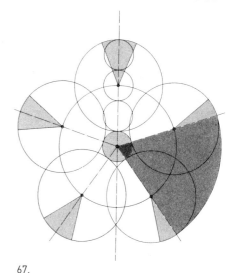

67.
Professor Thom's proposed basic geometry for the layout of Moel Ty Uchaf showing the fivefold symmetry together with the $^1/_5$ segment of a circle below (toned). The smaller toned areas are the segments of the circles used to determine the smaller perimeter curves — in Thom's opinion 'to establish a rational whole number perimeter.'

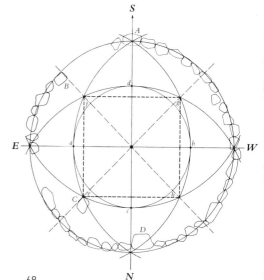

68.
The orientation procedures of the *Mānasāra Shilpa Shāstra* as applied to Moel Ty Uchaf. This *is* squaring the circle.

69.
Lanyon Quoit, Cornwall

Accepting Thom's proposed initial circle of 8 MY diameter as the first geometrical act, we can also take this as the primary circle according to the *Mānasāra Shilpa Shāstra* method (Fig. 20, p.54). After having obtained the east and west axes from the centre pole shadow the next part of the ritual, that of obtaining the solar cross, might follow a similar procedure: if we take point **a** on the eastern side of our central circle and make our radius the diameter of the primary circle we can inscribe an arc both ways from point **b** to the north and south. Similarly from point **b** as centre we can complete the 'fish' form and establish our north-south axis: this axis cuts the primary circle at points **c** and **d**. These two points become the centres for the east-west fish form, exactly crossing the first. We now have four points outside the original circle whose distance from the centre of that circle will be measured in incommensurable numbers as they are established from a geometric proportion by which the length of the longer axis, say north point to south point is $\sqrt{3}$ in relation to the diameter of our primary circle, taken as unity. What is most interesting is that if we draw a circle through these points (N, S, E and W) we obtain a circle which is only about 3 inches larger in diameter than Thom's proposed 14 MY circle! In other words this may have been a reduction from the proportional, to the numerically rational, as part of the symbolic ritual of squaring the circle.

In terms of the Hindu practice, certain points (*marmas*) are contained 'within' the stones and certain others are to be found within the space of a sacred building.[8] Here we have a proportional circle prior to the reduction to 14 MY intersecting all but five of the 41 bounding stones: hence in this sense it too is embodied in the construction. The next stage in the Hindu procedure is to 'square' the primary circle by joining the intersections of the fish form: when we do this by joining **e, f, g** and **h** we find a most accommodating reason for the single stone within the area, designated stone **C** (see Fig. 65, p.110). The 45° axis or diagonal of the square not only tangents this stone but the corner of the square itself terminates right beside the stone. Thom has called parallel phenomena the universal rule of being not *on* the centre but beside it, which also conforms with those *marmas* that must not be built *on* in the Hindu system. If we follow the other diagonal from **h** through **f** it continues until it tangents the stone designated **B** which is one side of the south-east gap. This analysis demonstrates that the three most venerated architectural proportional systems are embodied in this proto-temple.

Now we have to decide whether or not to follow Professor Thom in his belief that it is unlikely that Neolithic man knew the construction of the pentagon, which was not recorded officially until more than a thousand years later (by Euclid in *Magna Graecia*). However, we believe that the need for these early mathematician-astronomer-architects to establish a fivefold temple would have led them to discover the secret of dividing a circle into five. Conversely, having discovered the secret of the fivefold division of a circle, they applied it to their temple building.

It is very hard to imagine the sense of the miraculous that the discovery would have impressed on these early geometers, because the procedure is as simple as it is elusive and as elusive as it is precise and powerful. The face of almost every wild flower and herb that they confronted, from the buttercup to the periwinkle, would have challenged them to solve the riddle of how to make a fivefold division of a whole. Further evidence of the archaic Britons being fascinated by fivefold symmetry is the careful arrangement

70a–d.
The fivefold symmetry of a. the periwinkle, b. the buttercup, c. the corncockle and d. the helinium

71.
Crouched burial in the round
tumulus on Dunstable Downs.
There appear to be 144 fossils
with fivefold symmetry around
this person's skeleton. Maybe
the number is significant?

INTERMENT in ROVND TVMVLVS Nº 6 .
DVNSTABLE DOWNS

WORTHINGTON G. SMITH . MAR . 1887 .

of pentagonal fossilized sea urchin shells found arranged around
the skeletons in a circle during the excavations of the Barrow at
Dunstable Down, faithfully illustrated by W.G. Smith.

We have drawn out the procedure (Fig. 72a) that we expect would
have been followed had the builders known this secret. Starting with

a primary arc drawn with centre **c** and radius **ca**, the next operation is to place the trammel centre at **a** and without changing the radius cut the primary arc with a second one which cuts the first at points **x** and **y**. By joining **x** and **y** with a straight line (a cord in this case) point **b** midway between **c** and **a** is established. With centre **b** and radius **ca** point **d** is established (Fig. 72b) on the extension of **bx**.

Next we construct a vesica from **b** and **d** respectively which bisects **bd** at **e** (Fig. 72c). Taking **d** as a centre and with radius **de** we cut **dc** at **f**. With centre **c** and radius **cf** we draw an arc through to **g**. Then with the same radius and centre **a** we cut a similar arc from point **h** to point **j**. Point **h** is then the apex of a regular pentagon **hcgja** (Fig. 72d).

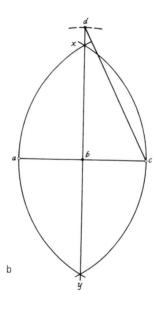

72a–d.
A 100% accurate method of constructing a pentagon from the *vesica pisces*

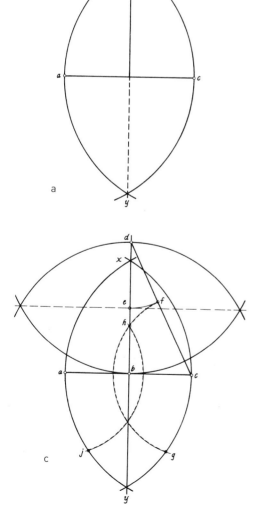

a

b

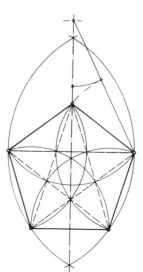

c

d

Returning to our study of Moel Ty Uchaf our drawing (Fig. 73) demonstrates the relationship between a smaller centre circle of one MY radius (shaded) and the fully drawn five outer circles. We have also shaded in the actual amount of each of those smaller circles used in the outer perimeter layout as proposed by Professor Thom. It is in the pattern of these shaded segments that the true bilateral symmetry becomes apparent — with point **k** as a pentagonal apex the opposite two circles have segments only half the size. Using the centre circle of one MY as a module we have continued inscribing these modules up the central axis to **g**, showing the numerically rational increments to the perimeter of Thom's geometry.

Using point **d** as a centre with a radius of $1^1/_2$ MY we can draw a circle which passes through **g** and just touches our centre 1 MY module circle. We proceed to draw the same size circles centres **r, s, t** and **k**, each of these circles touching the circumference of the shaded module circle.

73.
Geometrical analysis of Moel Ty Uchaf. The most remarkable use of fivefold geometry and a sevenfold star integrally. Could it be a temple to the planet we call Venus?

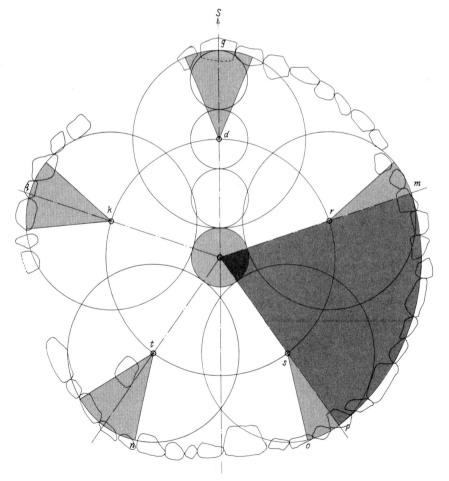

Starting from the centre of our module circle we draw central lines of symmetry through points **r, s, t** and **k** which cut our larger circles at points **m, p, l** and **q**. These points, with the exception of **q**, are the centres of the flattened curves of the whole temple's perimeter geometry. In the case of **g**, which is typical of **m, l** and **p** as centres, we proceed to draw a line through **s** to **o** and through **t** to **n**; with centre **g** the arc **no** is drawn opening out to the north. This brings us to a remarkable occurrence, the amount that the arc **no** 'opens up' from **m** would be, to a high degree of accuracy, *one seventh* of a full circle. This means if we join **g n** and **g o**, we have the arm of a seven-pointed star. The beauty of the construction is that from points **ts**, which coordinate them both, the arm of the five-pointed star is drawn to apex **d**. Both **d** and **g** are due south from the centre of the whole construction.

We can clearly see how the pentagonal symmetry of the site arose from a sighting of the star Deneb if we follow Thom; but the

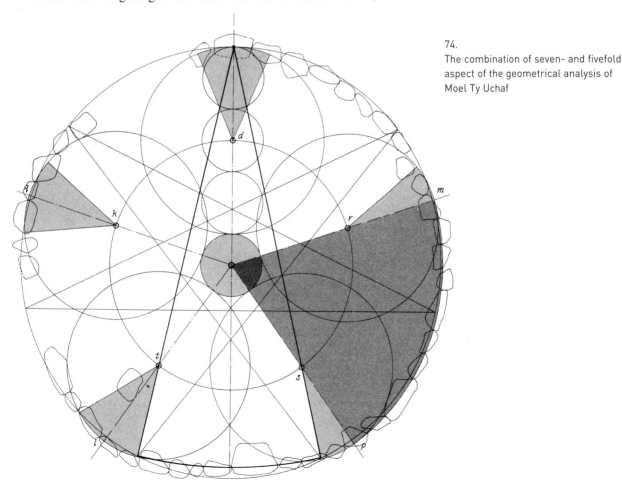

74.
The combination of seven- and fivefold aspect of the geometrical analysis of Moel Ty Uchaf

75.
The seven-pointed star inside the
stones of Moel Ty Uchaf. Note the
seven stones between each of the
points of the seven-pointed star.

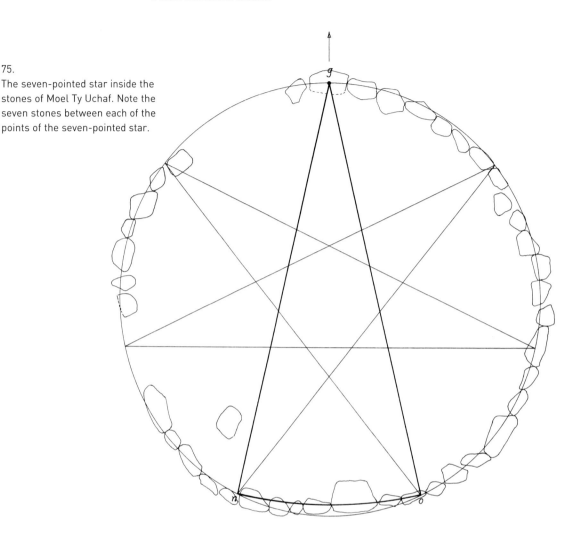

sevenfold symmetry must be treated, provisionally, as symbolic
until further work is done. We would expect its meaning to lie in
cosmic rhythms of a sevenfold nature, such as the quarter phases
of the Moon.

Possible astronomical reasons for the seven could be the days
of the week or a quarter cycle of the Moon and, as we have seen,
the visible 'wanderers' recorded in all ancient traditions were usually counted as five or seven. Returning to the dimensions of the
circle we find seven again embodied in the following way. The
Moel Ty Uchaf circle has a mean radius of 7 MY, is composed
of 42 stones (6×7) and has a 42$^1/_2$ (approx 6×7) MY perimeter.

Thus the fourness of the phases of the Moon and the seasons of the year, the five lesser wanderers (the planets) and the seven days of each quarter of the Moon are all expressed symbolically in the layout procedure of the temple as a whole. There is one more aspect of fiveness that could relate to the temple of the 'Hill of the Highest House,' one that could relate to its dedication. The Sun, Earth and Venus come into syzygy or conjunction five times during one complete cycle, thus setting up a pentagonal star *in time* in the solar system.

Bearing in mind that Neolithic culture was based on agriculture, it is logical that the temple should be dedicated to Venus, the goddess of fertility. The archetypal fiveness, the patterns of revolution of the planet Venus viewed from Earth and the significance of the conjunctions will be discussed in a later chapter.

We have demonstrated the elegance of Thom's proposals for obtaining the numerically rational perimeter which can be seen as the reconciliation between *pi,* the supra-rational, and the measurable, whole number perimeter. A veritable squaring of the circle.

76.
Cairn Holy II, Scotland, a beautiful example
of a 'roofed' space by the neolithic builders

5. Qualitative Number: Number as Rhythm, Cycle and Sequence

All that has by nature with systematic method been arranged
in the universe seems both in part and as a whole to have been
determined and ordered in accordance with number, by the
forethought and the mind of him that created all things.

    Nichomachus of Gerasa[1]

When God gave the Torah to Israel, He opened the seven
heavens to them, and they saw that nothing was there in reality
but his glory; He opened the seven abysses before their eyes,
then they saw that nothing was there but His glory. Meditate
on these things and you will understand that God's essence
is linked and connected with all worlds, and that all forms of
existence are linked and connected with all worlds, and that
all forms of existence are linked and connected with each other
but derived from His existence and essence.

    Moses de León[2]

The beginning of applied mathematics could be considered the achievement of the womenfolk of any given community, discovered in the principles of weaving, knotting, plaiting, braiding and even counting and storing the foods for the winter months. A particularly dramatic example of this mathematical ability is found in the memorizing of many highly complicated carpet patterns: in many communities in the Islamic countries of the Middle East a woman's status is founded on the number of carpet patterns she has memorized. One has only to picture some of the magnificent Persian carpets to be reminded of the extent of this accomplishment. From the threaded beads was presumably developed the facility of the abacus — following from the lost languages of knotted cords. A remnant of this language is found in the string finger games which have been recorded from the Torres straits in the Pacific to central Africa, from the Canadian Eskimos to the Navaho Indians. All appear to be remnants of a sign language previously carrying much

77.
Knotted string figures:

a.
'Ten Times,' first move. A derivative from the 'Turtle' pattern (Caroline Islands).

b.
Ten Times,' fourth move

c.
'Ten Times,' fifth move

d.
'Pygmy Diamonds,' fifth move. Known to the African Batwa pygmies, Congo Kasai Valley.

e.
'Brush House,' fifth and final move. Originated from the Pueblo Indian Antonio Abeita from Isleta, New Mexico. Also known at Zuni, New Mexico and called Pi-Cho-Wai, Ham-Pun-Nai — a brush house.

f.
'A six-pointed star,' formed from the 'Brush House.' Known to both the Pueblo and Klamath Indians.

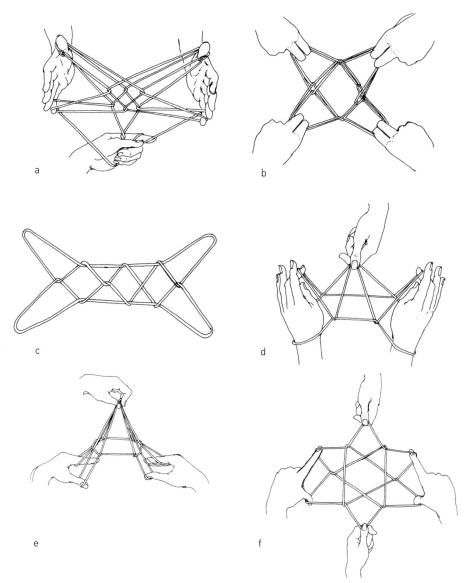

more complex reasoning. Lao Tsu in the eightieth verse of the *Tao Te Ching* even advocated: 'Let the people again knot cords and use them (in place of writing).'[3]

As far as the layouts of stone circles are concerned it is all but certain that knotted cords would have been the best way of performing the surveying and marking out, and of achieving the required numerical values of the perimeters. The cord also takes on a variety of mythological forms, the most explicit for our purposes being the theme repeated many times in the *Shatapatha Brahmana* that 'the Sun binds (*samavayata*) these worlds together by a thread, this thread is the same as the wind.' The connection between the thread and breath (wind) is found in the psycho-spiritual anatomy of tantra doctrine where the threads of Ida and Pingala wind their way round either side of the central column (*sushumna*) in the subtle body of mankind, and along these channels travel subtle breaths (*prana*). The *Shatapatha* also says: 'The Sun is the connecting link, since these worlds are attached to the Sun by the four points of the compass,' and Coomeraswamy reminds us of the myth from the *Sarabhanga Jātaka* where the keeper of light, Bodhisattva Jatipala 'standing at the centre of a field, at the four corners of which posts have been set up, attached a thread to the neck of his arrow and with one shot penetrates all four posts, the arrow passing a second time through the first post and then returning to his hand; thus indeed, he "sews" all things to himself by means of a single thread.'[4]

This line binding all things to the Sun is in one sense related to sunbeams and the shafts of light so well demonstrated in the interior of woods. As an example from British traditions we may instance the maypole with its tapes that connect and weave all participants to the maypole during the May dance. The sutra or sacred thread has its counterpart in the Hindu, Buddhist and Islamic scriptures, the strings of words weaving a worldly trace of the heavenly prototype: 'All this universe is strung upon me, as rows of gems upon a thread.'[5] No doubt the rosaries of Hinduism, Christianity and Islam hold similar symbolism as well as their practical role in remembrance.

Eliade found that the ideology of shamanism had developed a mythical version of paradise and the fall. Because the fall from paradise had broken the thread between mankind and the gods, the sacred rope became the property of privileged people, the limited few who were capable of controlling 'the best means of reaching Heaven in order to meet the Gods.'[6] One such group, due to their technical and intellectual capabilities, probably planned the stone circles. The following are some principles at a simple technical level which can be used to produce, by a system of whole number intervals, the kind of layouts implicit in the stone circles.

Take a thonged or woven rope and divide it by knotting, or knotting and beading in sequence, so that there are identical increments between the knots and certain significant numbers of length overall. For instance a length of twelve units, twelve also having a zodiacal and duodecimal significance, is the minimum measured length which can be triangulated into a three, four, five pattern to give a perfect 90° angle. In this triangle we can discern the archetypal numbers that constantly recur in our study: the first basic triad three, four and five, also gives us a particularly interesting conjunction of the two main significant numbers that occur in the shaman cosmology — seven from its first two parts (3+4=7) and nine from its last two parts (4+5=9).

An apposite example of the use of this triangle is shown in Thom's survey of the Druid temple near Inverness (Fig. 79). It can be seen from Thom's survey that a 3:4:5 MY triangle not only sets up the egg form but from the centre the circle is 9 MY to the furthest point north-west and 7 MY to the furthest point south east along the axis.[7]

The next important measured length of rope for our study is one with thirteen equal intervals. One explanation for the negative

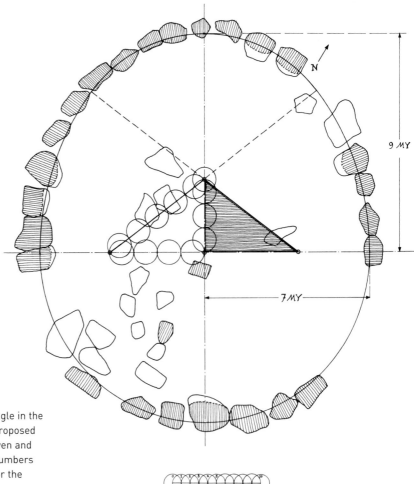

78.
The construction of a 3:4:5 right-angled triangle using a knotted cord. Based on twelve intervals.

79.
The use of the right-angled triangle in the setting out of Druid Temple as proposed by Professor Thom. Note the seven and the nine megalithic yards. The numbers were evidently very significant for the Neolithic builders.

9 MY

7 MY

N

value of thirteen in Christian superstition is due to the suppression of the thirteen-month lunar calendar when the Christian era brought in the twelve-month solar calendar. Although thirteen has lunar associations (there are thirteen 'darks' of the Moon, or new Moons, each year), it has also been related to the twelve signs of the zodiac together with the Sun — a symbolism which may relate to the maze at Chartres cathedral (Fig. 80) which is proportioned on a thirteen-pointed star.[8] If the rope with thirteen intervals is triangulated, this time into an isosceles triangle with sides four, five and four, two of the angles will divide a circle into seven with an accuracy of 0.1: a very good rule of thumb or practical method of laying out a heptagon or seven-pointed star (Fig. 81). Again, the 'composite' symbolism of the sides of the triangle is of interest as they total nine (4+5), both ways, in pairs. Curiously the next triangular sequence of whole numbers to make up a 90° angle consists of thirteen, twelve and five, a sequence apparently not unknown to the Neolithic peoples.

80.
A plan of the centre of Chartres maze showing the 13-pointed star on which it is proportioned. Also a possible Moon reference to the thirteen lunations in a single year.

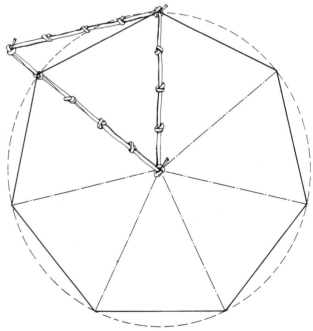

81.
The construction of a heptagon using a knotted cord, divided into thirteen intervals. Curious coincidence between thirteen annual Moons or lunations and the seven days of the week.

Knotted cords would be capable, depending on the nature of the knotting, of acting as straight edges, for sighting when pulled tight, as compasses or trammels when used in conjunction with two pointed stakes, and as measures by their knotted intervals, so their possible importance as the principal instrument of Neolithic constructional science is inestimable. None to our knowledge has survived, presumably due to their organic nature. According to the *Mānasāra Shilpa Shāstra* the specifications for the sacred sutra used in demarcation are cotton, Munja grass, silk and wool. Later, they may have taken the form of metal chains, again unrecognizable as specifically surveying or geometrical instruments because of the other uses to which they might have been put. The wearing of strings of beads, cords, and so on, around the various parts of the body is common to almost all mankind and takes on the possibility of a great range of meanings, symbolic, cosmetic and practical, according to the wearer.

Early computing systems could have been based on fruit stones or rounded pebbles of the reputed Pythagorean traditions (*calculus* comes from the Latin for a pebble from the earlier Greek *khalix*). We can see how such systems gave rise to the concept of qualitative number: directly such counting units were brought together in any other than a linear sequence the pattern and 'shape' of number was bound to show itself. It is a further speculation that when the abacus was formulated from threaded thongs, arithmetic divided from geometry and the split between quality and quantity was created, since the orthogonal 'lines' of the abacus prevent the number patterns forming into pentagons, hexagons and so on.

An investigation into the factor of shape in morphic number (a physical unit for each mathematical unit) soon gives rise to additional qualities, and hence symbolic values, of the patterns involved. We will use the concept of marbles because they are spherical; no doubt the ancients selected approximately spherical pebbles for this practice. One such marble symbolizes unity and therefore will not create any further patterns. Two marbles will not create a shape but they will demonstrate the most essential qualitative element of geometry — that of direction. Measure cannot take place unless it is in some direction — unless it is directed *toward* a specific point *from* a specific point. Direction is therefore qualitative spatially whereas homogeneous, purely quantitative space, which by definition admits of no specific direction as being any more important than any other, is unqualified. By this observation homogeneous space is immeasurable, as direction is necessary for measurement and direction immediately establishes a non-homogeneity to the space. Homogeneous space being immeasurable is therefore 'non-existent.'

The simple placing of two pebbles, when thoughtfully considered, produces the interesting conclusion that we *count* two, but *measure* one. That is, the distance between the two is one unit of measure whereas there are necessarily two pebbles to measure by. The significance here is that measurement is restricted to the domain of duality, of twoness. Measure itself, the third uniting factor, is intangible as it is the relationship between two things. It is almost as if we can recapitulate a very important early experience which tells us, more or less consciously, that the act of measuring can never give us unity — which is as true experientially as it is philosophically. The experience of unity is a transcending of duality or measurement. This is reflected in the 'old father time' image of Saturn (Chronos) carrying a sickle with its association of cutting up or sectioning, hence the words 'sect,' 'sector,' and so on. He is incapable of uniting in one direction but can be relied upon to divide into units of time and thereby becomes the father of time as a measure in the other direction.

It is only by 'standing outside' moving time that one can see the pattern that the planetary cycles make. This is aptly demonstrated in a spatial model (see Fig. 82) which freezes the trace of the time path of any of the planets and shows the beautiful symmetry of the flower-like patterns they make during each cycle, which will be dealt with in detail in a later chapter.

Geometric patterns, starting with the minimum threeness of a triangle, have a unique quality of their own in that their shape can remain unaltered although they can be enlarged to occupy virtually any amount of space. Five 'pips' can be placed together touching each other to form a pentagon and, without in any way affecting the essence of the pentagonal shape, these same pips can be placed well away from each other to make a very much larger pentagon. In geometry these are called similar figures for although quantity (size) is altered, essential quality is unaltered.

Number as quantity is specifically a one-for-one relationship, simply the items being counted. Number as quantity has the normal role of isolating exactitude, and thereby becomes a strict mechanical discipline. The value of this aspect of number to precision of calculation is almost inestimable. But it is in the qualitative aspect of number that 'rational' and 'irrational' are married. In other words the number of pips or units that make up the corners of a square remain

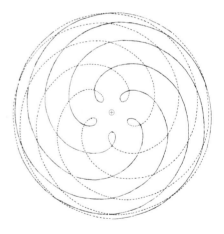

82.
The idealized path traced by Venus as viewed from the geocentric axis during an eight-year period. Remarkably similar to an apple sectioned through the pips horizontally.

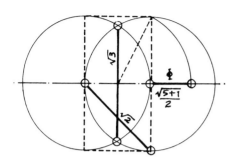

83.

The three primary proportional systems
as used universally in temple architecture,
all arising from the two overlapping circles
and the resulting 'vesica' form

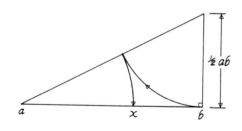

84.

The construction of the Golden Mean ratio
from the given line **ab**. This construction is
100% accurate.

simple and rational, but if they are placed accurately the distance
from one corner diagonally to the other can never be 'rational,' that
is, resolved into a whole number. This means that when four pips are
placed in a square and the pip itself is considered the unit of measure
it is impossible to express the distance across the square in simple,
rational increments of the basic pip. This rule holds good however
large one makes the square prior to the curved space of cosmic
dimensions. The diagonal of the square is the 'square root of two'
if the side measurement is one. This 'supra-rational' quality, as we
might call it, gave it a particular 'divinity' in traditional terms.[*]

There are three examples of these so-called irrationals, or 'transcendentals,' that seem to recur persistently through great periods of
temple building of mankind. The qualities of these three transcendentals are called proportional systems because of their harmonic
growth characteristics and, as we have seen in Chapter 4, they are
derived from the first three and most elementary number patterns
— the triangle, the square and the pentagon (see Fig. 83).

The last mentioned of these three, giving rise to the ratio 1 to
$(\sqrt{5}+1)\div2$, is known as the Golden Mean. This harmonic relationship is geometrically unique since a straight line **ab** divided at point
x in the ratio of the Golden Mean gives rise to the relationship **ab**
is to **ax** as **ax** is to **xb**. This means that the whole line is longer than
the first part in the same proportion as the first part is longer than
the remainder. Expressed mathematically.

$$\frac{ab}{ax} = \frac{ax}{xb} = \frac{\sqrt{5}+1}{2}$$

There was apparently an analogical connection in the ancient
Greek mind between this harmonic mean and human relationships;
the term Golden Mean was applied to human affairs in the maxim:
'Do unto others as you would have them do unto you.'

These three numerically irrational proportions do not exhaust the
series of transcendental numbers, but they are those, together with
pi, which occur most persistently in the controlling proportions
of ancient architectural monuments. If, as we have suggested, the
paradigm for a true temple lies in archetypal forms that have their

---

[*] This fact is also fundamental to Plato's exposition of recollection in his
   Meno dialogue.

correspondences in the patterns of heavenly bodies, then we would expect to find these proportions within those patterns, and we will return to this in a later chapter as it is a subject of special study.

The ancient approach to number was of quite a different order from the present-day one, due to a completely different orientation. Number geometry could provide insight into the Divine Intellect and structure of the metaphysical realms.

Due to the dangers of separation and specialization which give rise to 'severed' orders of one reality, the ancient sages took great care to treat arithmetic and geometry as the sciences of unification. This they achieved by integrating number, alphabet and sound values simultaneously. Consensus tradition indicates that the arts of writing and numbering were revealed to certain prophets (the forth-speakers of the tradition according to G.H. Mees) by the gods. Yet there was no doubt in the ancient mind that intelligibility was of a metaphysical order originating on an archetypal plane that was more or less available to mankind according to sensitivity, effectiveness of invocation or inspiration. The Promethean disaster was due to the reverse motivation of attempting to steal the fire of the gods, with its inevitably disastrous result.

The alphabets of the main revealed religions of the world have spontaneous number values to each letter. It is also apparent that the relationships between alphabets and number values could always be interpreted both demotic and hieratic levels. Although history is littered with examples of the misuse or distortion of priestly knowledge (T.S. Eliot's Madame Sosistis is a good modern example) this is by no means the norm. An example of the seriousness with which esoteric knowledge is treated is instanced by the shamans of the Papago Indians who were literally lynched if their prophecies were inaccurate. Archaic or traditional mankind knew that power was not the possession of the individual without divine sanction. Jagadguru Shankaracharya, who represents the Vedic tradition in its fullest sense, says that valid knowledge is obtainable by direct interior cognition through the spiritual discipline of yogic meditation.

Since Francis Bacon defined science as the study and testing of *exterior* phenomena, a definition that was never challenged by those with the knowledge to do so, present-day science and methods of obtaining and testing knowledge have become a complete reversal of the ancient wisdoms which insisted that knowledge became valid only to the extent that it led to the unification and self-realization of the person concerned. Or, as classical Platonic wisdom demands, that a thing be true, good and beautiful together. There was a final breaking-point in the Western philosophy and so-called Natural Science when the man of science was defined as one who observed, theorized, and tested *solely* exterior phenomena in the attempt (albeit self-contradictory) to establish an absolute objectivity by the subject.

Jagadguru Shankaracharya's remarkable book on Vedic mathematics was published in India and demonstrates that incredible mathematical feats can be performed mentally due, according to the author, to the inherent wisdom of the Vedas, the sacred scriptures of Hinduism. The author, in his prolegomena, describes the Hindu traditional approach to knowledge which is through *meditation*:*

> Immemorial tradition has it and historical research confirms the orthodox belief that the Sages, Seers, and Saints of ancient India who are accredited with having observed, studied and meditated in the Aranya — (that is, in forest-solitude) — on physical Nature around them and deduced their grand Vedantic Philosophy therefrom as the result not only of their theoretical reasonings but also of what may be more fittingly described as True Realization by means of Actual VISUALIZATION seem to have similarly observed, studied and meditated on the mysterious workings of numbers, figures etc. of the mathematical world (to wit Nature) around them and deduced their Mathematical Philosophy therefrom by a similar process of what one may, equally correctly, describe as processes of True Realization by means of Actual VISUALIZATION.[9] (Emphasis and capitals in the original text.)

The implications of this ancient yet perennial tradition are most provoking when one recalls the difficulty modern scholarship has in understanding the megalithic mind. This latter was evidently capable of great feats of orientation without written words or numbers — if the above techniques were used there would be no reason to externalize their calculations. We have chosen to look in some

---

* This word is used in the sense that the mind reduces its activity to single pointedness, and not as a process of thinking or mentation.

detail at two chapters of *Vedic Mathematics* which are significant to our study: 'The Vedic Numerical Code' and 'Recurring Decimals.' The author assures us that the formulae in this book were directly distilled from the Sutras of the Vedas by the convention of using 'the Sanskrit (*Devanagari*) alphabet to represent the various numbers.* And this they do, not in order to conceal knowledge but in order to facilitate the recording of their arguments.' This, he goes on to explain, facilitated their ability to memorize the sutras or verses, the basis of the oral tradition and the comparative traditions in the ancient Chinese and Druid triads.

The different ways of interpreting these ancient threads (sutras) of wisdom are aptly demonstrated by the author. We will choose examples from this study which relate to, and unite, our two significant numbers, seven and nine. In the first case we will look at Jagadguru's method of deriving a sequence of numbers which we can manipulate to express the fractions of seven in decimal notation.

Firstly, the Vedic approach is to find $^1/_7$ in decimals by simple division:

$$
\begin{array}{r}
0.142857 \\
7\,\overline{)\,1.0} \\
\underline{7} \\
30 \\
\underline{28} \\
20 \\
\underline{14} \\
60 \\
\underline{56} \\
40 \\
\underline{35} \\
50 \\
\underline{49} \\
1
\end{array}
$$

In the process of conversion we get a 'series' of remainders (3 is the first remainder after dividing 10 by 7) and these remainders appear in the sequence 3, 2, 6, 4, 5, 1. This is a recurring sequence which will repeat endlessly.

---

* This means each Sanskrit letter having a corresponding number value.

To save us going through the whole long division process Jagadguru says that even before the first digit emerges as a remainder, to remind us that the recurrence has begun, we should look for a uniform ratio. In this case that ratio is 3:1. 'At this point, we may note that inasmuch as the first dividend 10 (when divided by 7) gives us the first remainder 3, and, with a zero affixed to it, this 3 will become our second dividend and inasmuch as this process will be continuing indefinitely it stands to reason that there should be a uniform ratio.'

We have therefore a ratio by the simple rule of three and from this we may proceed to find the recurring sequence by multiplying by 3. From our first remainder (3) we obtain $3 \times 3 = 9$, but as we cannot have a remainder figure equal to or greater than our divisor (7) it becomes proper for us to divide this 9 by 7 to obtain our second remainder, 2. Multiplying this remainder by 3 gives us 6 which is the next number in our remainder sequence and confirms the geometrical progression (G.P.). Multiplying 6 by 3 gives us 18, which when divided by 7 gives a remainder of 4 and $4 \times 3 = 12$. Dividing 12 by 7 gives us 5, our fifth remainder! Multiplying 5 by 3 and dividing by 7 gives us 1 and as this was our first dividend we know that we have reached the end of our sequence and that the recurrence has begun. We could now write our sum:

$$
\begin{array}{r}
\text{G.P. } 132645 \\
\hline
7\,\overline{)1.0} \\
7 \\
\hline
3
\end{array}
$$

In other words, by knowing the ratio between the first dividend and the remainder and by using this as a multiplier we can create a geometric progression to get our result.

This preliminary process enables us to reach our objective which is to find the decimal expression of $1/7$ by a simple operation which we can do at sight *mentally*. Because we have the remainders 1, 3, 2, 6, 4, 5 all we have to do is mentally add a zero and divide each by 7. Thus we obtain 142857 which is our quotient or recurring decimal expression for $1/7$.

Jagadguru goes on to demonstrate an even easier method for attaining our objective by writing down the remainders as they occur and multiplying them by 7. By writing down only the last digit of each multiplication we obtain the following:

$3\times7=21$ and we put down 1
$2\times7=14$ and we put down 4
$6\times7=42$ and we put down 2
$4\times7=28$ and we put down 8
$5\times7=35$ and we put down 5
$1\times7=7$ and we put down 7

Thus $^1/_7$ equals 0.142857!

Jagadguru draws attention to an even more significant aspect of the calculations and that is that the two halves of our answer when added together sum to 9:

$$
\begin{array}{r}
142 \\
857 \\
\hline
999 \\
\hline
\end{array}
$$

This means that once half the answer is known the other half can be obtained by subtracting each of the digits from 9.

Another property of this number pattern which further links seven and nine — a recurring theme in this book — becomes apparent when we look again at the remainder sequence. Just as we found that when half the quotient was known the other half could be obtained by subtraction from 9, we find a similar phenomenon in the case of the remainder sequence but in this case we obtain the pattern:

$$
\begin{array}{r}
326 \\
451 \\
\hline
777 \\
\hline
\end{array}
$$

A fundamental theme of this book is the relation of time and number to the cosmology of the megalithic mind, and it is relevant at this point to investigate information contained within a Book of Hours. We believe that this contains the recording of an oral tradition similar in manner to that knowledge in the Vedas which Jagadguru has made explicit.

A Book of Hours is a prayer book which is based on the religious calendar of saints and festivals throughout the year and the most famous of these is the Book of Hours of Jean de France, Duc de Berry, which has been described as the most magnificent of late medieval manuscripts still extant. Included within this Book of Hours are twelve illuminations each representing one month of

85.
September, from the *Très Riches Heures* of the Duc de Berry, with Moon calculating letters in the second sequence out from the Sun of Apollo

the year. Each of these illuminations consists of two parts, as our illustration for the month of September shows: the lower part is a picture apposite to the month in question and the top semi-circular part contains calendaric and zodiacal information relevant to that month (Fig. 85). The inner ring on each of the twelve illuminations sets out the number of days in that month and the next ring out from this contains a series of letters. It is this sequence of letters with which we are concerned, and whose meaning we can obtain following the explanation of O. Neugebauer in his book *The Exact Sciences in Antiquity*. The semi-circle contains the letters of the alphabet from **a** to **t** (excluding **j** which may have been synonymous with **i**) in the following order: **b, k, s, g, p, d, m, a, i, r, f, o, c, l, t, h, q, e, n**. There is in fact a calligraphic error in the fifth letter which is written as an **f** instead of **p**; it will be seen from what follows that this must be an error.

By assigning a numerical value to each of the letters which appear in the sequence (as in the Vedic practice) the following values are obtained:

a	b	c	d	e	f	g	h	i	k	l	m	n	o	p	q	r	s	t
1	2	3	4	5	6	7	8	9	10	11	12	13	14	15	16	17	18	19

The sequence of letters as they appear in the Book of Hours then provides the following sequence of numbers:

b	k	s	g	p	d	m	a	i	r	f	o	c	l	t	h	q	e	n
2	10	18	7	15	4	12	1	9	17	6	14	3	11	19	8	16	5	13

Neugebauer discovered that this sequence follows a simple law: add 8 to the first number to obtain the second and so on through the series, except that when the sum exceeds 19 one subtracts 19 to obtain the next number in the sequence. In the last place we have $5+8=13$ which would be followed by $13+8=21$ and $21-19=2$. This is the first number on our list and we can see, therefore, that the list repeats itself after 19 steps.

The significance of a 19-year cycle in calendaric calculations was first proposed by Meton in the fifth century BC; the purpose of this cycle was to link the solar and lunar years. A lunar month (lunation) is the period between successive conjunctions of the Sun and Moon and is about $29^1/2$ days. Consequently 12 lunar months amount to 354 days which is about 11 days less than the solar year. Meton proposed that 19 solar years equalled 235 lunar months or 6,940 days (the correct lengths are 6,939.69 and 6,939.61 days respectively). Meton therefore showed that the new Moon falls on the same day every nineteen years; that is, if the new Moon falls on the first day of January in a given year then there will be a new Moon on the first of January nineteen years later. This 19-year or Metonic cycle is accurate to the extent that only after 310 Julian years do the cyclically computed new Moons fall one day earlier than they should.

This cycle not only formed the basis of the Seleucid calendar but was also the foundation of the Jewish and Christian calendars and was used in particular to establish the date of the key Christian festival — Easter. It was therefore by means of this cycle that the contemporaries of the Duc de Berry solved the problem of establishing the dates of the new Moons, at least for religious purposes.

Unfortunately, the Book of Hours was never completed and the calendaric information for the months of January, April, May and August is missing from the illuminations for these months. However, if we choose a year on which the first new Moon falls on 19 January as the first year of the Metonic cycle then, by proceeding through the year with successive 29- and 30-day lunations — with the occasional addition of one day so that two 30-day lunations follow one another — we would find that the new Moon would fall on the following days of the year: 18 February, 19 March, 18 April, 17 May, 16 June, 16 July, 14 August, 13 September, 12 October, 11 November and 10 December. In the Book of Hours we find the letter 'a' opposite each of these days in the relevant illumination excluding, of course, those which were never completed.

Continuing the process of calculation into the second year we arrive at 9 January for the first new Moon of the year and the date obtained for September is the second. As can be seen in the illustration the letter 'b' is opposite 2 September. The continuation of this process throughout the 19-year cycle leads to the arrangement of letters, representing numbers from $a=1$ to $t=19$, exactly in the form set down in the Book of Hours.

Therefore, in order to know on which date the new Moon is supposed to fall it is only necessary to know which number the present year has in the 19-year cycle. This number is known as the 'golden number' because, as one thirteenth-century scholar expressed it, 'this number excels all other lunar ratios as gold excels all other metals.'

The connecting factor between these widely spread and ancient cultures is the correspondence between letters and numbers which not only enabled their users to employ certain kinds of mental mathematical short-cut techniques for calendaric purposes, but were considered the archetypal basis underlying all cosmic phenomena.

Returning now to the Vedic mathematics explicated in Jagadguru Shankaracharya's book and to the connection between seven and nine, we find a beautiful cyclic example for the expression of the fractions of seven in decimals. By using the Vedic practice already discussed we obtain the following:

$$^1/_7 = 0.142857$$
$$^2/_7 = 0.285714$$
$$^3/_7 = 0.428571$$
$$^4/_7 = 0.571428$$
$$^5/_7 = 0.714285$$
$$^6/_7 = 0.857142$$

We can see that not only do the same six digits appear in each of the above decimals but also that they appear in the same sequence and in the same direction in every case. Therefore, in order to write down the decimal equivalent of any of these vulgar fractions, we need to know only the sequence of numbers and the starting-point in the sequence for any particular fraction. Jagadguru suggests a simple rule for determining this: each decimal equivalent starts with the number equal or nearest to the numerator of the vulgar fraction. Having obtained 0.142857 as the decimal equivalent of $^1/_7$ it becomes a simple matter to write down the equivalents of the other fractions: $^2/_7$ begins with 2 and we write down 0.285714; there being no 3 in the answers $^3/_7$ must begin with 4 and we write down 0.428571; $^4/_7$ begins with 5, $^5/_7$ with 7 and $^6/_7$ with 8 and we can write out the whole decimal in each case.

Another method given by Jagadguru is even simpler: multiply the numerator by the denominator and the last number of the product is the last number of the sequence for that fraction. Thus, 7×2=14 so the sequence for $^2/_7$ must end in 4 and we can write down 0.285714.

This sequence can be presented graphically so that the geometric form of these decimal equivalents of the fractions of seven can be seen in its recurring shape (Fig. 86). The numbers 1 to 9 are placed equidistantly round a circle following a clockwise direction and the numbers are then joined to trace out the flow pattern of the recurrent decimal sequence. In the illustration we have shown the starting-points for the fractions from 1 to 6 so that by following the line from any of these starting-points we are able to read off the decimal equivalent of any of the fractions.

So, as an example, if we want the recurring decimal for $^1/_7$, we begin at 1 and follow the dashed line pattern after placing our starting number behind the decimal point. Hence we get 0.142857.

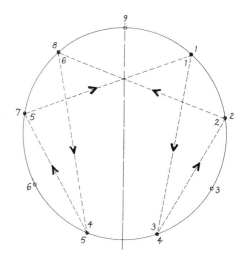

86.
The graphic presentation of the decimal equivalents of seven

If we take 6 on our inner face to correspond to $^6/_7$ we simply follow the dashed line in the correct direction after placing the outer
number first, 0.857142, and we get the correct recurrent decimal for
the fraction $^6/_7$. This shows a unique correlation between nine and
seven graphically and numerically and can be taken as an indication
of the integrative attitude of the ancient science of correspondences.
The standing stone circles embody both number and geometric patterns and are simultaneously aligned to Sun and Moon 'horizons' at
significant times of the year.

If we accept that the metaphysical precedes and is the source of
the physical — the first principle of traditional societies — then we
can see that the stone circles, as true temples, would be expected to
embody the archetypal number patterns underlying creation as well
as be aligned to the significant positions of Sun and Moon rises
in the cycle of the year; as one (the created order) was the outer
expression of the other (the underlying principles) and both confirm
the unity of existence and experience.

6. Templates, Breastplates and Cosmic Calculation

*You should prepare a necklace of otter skin, and from it there
should hang a circle with a cross in the centre. At the four
places where the cross meets the circle there should hang
eagle feathers which represent the four Powers of the Universe
and the four ages. At the centre of the circle you should tie a
plume taken from the breast of the eagle, for this is the place
which is nearest to the heart and centre of the sacred bird.
This plume will be for Wakan Tanka, who dwells at the depths
of the heavens, and who is the centre of all things.*

Kablaya, a holy man of the Oglala, instructing Black Elk on the Sun
Dance.[1]

*Now, that golden Person who is within the Sun, who looks
down upon this Earth from his golden place, is even He who
dwells within the lotus of the heart ...*

Maitri Upanishad vi.1

Man's heart is the central point and heaven the circumference.

Shabistani, *The Secret Rose Garden*

*Wisdom without action hath its seat in the mouth; but by
means of action, it becometh fixed in the heart.*

From the *Shekel Hakodesh.*[2]

As the idea of megalithic astronomy gains strength, both in the
minds of the archaeologists and in the new facts emerging from
each new investigation, the questions must follow: how did they
learn, practise and record their knowledge? What tools did they
require apart from an extremely well-trained memory?

It is reasonable to suppose that the megalithic astronomers
practised geometry at hand scale; this would have made basic
economic sense. One would hardly begin a massive stone alignment

87.
Set of stone spheres with tetrahedral symmetry and incised with spiral patternings

programme without first verifying that one's intentions and calculations were accurate — both in a 'drawn' sense and in some sort of miniature three-dimensional model. The use of strands of hair, split straw, finely whittled twigs and a clay surface could have rendered extremely accurate miniature sighting models which could have been set up at the centre of a prospective stone circle. Practical experiments have been carried out using a clay tablet as a 'ground' for geometrical drawing.* The results were satisfactory enough to indicate that this would have been an adequate draughting method in materials readily available to the megalithic community.

In the next two chapters we will investigate in depth two kinds of objects which relate to the megalithic stone building period — both of which might be regarded as tools for the kind of conceptuality which would be necessary for the astronomical alignments and 'ground-geometry' apparent in the stone circles.

---

* These were demonstrated in the British Arts Council film *Reflection* produced in 1978.

The first are 'plates' and relate primarily to the two-dimensional geometry of flat shapes and symmetrical divisions of a circle; the second relate to the fundamental three-dimensional divisions, or spherical geometry.

Both are physical objects which have been unearthed for many years and which reside in the museums of Britain — we will scrutinize them in depth, keeping in mind the background of cosmology we have explored.

These 'physical' objects will be put to the test to see what kind of mathematical properties they may have in addition to their symbolic and artistic value. The objects in question are the gold breastplates from Clandon and Bush Barrows and the carved stone spheres of Scotland.

We shall take the breastplates first, as we believe they can be viewed as part of a universal tradition. In this tradition their use signifies authority and a divine mandate to the wearer, and their occurrence in different forms may be found with this significance in many different cultures. Comparisons become important when the primary principles are the same, that is when the symbolism and physical function are united in a cosmology: the meeting ground, appropriately, lies in the mathematics or the number and geometry aspect of these objects.

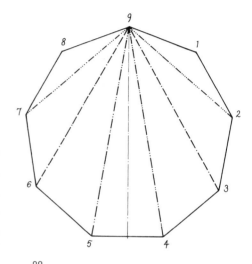

88.
Some angular properties of the enneagon

Before studying the breastplates themselves we must look at some of the properties of the number nine and the ninefold division of a circle, recalling the connection with the cosmology discussed earlier. In our illustration (Fig. 88) we have numbered the points and have joined the topmost point, marked nine, by a line to each of the other points of the ninefold division, creating a set of seven angles at the top.

If we start with the most acute or sharpest central angle, 4/9/5, it can be seen that the other angles symmetrically either side of this central angle are made up from this angle in sets. 3/9/6 is *three* such angles, 2/9/7 is *five* such angles and 1/9/8 is *seven* such angles. If we take the two numbers at the terminals of each of the angles we find that they all sum to 9, and according to divergence from the basic angle, the greater the angle the greater the difference between the digits.

We are now going to single out (Fig. 89) the angle 2/9/7 and add lines joining 2 to 5 and 7 to 4 thus creating a rhombic shape with a reflection of the angle 2/9/7 within the circle. 2/9/7 and its reflection are composed of five of the original angles (4/9/5, Fig. 88) and the two smaller angles of the rhomb are made up of four such basic angles.

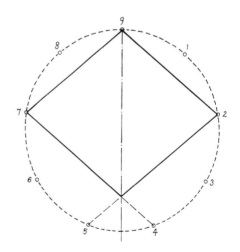

89.
The development of a rhombic figure from the enneagon

This rhomb separated out has the special property of dividing the circle into two ninths of its circumference and this is achieved simply by placing the sharper angle of the rhomb at the centre of any circle — in our illustration (Fig. 90) the rhomb is proportional to the circle but it can, of course, be used to divide a circle of any size. Such a rhomb in bodily form would act as a very practical *template* for constructing a ninefold division of a circle. It would have to be placed eight times adjacently and marked off to give all nine radii. In terms of the practical application that such a template would have, the extensive research by E. Moessell into the metal angles unearthed in Egypt led him to believe that these were used by master builders of ancient Egypt in establishing the overall proportions and in the details of their buildings.[3] This tradition has been maintained until today in the form of the 90° mason square and the 30° 60° 90° set square and 45° 45° 90° set square of the draughtsman.

It is in their own geometry that we find a direct connection between two breastplates unearthed from the Bronze Age barrows of Clandon in Dorset and one from Bush Barrow near Stonehenge, and the preceding geometry (see Figs. 109 and 110, p.148). The one from Clandon is now in Dorchester Museum, and the other from Bush Barrow together with a smaller gold rhomb are on show in the British Museum. The smaller of the Bush Barrow rhombs may not qualify in quite the same sense as the larger rhombs as it is of quite a different technical quality. This does not diminish the geometry, however.

90.
A $^2/_9$ rhomb used as a template for the ninefold division of a circle

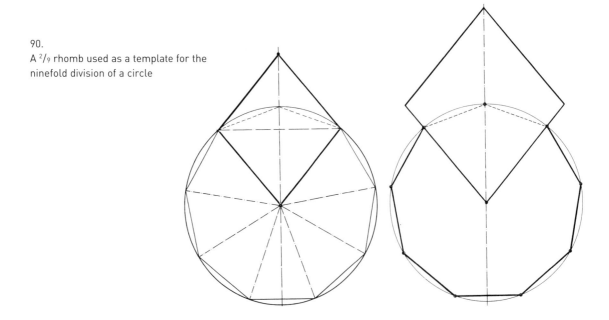

The Bush Barrow burial mound, not far from Stonehenge, is where a gold breastplate was found, decorating a person of respect and authority, possibly a chieftain. It is possible that this man was directly connected with the astronomer-priests who planned the final layout of Stonehenge. His own learning is not likely to have been that much less than the other leaders of his culture, and he may even have had some direct responsibility for the last period of buildings at Stonehenge. The question must arise, 'Did the crafts-man who made this breastplate know he was creating a template for a ninefold division of a circle?' There are various reasons which support the theory that he did. Firstly the object was finely worked, with great precision. Secondly it was worn as a sign of authority, and the third reason is the appropriateness of its position on his body. Not least is the proximity in time and space to Stonehenge itself, where it is increasingly obvious with each successive survey that great geometrical skill was employed by the builders.

The smaller of the two Bush Barrow gold rhombs is little bigger than the end of a man's thumb, but is geometrically interesting as it is made up of two equilateral triangles. This in itself holds no great surprise as it is the most simple of the diamond shapes to make with a compass. If two circles of the same size are drawn so that the centre of one lies exactly on the edge of the other, the shape created by straight lines from the two intersections and the two centres makes up this particular diamond shape. (The primal significance of this geometric gesture was described in the manuscript on Hindu temple founding.)

This elementary piece of geometry is so simple yet so impor-tant that it qualified as the first theorem of Euclid's *Elements*. Its property which is relevant here is that it can act as a template. If one of the sharper points of this rhomb is placed on the centre of a circle it makes a one sixth division of the circle or one side of a regular hexagon. If the more blunt angle was placed at the circle's centre, the circle would be divided into three or two sixths. The relation between these simple operative facts, and the construction of many of the stone circles increased our suspicion that there was a connection between these templates and the greater mathematics of the layouts of the stone circles. The importance of the hexagonal division for the construction of the Castle Rigg circle has already been discussed. Not only this, but little has been put forward as to how megalithic builders worked out their plans before initiating the massive constructions. Small versions have always been, and still remain, the rule when working out the plans for a large building

project. There is no reason to believe the Neolithic builders were an exception — so the notion of tools becomes relevant. Although we have here in the gold rhombs possible implements of a later period, the principle of the use of rhombs to record critical angles may well have been inherited from a wooden or stone predecessor. Further, as it is perceptively obvious that the heavens circulate or surround the earthly environment, it is equally obvious that the intervals on this circuit, the constellations — in whatever grouping — could best be represented on a circle. Therefore orderly divisions of a circle would be the next challenge to astronomy-minded men.

At first glance there is nothing particularly significant about the shape of the breastplates either — it is the workmanship and delicate precision that first catch one's attention and this latter has led to the hypothesis that they were the workmanship of a single craftsman. In fact, because all three of these gold diamond shapes are different, little attention seems to have been afforded to the possible significance of their angles. Apart from geometric analysis which will be used to suggest a significance, there is also the particular position on the human body in which they were found — over the heart. The heart is, in traditional psychology, the seat of the soul; a subtle counterpart to the central physical organ controlling the circulatory system of the human body. Sacred geometry and the divisions of the temple space are at the heart or centre of the definition and meaning of Temple. Differentiation correctly starts from a unifying centre as sunbeams diverge from the Sun.

To develop this idea, we have to return to the principle of cross-cultural parallels. Because of the age of the records from ancient China and the extent of research of modern sinologists, it is worthwhile to trace the significance of the rhomb and heart in the earliest written Chinese records. In particular, sinologist Carl Hentze has laid great stress on the importance of the rhomb-shaped stone appearing on ancient Chinese bronze vessels (see Fig. 92).[4] This lozenge-shaped object, depicted as being borne between two hands, has a remarkable resemblance to the rhombs of Bush and Clandon Barrows — even, as far as one can gauge, the size in relation to the hands is similar. Hentze identifies one important aspect of the meaning of this figure as *yu* ('previous stone') which in context, he says, also indicates 'wholeness' and the 'total world.' We might work around the translation 'previous stone' and suggest possible alternative interpretations, for instance 'original' or 'archetypal' stone, signifying 'in the beginning' or the paradigmatic 'originating' stone, that is, that which simultaneously centres and archetypally divides space and time into its 'original' divisions. On investigating the earliest meaning given to this pictogram, it was discovered that there are two derivations. The first was *chii* which means to offer or receive sacrificial offerings; the second was *lung* meaning to play or handle. Wieger, more specifically, and curiously, gives the meaning as two hands playing with a jade ball (Figs. 93 and 94).[5]

In the transition from pictograms to the convention of character writing certain elaborations and variations developed, two of which concern us here. Both have the meaning *hsuan* ('to calculate'). The first (Fig. 95) shows four hands using an abacus of the bamboo variety (according to Wieger), the second (Fig. 96) shows the character for jade in the centre (as with *lung*, above) which had been described as a jade sphere. Can we assume calculation on a sphere in this case? The second character also has the meaning 'to plan.' Another curious association with the jade character is the word *heng* (Fig. 97) which is described in Matthews as: 'Part of an astronomical instrument used in very ancient times.'[6] The jade radical is found yet again in Kung writing coupled with the character meaning 'all' to give 'a stone sceptre' or official insignia. This latter recalls the insignia known as a Pi (Fig. 98). Only the Emperor of China was permitted to wear this polished stone 'instrument' on his breast, both as a sign of his worldly authority and as his heavenly

92.
Yu

93.
Chii

94.
Lung neng

95.
Hsuan

96.
Another version
of *hsuan*

97.
Heng

98.
Pi

99.
Photograph of a jade Pi

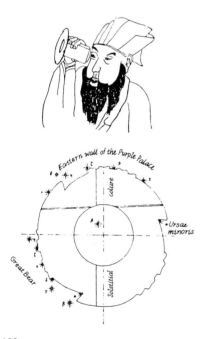

100.
The use of a Pi as a circumpolar sighting template

mandate (Fig. 99). This connection was accomplished by using the Pi as a circumpolar sighting template.[7] This small disc, which later became synonymous with the symbol of heaven (the circle), was attached to the end of a squared tube (earth symbol). It was used by centring on the Pole Star, and aligning the serrations around the outer edge to the stars of the Great Bear or Big Dipper constellation. As this constellation rotates once per year, the relative position of the horizon to the constellation indicates the time of year and thus could be estimated more or less accurately by eye (Fig. 100).

Hentze's own conviction is that the two triangles making up the jade rhomb represent the 'upright and inverse worlds' or the world in its entirety which is '... that of the living and the dead.' As we have discussed, the shamans also expressed the number of heavens as reflected in as many hells and underworlds. Could there then be a connection between this jade rhomb and the gold rhomb found at Bush Barrow in the sense that it could accurately divide a circle into a determined number of parts, bearing in mind the cosmological indications? The value of this exercise would be to make a diagrammatic image of the whole 'circle' of the heavens as a background against which to chart the movements of the planets. This means that both the Pi and the jade rhomb could have been equally accurate astronomical tools. And the jade spheres cannot but leave one wondering about possible parallels with the stone polyhedrons from Scotland, which are discussed in the following chapter. There is a living craft tradition today in China that carves polygonal spheres within spheres from ivory as a model of the cosmos.

There is another remarkable coincidence in relation to the position in which the precious gold breastplates were found on the bodies of the buried leaders, rulers or priest-kings in Bush and Clandon Barrows. Karlgren, another sino-etymologist, elaborates on the very ancient (c. 1122–770 BC) Chinese character *mien* ('precious stone') which is clearly pictorial and is made up of two images side by side (see Fig. 101).[8] The first means a prince, king, or ruler and the second is anthropomorphic and descriptively a person with a half-Moon image on the centre of the chest triangle. Karlgren comments on a parallel image of the same group: 'The graph shows a man with tattooing on the breast.' We would prefer a rather more subtle and involved reason for the association of the breast and heart as shown in Karlgren graph no. 475f (see Fig. 102) where the image (and character for heart) is clearly discernible. It is of interest here to point out that the ancient Chinese character for heart also signified mind, and was rooted in their belief that heart and mind were inseparable — the seat of the intellect was in the heart.

Whilst still with Karlgren, there is another graph of uncertain meaning which is *nie* in Figure 103 a or b form. Karlgren says this was used synonymously in the first millennium BC with graph *chii* or as in Figure 104, which means to hold, grasp, or take, visually interpreted by Karlgren as a manacled man and manacles respectively. The similarity to the lozenge strikes us, though possibly in arc form as in the fish-shape of the second stage in the temple founding ceremony. If this seems too fanciful a way to interpret a man taking hold of his position or orientation, we will cite another equally ancient character (c. 1122–770 BC), *liang,* meaning to measure and heavy (see Fig. 105). Although its upper image looks quite presentably like the graph for the Sun, Karlgren insists that it is an object of uncertain meaning. Reinforcing our interpretation, there is the oldest image for the EAST or place of honour, the place of the rising Sun presented thus (see Fig. 106a–b) = *tung* (c. 1122–950 BC). It may be that both *tung,* in terms of directing to the sunrise, and *liang,* as measuring with the sunrise (see Fig. 107), can be jointly interpreted to express an orientational and astronomical function.

Curiously, another version of *tung* developing from the above graph means 'rainbow' (see Fig. 108a), the largest and most dramatically subtle of natural geometric phenomena — seemingly confirming the arc value of the graphic image.[*] To conclude our summary search into ancient Chinese graphics for clues, we find the most ancient symbol for 'sunrise' (see Fig. 108b) having the most unusually heavy base — could this be the Sun rising over a mid-distant marker stone?

If we now look at the Bush Barrow breastplate (Fig. 109) which is in very good condition, and continue our investigation of its mathematical properties, we find although its outer perimeter tends very slightly toward curves, which could be due to the pressure in the grave over the millennia, we can still take accurate measurements of its angles. The angles subtended by the edges at the two sharpest points are to a fair degree of accuracy 80°. However as the angle is repeated three more times, one within the

---

[*] Also significantly the rainbow was used as a symbol by the Siberian shamans as a bridge to cross into the realm of the gods.

101.
Mien

102.
Yin

103a.   103b.
Nie   *Nie*

104.
Chii

105.
Liang

106a.   106b.
Tung   *Tung*

107.
Liang

108a.   108b.
Tung   *Tung*

other, we can measure more accurately these inner rhombs. The angle is, to within less than half a degree, 80°. If we divide 360° by 80° we find it goes in 4^1/$_2$ times. As we have already noted, if the rhomb is placed on a circle with the 80° angle at the centre it would divide the circle exactly into two ninths. Therefore the Bush Barrow breastplate could also be defined as a template; one which enables a careful user to achieve the division of a circle into *nine* equal parts. Any connection between Bush Barrow and the architects of Allan Water would be very hard to substantiate geographically, but a connection through the megalithic *collegia fabriorum,* which must have existed in some form to give the standardization implied by the consistency of Thom's findings, is a possibility that cannot be ruled out. Whatever the case, what is evident is that this gold plate unearthed at Bush Barrow placed over the heart of the principal of the burial has a precise aspect connecting it with the significant number nine and the possible use as a template in the temple founding sense.

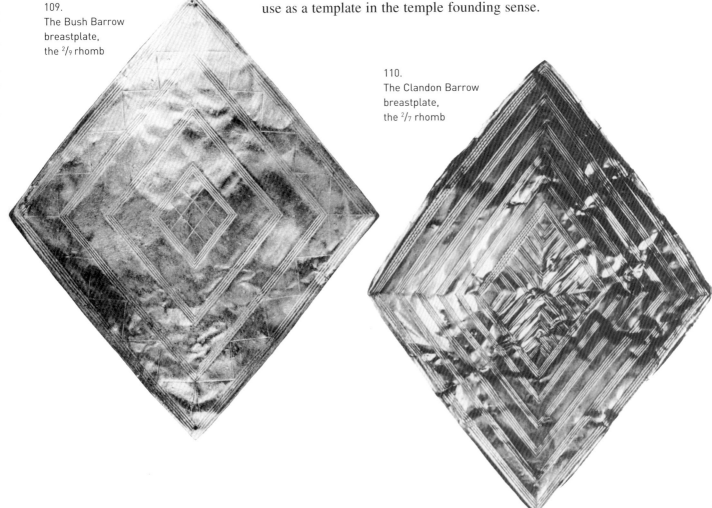

109.
The Bush Barrow
breastplate,
the ^{2}/$_9$ rhomb

110.
The Clandon Barrow
breastplate,
the ^{2}/$_7$ rhomb

The third golden rhomb, the Clandon Barrow breastplate from Dorset (Fig. 110), unfortunately has suffered more battering through the passage of time than the Bush Barrow template but not too much to obliterate the information we need: the key angles. Firstly, we discover on close scrutiny that the precision of this plate is not quite as consistent as the larger Bush Barrow plate, yet if we measure the five concentric wider angles of the internal rhombs (we do not include the outer angle which has suffered most from external distortion), they are consistently $102\,^3/_4°$. When this apparently obscure angle is placed on the centre of a circle it divides the circle into *two sevenths* to an accuracy of less than $^1/_4$ of a degree.[*]

111.
The Hurlers, a group of three stone circles, Bodmin Moor, Cornwall

---

[*] The true angle would be 102° 51' 25" which is the accurate two sevenths of 360° on the total circle.

112.

A schematic freehand sketch of the Bush Barrow template demonstrating the numerical aspect of the pattern divisions. The ancient Chinese, Hebrew, Arabic and Jain 'magic square' number sequence (summing 15) has been placed speculatively into the ninefold division of the centre shape. Do the four sides of the nine angles relate through 36 to the ancient convention for dividing the whole circle into 360 degrees? Does the pattern on both the edge and centre hint at the usage of a decimal base to megalithic or Wessex mathematics? How calendaric could this plate be?

But before our enthusiasm for this result colours our judgment, we have to explain the fact that some of the angles on the opposite side of the plate differ from this result by as much as 2°. One possible solution to this inconsistency could lie in the fact that both the larger breastplates have an unusually large lip or turned-around outer edge. Bearing in mind the preciousness and hard-earned nature of the material it would be too easy to pass it off as an excess of stiffening; a more practical possibility is that the plates were covers or metal receptacles for other plates.[*] These other templates could have been of less durable, probably organic, material, long since deteriorated. Such a solution could be related to the fact that the organic or wooden rhomb was the working tool for practical mathematics whilst the precious covering was the 'sacred' receptacle.[†]

The unavoidable fact is that each of the three surviving gold rhombs, although differing in size, has inherent in its shape special divisions of a circle: two sixths, two ninths and two sevenths respectively. Not only are these last two particularly difficult geometrical divisions of a circle but they both occur by implication in the surveys of the stone circles: Allan Water as we have already mentioned embodies the ninefold division, and both Borrowstone Rig and Moel Ty Uchaf contain the seven. A reinforcement to this connection between the plates and the stone circles lies in the fact that both the Borrowstone Rig and the Allan Water geometries contain two sevenths and two ninths of their circles respectively.

Added to this, the outer band of the larger Bush Barrow template is divided into *nine* triangular compartments per edge, as is the centre in a rhombic grid of nine compartments similar to the Magic Square division: by the placing of the first nine digits in such a 'square' in a particular manner both horizontally, vertically and diagonally they sum to 15 (Fig. 112). Peoples as distinct as the Arab Muslims and Jains of India as well as the Chinese authors of *I Ching* and the Tibetan Buddhists have all allotted transcendental properties to this number arrangement.

---

[*] There is evidence of wooden rhombs which were inside these gold containing rhombs.

[†] There is a curious reinforcement to this idea in the two mysterious objects that were contained within the breastplate of Aaron, called the Urmin and Thummin. No explanation is given as to their precise nature but they were consulted by the priest to obtain special kinds of knowledge. (See Exodus 28,30.)

We believe that embodied here in this breastplate are a series of very important philosophical values all relating to the number nine. Equally there are perennial philosophical values associated with the sixfold divisions embodied in the smallest gold rhomb also found at Bush Barrow (Fig. 113).

The sixfold division of a whole has a primordial value in all three Abrahamic monotheistic religions (Judaism, Christianity and Islam): the number of days of creation are six, in Judaism, Christianity and Islam. In the most ancient Chinese document known as the 'Classic of Change' *(I Ching)* is embodied, according to sinologist Joseph Needham,[9] all the accumulative knowledge of many centuries of Chinese science. The opening passages of this classic deal with the pattern of *six* lines, the hexagram, called *ch'ien* (the creative), considered to be the source of all the other sixty-four hexagrams (Fig. 114).

The most immediate cross-cultural comparison to come to hand is the material of the Old Testament where we have Solomon's proverb: 'Let not mercy and truth forsake thee: bind them about thy neck; write them upon the table of thine heart.' (Proverbs 3,3). This exhortation contains two very important concepts which make a possible comparison with the Bronze Age British breastplates. The first is that mercy and truth are to be associated with a tablet; the second the association with wearing the truth upon the heart. The Jewish high priest traditionally wears a breastplate into which are set twelve appropriate semi-precious or precious stones. This exhortation of Solomon's is not isolated as he says further: 'My Son, keep thy Father's commandment, and forsake not the law of thy Mother: bind them continually upon the heart and tie them about thy neck.' (Solomon 6,20–21) The tradition of the breastplate is found in Exodus 34,3:

3 'And they did beat the gold into thin plates ...
8 And he made the breastplate of cunning work ...
9 It was four-square; they made the breastplate double a span was the length thereof, and a span was the breadth thereof, *being* double.
10 And they set in it in four rows of stones: *the first* row was a sardis (or ruby), a topaz, and a carbuncle: this was the first row.
11 And the second row, an emerald, a sapphire, and a diamond.
12 And the third row, a ligure, an agate, and an amethyst.
13 And the fourth row, a beryl, an onyx, and a jasper: *they* were enclosed in pouches of gold in their enclosings.

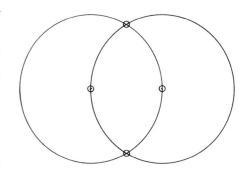

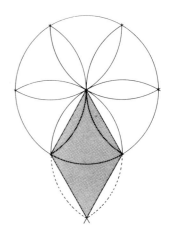

113.
The sixfold division embodied in the smallest Bush Barrow gold plate

114.
The creative principle of the *I Ching*, an initial sixness

7	26	8	19	16	35
33	28	32	5	9	4
20	25	6	31	12	17
2	21	18	29	11	30
34	10	23	14	27	3
15	1	24	13	36	22

115.
The cosmological arrangement of the square of the Sun. The arrangement according to Frederick Bligh Bond as derived from the numerical values of the placing of the tribes in the camp of the Israelites. The total sum of all digits is 666, the sum down or across any line is 111.

14 And the stones *were* according to the names of the children of Israel, twelve according to their names, like the engravings of a signet, every one with its name according to the twelve tribes.'

Here again is the tradition of correspondences: as with the metals, this time precious stones are corresponded with the tribes of Israel. Earlier in Exodus (28,15) we find the breastplate called the 'breastplate of judgment' followed by the phrase 'with cunning work' making a link between the value system of divine judgment and cleverness or skill, both qualities that would be expected if the breastplate were associated with astronomical wisdom and knowledge. This we will return to shortly. Later in this same passage the position and symbolism of the breastplate is reaffirmed (28,29):

> And Aaron shall bear the names of the children of
> Israel in the breastplate of judgment upon his heart,
> when he goeth in unto the holy place for a memorial
> before the Lord continually.

After this passage immediately follows the enigmatic reference to the Urim and Thummin already mentioned above:

> And thou shalt put in the breastplate of judgment the
> Urim and Thummin; and they shall be upon Aaron's
> heart when he goeth before the Lord ...[*]

---

[*] This mysterious pair of objects is mentioned again six times, in Leviticus 8,8; Numbers 27,21 where a judgment before Eleazar was counselled ... 'after the judgment of Urim' and in Deuteronomy 33,8. When Moses before his death gave his belongings to the leaders of the twelve tribes he said to Levi 'Let thy Thummim and thy Urim be with thy holy one ...' When we come to the passage in 1 Samuel 28,6 we find even more oracular implications: 'And when Saul inquired of the Lord and the Lord answered him not, neither by dreams, nor by Urim, nor by prophets. Then Saul said unto his servants, seek me a woman that hath a familiar spirit, that I may go to her, and enquire of her.' Next in Ezra 2,63 we return to the mystery, as what we learn is merely that the Urim and Thummim are either the mark of a true priest, or that only a priest may have such objects: 'The Governor said unto them, That they should not eat of the most holy things till there stood up a priest with Urim and Thummim ....' Finally Nehemiah relates exactly the same situation (7,65): the need of a priest with Urim and Thummim to cleanse the people concerned.

An analysis of the symbolism of the twelvefold system represented by the twelve tribes of Israel has been taken by many scholars to have an astronomical connection. We will choose one such biblical scholar and relate his findings in detail as they have direct bearing on our thesis of the astronomical connection between template, temple and the 'contemplation of the first principles and the cosmos' proper to the use of a temple. Frederick Bligh Bond was both a professional architect and an archaeologist as well as a student of the Old and New Testaments, and his interest was in the 'inner mathematics' of the Bible, similar to the technique advocated by Jagadguru Shankaracharya for the deeper understanding of the Vedas. It is a commonly accepted fact that Hebrew, Greek, Arabic and certain Gothic alphabets, like the Sanskrit, had numerical values for each of their letters.

In a private and unpublished paper Bond states his convictions that the chapters under the heading 'Book of Numbers' in the Old Testament contain important mathematical formulae which have direct bearing on the mathematical methods used by the ancient Jewish priests to calculate their calendar. To summarize Bond's reasoning:

1. He believed it clear that both numerical and geometrical principles were indicated in the 'Book of Numbers.'
2. He accepts certain premises, namely:
   — a. that the form of Heavenly things are to be taken as spherical or circular; whilst
   — b. the form of the Earthly reflection of these principles will be square or cubic, but there must be an *arithmetic mean* or symbol by which Heavenly form can be expressed in Earthly terms (remember the incommensurability of the circle, through the value of *pi,* and rational increments of the megalithic yards that are central in Thom's thesis on 'flattening' the Neolithic circles);
   — c. this reconciling number is obtained by the original chapter and Parashioth divisions, being 36 and 10 respectively;
   — d. the number 36 (6×6) when related to the circle gives the most 'perfect' division, the 360°, which is directly related to the 36-fold division into the 12 zodiacal houses and 36 decanates of ancient astronomy;
   — e. this is expressed in earthly 'square' form in the geometry of the camp of the Israelites, the 6×6 division of a square into 36 sub-unit squares (and is incidentally known as the 'square of the Sun').

6	32	3	34	35	1
7	11	27	28	8	30
24	14	16	15	23	19
13	20	22	21	17	18
25	29	10	9	26	12
36	5	33	4	2	31

116.

Another arrangement of the square of the Sun according to Wallis-Budge

Bond goes on to demonstrate the numerical properties of this arrangement of numbers, which operate in a remarkable way:

— the numbers from 1 to 36 are displaced in the squares so that they sum to 111 per line, vertically and horizontally;
— each set of 6 lines horizontally or vertically sums 666 (a solar number according to both Bond and Wallis-Budge), which is also the sum of the numbers from 1 to 36;[10]
— further solar and calendaric significance is posited by Bond in the sum of the peripheral 20 cells which is 365, the days of the solar year in whole numbers, and it is this property of his arrangement that significantly differs from Wallis-Budge's.

Bond goes on to point out that 666 is 18 times 37, which he explains gives rise to the special relation between 36 and 37 in the ancient Judaic tradition: which allows the addition or subtraction of unity, the 'number of completion,' from a given number to demonstrate special relationships. We will see the value of this number in the adjustment between solar and lunar rhythms presently. Bond finds the number 37 of particular significance throughout his numerical studies of the ancient Jewish scriptural mathematics. It is a point of astronomical interest to add here that Jupiter moves through 37° of the 360° of the sky during one year.

Next he explains the relationship between the geometries of circle and square and says that the 'squaring of the circle' can be considered the rationalizing in earthly terms of the circular movements of the heavens. As we have seen the outer 20 cells of the square total 365, but in the other arrangement given by Wallis-Budge the outer numbers total 370 (10×37). Biblical students such as Dr Milo Mohan, Bond points out, have shown that there is a connection between biblical prophetic eras and the need for an intercalary year, which he has called the 'Diluvian Year.'

The method of using this mathematical arrangement is derived directly from the numbers of the twelve tribes of Israel, which in turn relates it to the stones of the breastplate, the more so as Wallis-Budge demonstrates this particular arrangement is to be engraved on a gold plate, the metal of the Sun, in the following way. Because we must reckon in whole days, from dawn to the next dawn, we make the solar year 365 days, but as we and the ancients knew, this leaves a shortage of a quarter of a day in each year, so in twenty years five days would be lost. The correction of five days must be made in the 21st year, which will therefore be a year of 370 days. Bond sums this up in relation to our 'Magic' square as:

20 years at 365 days each=7,300 days
1 year at 370 days   = 370
                         7,670 days (or 21×365.24 days)

This is quite good, but using the 19-year Metonic cycle of solar lunar concurrence is better:

19 years at 365 days each=6,935 days
        1 year at 370 days = 370
                         7,305 days (or 20 years of
                                  365.25 days)

This brings the numerical arrangement of 36 squares (numerically derived by Bond from the names of the twelve tribes, twelve captains and twelve fathers of captains) with its characteristic twenty outer cells into line as a tool for accurate cosmic and calendaric calculation. This is confirmed in its relation to the breastplate by the nature of the metal, gold, and the engraving of the twelve tribes, which in their full representative numbers become 36 in the 'Book of Numbers.' And finally, there is a direct confirmation of Bond's symbolism from Josephus:

> He also appointed the breastplate to be placed in the
> Middle of the Ephod, to resemble the earth, for that
> has the very middle place of the world ... And for the
> twelve stones, whether we understand by them the
> months, or whether we understand the like number of
> the signs of that circle the Greeks call the zodiac, we
> shall not be mistaken in their meaning.[11]

Almost halfway between the ancient British templates and the jades of ancient China is the site of an early Bronze Age burial in Alaca Huyuk, Turkey. In 1937 thirteen royal tombs were uncovered. These are described by Jaquetta Hawkes as one of the most spectacular finds yet made in Anatolia. Within the twenty-foot by ten-foot graves, lined with stone and covered by an elaborate timber canopy, lay the bodies of kings and queens surrounded by many ritual objects. The bodies themselves were decked in their personal

117.
A gold flagon, chalice and pin, brooch,
bracelet ornament and copper Sun disc.
From the tombs of Alaca Huyuk.

118.
An early Bronze Age gold buckle found
at Alaca Huyuk. Note the central rhomb.

possessions, weapons by the men and domestic toilet articles and
jewellery by the women.

It is the so-called gold buckle worn on the breast of one of the
'kings' that caught our attention, as it appeared to have significance
beyond its obvious function as a breast-buckle.

It is illustrated admirably placed in front of one of the bronze
grilles in Lloyd's *Early Highland Peoples of Anatolia* (Fig. 117).
Here we see a double circle form, rather like a figure eight in profile, made from beaten gold, with two holes at the respective centres
of the circles (Fig. 118). Through the hole is threaded a gold pin
with geometrically radial fins at its head; it was apparently used as
a buckle by threading the pin alternately through the gold plate and
the garment below (see Fig. 117).

The double circle plate has two kinds of decorative articulation:
the strongest pattern is seven circles with central raised points, three
each in the respective upper and lower circles and one exactly on
the area joining them. The second decorative feature is the small
bump-like protrusions surrounding the perimeter and even more
interesting, a pair of diagonal lines of similar small relief knobs
making a rhomb across the centre.

In terms of both the British templates and the circumpolar sighting jade template from China, this particular breastplate can only be
considered a degenerate form of geometry. It is well to remember

that this is the common fate of such objects. When their more profound significance is lost or obscured they degenerate into decorative insignia of power, instead of being an instrument of power in
themselves. The Emporial Pi in ancient China is a perfect example
of this, for the later Emperors apparently did not know why they
were wearing the jade ring on their breasts apart from the fact that
it was a traditional symbol. These rings even became smooth-edged
and therefore would have been useless for their original function of
sighting the circumpolar stars.

To return to the Alaca Huyuk gold plate, although precise measurement has yet to be made, it is not expected to yield anything that
could be taken as geometrically precise. If our thesis is correct and
this is a degenerate form, retaining the symbolism but with relaxed
precision, we would expect to find only an approximation to a two-
sevenths rhomb. The clue to this is in the seven embossed circles
and the fact that the rhomb itself is defined by seven small knobs
on each side of the central overlapping rhomb. The central pin, as
a miniature ontological axis, has a hexagonal set of fins at its head
and penetrates through the centre of the upper and lower circles as
a symbol of an axis uniting the Heavenly and Earthly realms (see
Fig. 121). It echoes the symbolism of the shaman's pole.

What cannot escape notice is the larger grille made from
bronze and apparently less than 12 inches across (Fig. 119). It is
ovoid in shape with 54 (6×9) holes in it in a geometric pattern.
Attached to the top face is a projecting loop from which hangs a
circular metal disc with eight radial segmental holes cut into it.
This smaller hanging disc is approximately ¼ the width of the
larger axis of the main grille. On closer inspection the reduction
on the vertical axis of the larger grille, to make it into an oval,
determines the shape of the contained rhomb within and thereby
the characteristic shapes of the 54 triangular holes. The whole
oval is dominated by a major rhomb from top to sides and to
base. This base point is lost in the rectangular forking presumably
for fixing the grille onto the burial structure. This rhomb would
have been a perfect square had the oval been a circle, but what
is interesting from our point of view is that the rhomb approxi-
mates very fairly to the 40° of the two-ninths rhomb of the Bush
Barrow template. It is noticeable that the only other numerical
value embodied in the object is the 54 (6×9) holes cut through
it, and this number has a deliberation about it because the bottom
two triangles, which have been omitted, would have made it 56 or

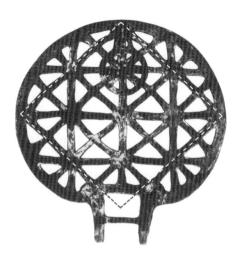

119.
A copper grille 'Sun disc' from Alaca Huyuk
with Bush Barrow template superimposed

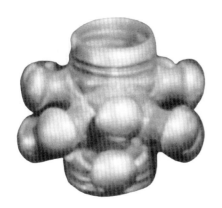

120.
An ornament from Alaca Huyuk showing twelve hemispherical projections arranged symmetrically

8×7. The difference between the small circle and larger ovoid is another mark of deliberate differentiation.

Further confirmation of how widespread was mathematical knowledge of the time lies in a small object, also made of gold, in the same illustration of Lloyd's book. This has a remarkable structural resemblance to the stone ball in the Ashmolean museum at Oxford. The object has twelve hemispherical projections standing out from a cylindrical axis (Fig. 122). The twelve projections are arranged in beautiful symmetry, three sets of four, in a manner similar to the cuboctahedral pattern frequently found among the Scottish Neolithic spheres (the subject of the next chapter). But it has the addition of two openings through which the hole passes, thus becoming a fourteen-headed object which we have discussed at length in the descriptions of the carved stone spheres.

In addition to this geometric object is an exquisite gold pin (see *Early Highland Peoples of Anatolia,* p.26) also in Ankara Museum (Fig. 123). This has a fine polyhedral head. On it there are circular beadlike discs for each face of a cube, on which a gold symmetrical cross had been added with a centre stud. Five of the faces of the cube are thus represented, with the sixth extending to become the blade of the pin. As Lloyd remarks, these early Bronze Age objects demonstrate that in Anatolia at that time there were few processes of metal work unknown to the craftsmen. We would add that there was probably also much mathematical knowledge of one kind or another.

Conclusion

Whatever shortcomings or speculative aspects there are to our interpretations and cross-cultural comparisons, what cannot be avoided is the remarkable coincidence between: (a) the three gold rhombs having geometrically significant angles; (b) these angles

121.
A gold pin from Alaca Huyuk

being two sixths, two sevenths and two ninths of a complete circle respectively; and (c) in relation to the megalithic mathematics of the inhabitants of Britain that these geometrical proportions should be evident in certain of the stone circle (temple) layouts.

We believe there is sufficient evidence to consider these objects as templates or the containers of working templates (see Figs. 122–24).

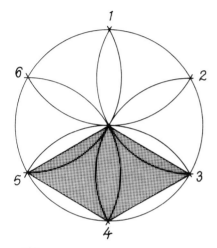

122.
The smaller Bush Barrow template as the divisor of a circle into $^2/_6$ or $^1/_6$

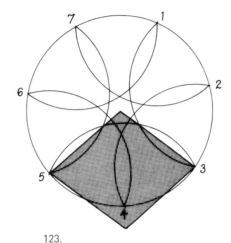

123.
The Clandon Barrow template as the divisor of a circle into $^2/_7$

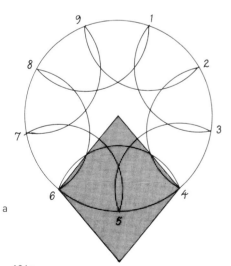

a

124a.
The larger Bush Barrow template as the divisor of a circle into $^2/_9$

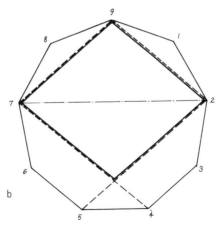

b

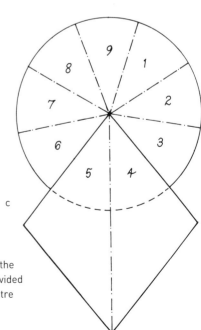

c

124b–c.
The resultant template as a function of tracing the number pattern 9, 2, 5, 4, 7, 9, and **c**, a circle divided by the template with its point placed on the centre

125.
Stonehenge by moonlight

7. Platonic Spheres —
A Millennium Before Plato

Thus open out the Tao, and it envelops all space: and yet how small it is, not enough to fill the hand!

> Huai Nan Tzu d. 122 BC[1]

Knowledge is simple recollection.

> Plato *(Phaedo* 72.E)

Our master is Plato, especially in his works Timaeus *and* Phaedo; *whereas Aristotle remains the loadstar of those who seek truth by the empirical method ... this mystic Platonic method is a different kind of philosophy and a shorter way than that of the peripatetics, which loses itself in secondary questions.*

> Suhrawardi d. 1191[2]

Raise the stone and there thou shalt find me.

> *Oxyrhynchus Papyri.* The Gospel according to Thomas (log.77)

Know oh brother ... that the study of sensible geometry leads to skill in all the practical arts, while the study of intelligible geometry leads to skill in the intellectual arts because this science is one of the gates through which we move to the knowledge of the essence of the soul, and that is the root of all knowledge.

> From the *Rasa 'il* by the Brotherhood of Purity (Trans. S.H. Nasr)

Prehistoric solid geometry:
Introduction to the carved stone spheres

The many recent discoveries which indicate the mathematical abilities of Britain's Neolithic peoples could be put forward to claim that the history of mathematics need be rewritten. Such a claim would no doubt be met with scepticism, especially if it were shown that

126.
Set of stone spheres with tetrahedral
symmetry. The central front one has white
tape added to clarify the symmetry.

the evidence for such an assertion had been staring us in the face for
over one hundred years. However, a new approach to the material
would seem to indicate that this may not be far from the truth.

When archaeologists were confronted in the second half of the
last century with beautiful and precise solid geometrical figures, veritable works of art carved in stone, they were either reluctant to recognize their sophisticated symmetry or lacked the perceptual ability to
fully appreciate it. It seems they simply didn't believe that the archaic
inhabitants of Britain were capable of making or even conceiving
such sophisticated mathematical forms. Without speculating on what
these objects may have meant to the makers, we intend to discuss
their mathematical significance. There is no doubt they were of considerable value to their makers due to the dedication and concentrated
skill devoted to their carving — many are of granite and would have
taken months to complete. As we have noted with the stone circles,
the same forms could more easily have been created from timber, so
'permanence' was apparently of the essence.

The mathematical content, in terms of the sophistication of the
concepts exhibited in the forms of the stones, can be estimated by

studying the laws of space division and symmetry. We can also refer to the earliest recorded awareness of these 'figures,' and the remarkable fact is that these Neolithic objects display the regular mathematical symmetries normally associated with the Platonic solids, yet appear to be at least a thousand years before the time of either Pythagoras or Plato. There are no written records, to our knowledge, that refer to these basic solid geometrical forms prior to those implied in the *Timaeus* of Plato. Yet it would be a great shortcoming to assume the facts contained in this cosmology were the invention of Plato himself. It seems far more likely that the dialogue form of the *Timaeus* was deliberately chosen to convey the fact that the reader was being privileged to 'sit in' on an ancient oral tradition.

Let us turn to the *Timaeus* by Plato and sift through the evidence as presented in this earliest of written sources. Timaeus himself

127.
Platonic set of carved Neolithic spheres with coloured tape to show their symmetries. Modern plastic dice of corresponding symmetries have been placed on the inside of the circle:

green = tetrahedron
red = octahedron
yellow = icosahedron
white (red numbers) = cube
white = dodecahedron

128.
A beautifully incised tetrahedral
Neolithic sphere

was believed to represent the views of the Pythagoreans who were, according to Aristotle, transmitters of an oral tradition.

Plato expressed the cosmology in geometric symbolism in the discourse of the *Timaeus,* and a graphic commentary on this aspect of the symbolism will be most useful for an understanding of the relationship to the stone models. This symbolism reduces the essence of earth, water, air and fire, the basic elements of our sensorial experience, to equally essential geometric figures.

Plato discusses the doctrine that states that the essential relationships between phenomena are triangular or triadic sets and as such represent the act of the artificer of the universe when bringing 'beautiful order' into the four elements.* These triadic

---

* The Thomas Taylor translation of the *Timaeus* will be used because of its distinctive inner sympathy with Plato.[3]

a

b

relationships reflect the three prior subsistences; being, place and generation. And when the creator ordered the primary chaotic mixture, fire and earth, water and air, he did so with forms and numbers. As Plato states, 'every species of body possesses profundity. It is necessary that every depth should comprehend the nature of a plane,' that is, that all solidity can be expressed in the planes that bound it. And, as the basis of rectitude, the ultimate polygon that every plane can be reduced to is a triangle; therefore we should look to the triangle for our essential sets of relationship (Figs. 129a–c).

> But all triangles originate from two species; one
> of which possesses one right angle, and two acute
> angles. And the other one of these contains one right
> angle distributed with equal sides; but in the first
> unequal angles are distributed with unequal sides.[4]

To avoid accusing Plato of deliberate obscurity on the one hand or inaccuracy on the other it is very important to remember that he is talking in a symbolic manner as well as in precise geometric terms. Having clearly stated that the four elements are the basis of our world, he later says, 'There is also a certain fifth composition which Divinity employed in the fabrication of the universe ...'[5] This is a clear indication that the five solid figures that bear Plato's name (the tetrahedron, octahedron, icosahedron, cube and pentagonal

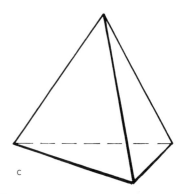

c

129a–c.
a.
The spherical version of tetrahedral symmetry as carved by the Scottish Neolithic community at least a millennium before Plato

b.
A further version of the same basic symmetry made up of four spherical pebbles in pyramidal form

c.
The planar version of the same symmetry as described by Plato in his *Timaeus*, the true pyramid with four triangular faces

In all cases the mathematical law of symmetry is constant — four kinds of event equally distributed in space, yet in form each is quite distinct.

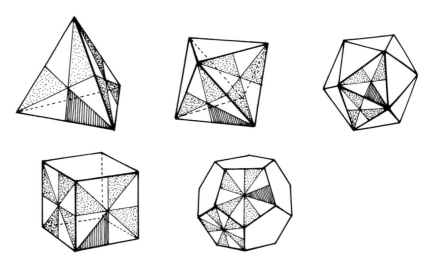

130.

The Platonic solids: their component faces and inherent symmetries. Also shown is the smallest single triangle of which each can be composed. Left to right: tetrahedron, octahedron, icosahedron, cube and dodecahedron.

dodecahedron) were known to him (Fig. 130). Strictly speaking *three* basic triangles are required to fabricate these five solids which are: the half-equilateral triangle, the half square and the one-tenth of a regular pentagon (Fig. 131). 'We ought therefore to choose the most beautiful,' he says, 'if we wish to commence our investigation in a becoming manner. And if any one shall assert that he has chosen something more beautiful for the composition of these regular figures for each of the elements, earth, water, air and fire, we shall suffer his opinion to prevail; considering him not as an enemy, but as a friend.'[6] This passage has a particular kind of double meaning related to the earlier passage where he summarizes the principles by which the origin of the elements relate to each other. 'The supernal principles of these indeed are known to Divinity, and to the man who is in friendship with Divinity.' Hence the term 'friend' would seem to have a special meaning, referring to the kind of consciousness of or relationship with Divinity the 'friend' in question has achieved.

More specifically if all five of the Platonic bodies in their planar form are reduced to their most elementary constituent we have not two but three triangles as we have shown. But Plato suggests that one proceeds to find the most beautiful — and arrives at the half-

131.

The three basic triangles:

— the half-equilateral (30° 60° 90°)
— the half-square (45° 45° 90°)
— the tenth-pentagon (36° 54° 90°)

All shown in vertical shaded lines in the three shapes.

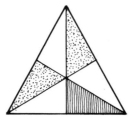
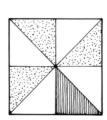
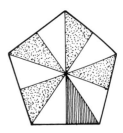

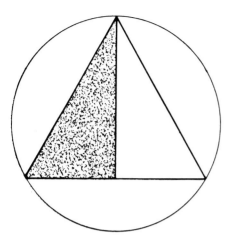 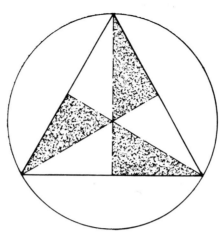 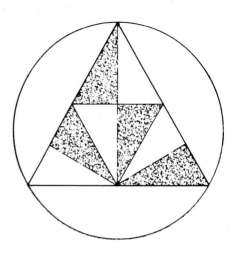

equilateral triangle,* the scalene whose angles are 90° 60° 30° — and it is this that is necessary in making up the prime solid body symbolic of fire: the tetrahedron. Whereas the isosceles triangle, whose angles are 90° 45° 45°, is the one needed to make up the cube, the symbolic body of the earth. In fact it is left to a 'friend' of divinity to discover that the third triangle is the scalene composed of 90° 54° 36° needed to make up the pentagonal dodecahedron of twelve faces symbolizing the heavens or whole. The essential difference here is that this element, sometimes called the ether, is of a different nature from earth, water, air and fire which are apparent to the senses.

Plato's primary triangle, the one with the angles of 60° 30° 90°, can create by symmetrical arrangement the remaining two regular triangulated solids that are possible and permissible in three-dimensional space, the octahedron and the icosahedron relating to air and water respectively. Doubling, by reflection, this prime triangle results in the equilateral triangle. By the principle of similar figures we can demonstrate how the pairing of right- and left-handed versions of the prime triangle can make up the equilateral triangle from one pair, three pairs and four pairs (Fig. 132). By following Plato's cosmic symbolism these triangles can be assembled to construct whole, 'round' regular systems known as the five

132.
The equilateral produced by pairing left and right-hand versions of the prime triangle. Left to right: one pair, three pairs, four pairs.

---

* And this is debatable as the half square has the virtue of balance in the equality of its sides but the half-equilateral triangle chosen by Plato has the triadic consistency of having three sides and three angles whereas the half square has *two* kinds of side and *two* kinds of angle.

133a–b.

a.
A stone sphere with both cubic and octahedral symmetry

b.
Highly polished cubic sphere with octahedral symmetry marked in blue tape

134a–b.

a.
A beautiful example of an octahedron and cube together

b.
Set of dual solids all exhibiting cubic and octahedral symmetry together

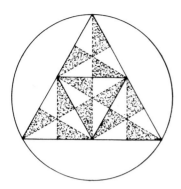

135.
The net of the tetrahedron
composed of 24 basic scalene
30° 60° 90° triangles

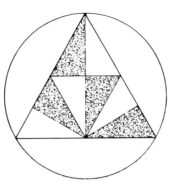

136.
The net of the tetrahedron composed
of 8 half-equilateral triangles

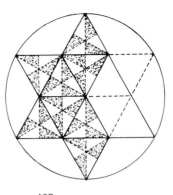

137.
The net of the octahedron composed
of 48 basic scalene triangles

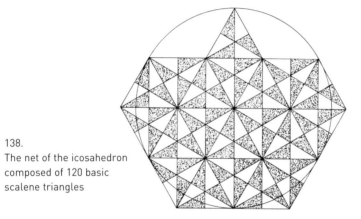

138.
The net of the icosahedron
composed of 120 basic
scalene triangles

Platonic solids. In fact only three such systems of totally regular assemblies of equilateral triangles are possible: the tetrahedron, the octahedron and the icosahedron, with four, eight, and twenty triangles respectively.

Firstly, the most simple, the four-faced tetrahedron (the symbol of fire), made up by 24 of the smallest basic scalene 90° 60° 30° triangles, although the same figure can be made up of eight of the half-equilateral triangles (Figs. 135–37). Secondly the eight-faced octahedron symbolizing air, made up of 48 of the smaller triangles (Fig. 137); this same figure can be made up of 16 half-equilateral triangles. To complete the triad there is the twenty-faced icosahedron (Fig. 138). The remaining two Platonic figures, the cube and the dodecahedron, are constituted as follows: the cube can be made

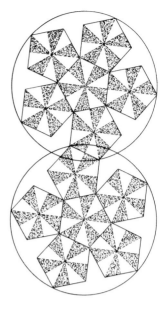

139.
The net or composition of the cube

140.
The net or composition of the
dodecahedron

up of 12, 24 or 48 half-squares (Fig. 139); the dodecahedron can be made up of 60 pairs of its characteristic triangle (Fig. 140).[7]

It will be noticed that by dividing Plato's basic equilateral triangle in half he arrives at constructions which are based on multiples of eight: tetrahedron 8, octahedron 2×8, icosahedron 5×8 (Fig. 141). In summary, the regular symmetries in three-dimensional space are based on: the twofold, a single mirror reflection; the threefold, in which the parts are similar in three equal directions; and the fourfold, in which the same reflection principle is true in four directions. Finally we have the fivefold symmetry in which the axis of similarity is in five directions.

141.
The symmetry of the tetrahedron,
the octahedron and the
icosahedron showing multiples of
eight half-equilateral triangles

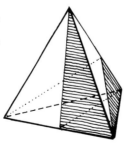

In three-dimensional assemblies (Figs. 142–44), the tetrahedron embodies the symmetries of two- and three-foldness; the octahedron embodies the symmetries of two, three- and four-foldness, as does its dual (see Fig. 143b) the cube (symbol of earth) which is generated by the conjunction of the isosceles triangles gathered into groups of four with their right angles in the centre. The icosahedron embodies the regular symmetries of two-, three- and fivefold symmetry, as does the pentagonal dodecahedron, its dual, thus completing the five regular solids: one constructed of squares, three of equilateral triangles, and one of regular pentagons.

If we now investigate further the 'certain fifth composition' we find that the number of basic elements needed for the conjunction

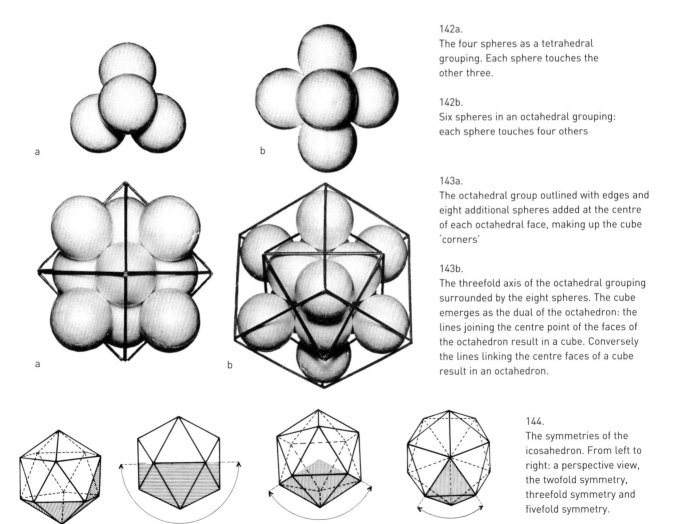

142a.
The four spheres as a tetrahedral grouping. Each sphere touches the other three.

142b.
Six spheres in an octahedral grouping: each sphere touches four others

143a.
The octahedral group outlined with edges and eight additional spheres added at the centre of each octahedral face, making up the cube 'corners'

143b.
The threefold axis of the octahedral grouping surrounded by the eight spheres. The cube emerges as the dual of the octahedron: the lines joining the centre point of the faces of the octahedron result in a cube. Conversely the lines linking the centre faces of a cube result in an octahedron.

144.
The symmetries of the icosahedron. From left to right: a perspective view, the twofold symmetry, threefold symmetry and fivefold symmetry.

or construction of the element water (120 of 90° 60° 30° mirrored triangles) equals the number of basic elements needed to make up the 'universe' (120 of 90° 54° 36° triangles mirrored to each other). This clue, when related to a comment made after the construction of the first solid, the tetrahedron symbolizing fire, leads us to the solution of an age-old problem. This solution could be the basis for accusing Plato of blurring the fact that three basic triangles are necessary if we are building *planar* figures. The important comment is that 'the first solid species was constituted, distributive of the whole *circumference* into equal and similar parts.'[8] (The italics are the present author's.)

If *circumference* is interpreted literally, we are also dealing with a spherical surface. This not only satisfies the principle that it is the sphere that is the 'fairest form' for the universe, the differentiated elements as such being merely perceived but none the less essential subdivisions of that unity in which their reality lies. To return to the

145.
Sphere with simultaneous icosahedral and dodecahedral symmetry. The blue tapes emphasize the icosahedron edges.

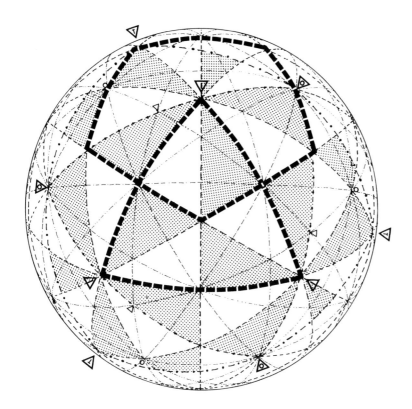

146.
The reciprocity of the icosahedron and the dodecahedron. The bold triangle divides the sphere into 20 equal areas — the spherical icosahedron — and there are 6 component triangles per area making a total of 120. The bold pentagon divides the sphere's surface into 12 equal parts — the spherical dodecahedron — with 10 component triangles per face making a total of 120 for the whole sphere.

significance of numbers of elements in the dodecahedron and icosa-hedron, we see that if a spherical surface is divided into the greatest number of equal triangles the result is 120. Most significantly Plato *does not ever give specific angles.* Therefore, when it is learnt that these 120 parts are both the composite symmetry of the icosahedron and dodecahedron we realize that indeed there are only two kinds of triangle *on the sphere* which encompass exactly the spherical projection of all five regular figures. The implications are that Plato was merely giving an introduction to a whole esoteric science of both plane and spherical geometry as a cosmology: 'Since our eyes often open the way to the understanding of a problem, it would be as well to draw a diagram' (see Fig. 146).[9]

This projection of symmetrical lines on the surface of the sphere demonstrates certain essential factors bearing on the interpretation of Platonic cosmology as outlined in the *Timaeus*. Firstly all lines seen in the drawing are parts of similar sized circles — that is the circle that divides the sphere in two equal halves — this particular circle on any given sphere is called a 'great' circle.

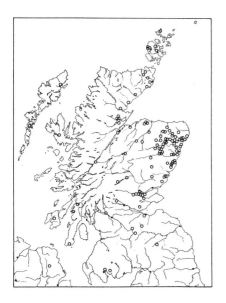

147.
Sites of the discovery of the Scottish Neolithic stone spheres

The number of great circles on this drawing is directly related to the minimal number necessary to subdivide the sphere into the greatest number of equal parts. This means that a set of significant crossing-over points of the great circles lie at equal distances from each other; the pattern enclosed in these crossing-over points creates the twenty faces of equilateral spherical triangles and is known as the spherical icosahedron. The twelve nodal points of the icosahedron are also the centres of the faces of the pentagon spherical dodecahedron. This demonstrates clearly that each of the component one-sixth of an equilateral triangle elements are identically the same components that make up the spherical pentagonal face of the spherical dodecahedron. This confirms Plato's assertion that only *two* triangles are necessary to create the set of symmetrically regular figures if their common source is the containing sphere of unity. However the triangle which is on twentieth of the sphere's surface is the 'fairest' in the sense that it can be seen to be responsible for establishing the unity between all five of the Platonic figures on the sphere.

Having confirmed that Plato knew the rules of regularity in space, without literally spelling it out, we can begin to appreciate the full implications of the British Neolithic geometric spheres. They represent a quite amazing achievement of balance between one symmetry and its two expressions — known as the regular duals. It is in the dual aspect of the regular figures that the pre-Pythagorean Scottish versions become so remarkable. We never

148.
The spherical dodecahedron and icosahedron both shown in relation to the cubic symmetry which is defined by the diamond-shaped tape

149.
The 'spherical' cube and its dual,
the octahedron, modelled and on a
Scottish sphere

find the straight-edged and flat faceted versions of the mathematical symmetries which we have been led to expect from the Greek tradition, but in their place the duality of cube and octahedron are displayed *simultaneously* (Fig. 149).

The way in which it becomes possible to present two figures simultaneously is through what are known as 'small' and 'great' circles. On the sphere, the divisions of symmetry are defined mathematically as 'great' circles when their centres coincide with the centre of the sphere and describe the largest possible orbit on the sphere's surface, that is, the circumference. 'Small' circles are all the remaining complete circles that can be inscribed on the sphere. As these are theoretically indefinite in number we can shorten the list by taking those which occur symmetrically and regularly around the whole surface. As we might expect, these also coincide with the circles drawn within the faces of the Platonic figures, for instance, the cube will have six small circles, one for each face. The three fundamental spherical models to exhibit the essential three-dimensional symmetries would be: first, the spherical tetrahedron; second, the joint spherical octahedron and cube; and third, the joint spherical icosahedron and dodecahedron. These three spherical models all exist among the Scottish finds, and, in the opinion of the present author, qualitatively stand as the supreme achievement in these hand-sized objects.

Given the original carvers were not working by pure inspiration, we suggest that they wove a flexible thonging around the prospective stone sphere to establish the salient great circles as their basic guide to symmetry. This calls our attention to another curious

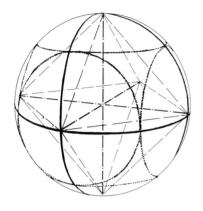

150.

The basic symmetry of octahedral geometry: the 'small' circles are centred on the points of the octahedron and become simultaneously circles in the face of the cube within the same sphere. The octahedron is shown in dotted line with its surface symmetry in thick line.

property to emerge from these regular great circle divisions of the sphere's surface, and that is the fact that *seven* particular polyhedrons or solid figures result. Simultaneously with the five Platonic figures there are two more which are formed by the union of the cube and the octahedron: this is the fourteen-faced cuboctahedron. And between the icosahedron and dodecahedron is a figure also made up of pure great circles, which is the icosidodecahedron of thirty-two faces. These latter two figures are categorized as semi-regular solids since they have two kinds of faces, whereas the regular solids have only one.

But this is not all. Two more figures are present, which make up a set of *nine*. These last two have similar faces to each other but are categorized as of a lesser symmetry than the two semi-regular figures above and are their duals. The first is known as the rhombic dodecahedron; it has twelve diamond faces and is the dual of the cuboctahedron. The second is known as the rhombic triacontahedron which has thirty 'diamond' faces and is the dual of the icosidodecahedron. Thus there is yet another recurrence of the significant numbers five, seven and nine, this time in terms of regularity and symmetry in the major archetypal divisions of the unitary sphere.

Since 1850 these small carved polyhedrons or incised spheres, so often carved in Britain's hardest stone, which include all the symmetries represented by the Platonic solids, have emerged from archaeological diggings, cairns or been discovered in open fields,

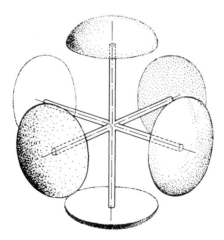

151.

Octahedral small circles protruding on the x, y and z axes in relation to certain of the Scottish spheres

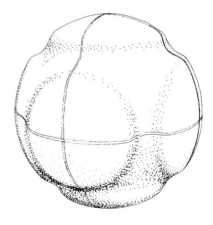

152.

The octahedral symmetry drawn on a stone 'sphere' to demonstrate its mathematical basis yet, inexplicably, nobody seems to have found them mathematically significant. At this moment of writing the author has, during the day, handled five of these remarkable objects in the Ashmolean Museum, Oxford. Although the curator of the prehistoric department was most helpful and polite, nevertheless he had not deemed the spheres important enough to be on show but kept them in a drawer marked 'Scotland' with other 'lesser' objects. Of the five, three were carved of granite or a similar very hard stone, one apparently of sandstone and the fifth, the most complex, of an unrecognizable stone. The striking fact was that there were two spherical tetrahedrons symmetrically outlined and embossed in small circles on the surfaces of a sphere: one of them close to the spherical form, the other cut away to leave the small circles standing out in considerable relief. Here also were two versions of the fourfold symmetry represented by the cube together with the octahedron, which could be described as cuboctahedra. This is a most beautiful and ingenious interpretation of the *x, y, z* axes at 90° to each other in three-dimensional form. The 'faces' of the cube, which are also the 'points' of the octahedron, are worked into circular form following a sixfold division of the sphere. The intervening spaces, the corners of the cube, are left projecting and define the eight cubic corners of the form. Here were two spherical cuboctahedra presumably fabricated over a millennium before Plato, the man some experts call the discoverer, was born!

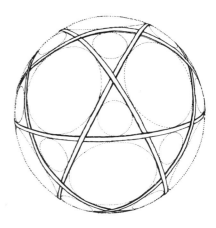

153.
Straps of leather thonging defining the fivefold symmetry on a stone sphere

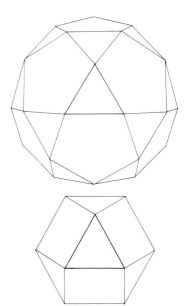

154.
The icosidodecahedron and the cuboctahedron both are made up of continuous 'great' circles which could have been made of thonging

155.
Spherical set exhibiting dual cubic and octahedral symmetries together

I was rapt in admiration as I turned over these remarkable stone objects when another was handed to me which I took to be an icosahedron. This was a far more complicated and skilled piece of carving and seemed to have the twelve characteristic projections of the icosahedron. Each of these bumps protruded like small rounded mountains from the sphere. On careful scrutiny, after establishing apparent fivefold symmetry on a number of the axes, a count-up of the projections revealed 14! So it was not an icosahedron (Fig. 156).

Careful analysis revealed the carver's strategy which was to polarize seven points above the meridian, and seven below, equally spaced. This gave the beautiful artefact a sixfold symmetry at its two poles: a central axial protuberance surrounded symmetrically by six others. The only other place where I had seen anything remotely similar was among the Egyptian antiquities in the British Museum, a stone icosahedron dice, to which we will return later. On investigation it turned out that the majority of the three hundred or more of these objects found so far were of octahedral symmetry, the next highest percentage were of tetrahedral. Next in numerical order came those with seven faces or protrusions which, in a previous publication, we called, in its symmetrical aspect, the 'twin icosacap.'[10] Following these

156.
A carved stone ball with 14 nodes

came representatives of a variety of symmetries yet including the twelve-faceted dodecahedral or icosahedral symmetry. The repeated occurrence of the figure with the seven protrusions suggests a similar symbolism to that of the seven heavens, the seven-pointed star, the seven planets and the seven metals of the later cosmological systems.

Leaving the social function of these stone objects aside, because interpretations become subjective and finally land in that wastepaper-basket of a word, 'cultic,' into which all difficulties are thrown, what we have are objects clearly indicative of a degree of a mathematical ability so far denied to Neolithic man by any archaeologist or mathematical historian. We only 'know' that the Neolithic producer of these objects had such a knowledge of three-dimensional mathematics because of the objects themselves. When one inspects the great variety of these intricate and intelligent objects one marvels at the time, patience and skill employed in their making. Here we have the hardest stone found in Scotland being chosen to create beautiful mathematical symmetries for no apparent utilitarian use! It is just this latter aspect of the objects that has baffled archaeologists to date. However their very existence demonstrates a degree of mathematical awareness which the old school of archaeology still remains reluctant to concede to Neolithic peoples.

We believe they can demonstrably be taken to reinforce Thom's calculations and proposals which were so tardily received by the majority of the archaeological fraternity. The study of the heavens is, after all a spherical activity, needing an understanding of spherical coordinates. If the Neolithic inhabitants of Scotland had constructed Maes Howe before the pyramids were built by the Ancient Egyptians why could they not be studying the laws of three-dimensional coordinates? Is it not more than a coincidence that Plato as well as Ptolemy, Kepler and al-Kindi* attributed cosmic significance to these figures?

Not every ancient stone ball found in Scotland will be a mathematically significant form, as all expressed traditions suffer the law of degeneration: no doubt the later ones deteriorated into decorative

---

* Al-Kindi, latinized to Alkindus, was born around 805 in Kufah. An Islamic philosopher of pure Arab descent, he wrote a treatise on the Platonic solids called *On the Reasons why the Ancients ascribed the Five Figures to the Elements*.

157.

Egyptian icosahedral dice used for consulting the spirit world by making words from the Greek letters on each face when cast

expressions as the forms separated from the knowledge for those who knew how to use it. Should any reader still doubt the necessary symmetric imagination to create one of these mathematical 'handfuls,' they are challenged to find a suitable stone for themselves and proceed first to make it spherical and then describe *four* equal small circles on its surface and carve these into relief form — with nothing but other pieces of stone to carve with.

The circular divisions of the sphere, particularly 'great circles,' which are the largest circles one can inscribe on a sphere, have the effect of least interference to the unity of the sphere yet differentiating the divisions, regular or irregular, that can be made on that sphere. Each great circle 'orbits' the sphere in a literally cyclic manner, a continuous path analogous to the paths of the planets, Sun and Moon around the Earth. At the same time they retain the transcendental quantity of *pi*. Polyhedrons with edges and flat surfaces, like the great pyramids of Egypt and the figures of the Greek mathematicians, are of the nature of the measurable because of the flatness and straightness of their forms. If the flattened circle geometry of the stone-circle temples can be described as proto-geometry, we could similarly call these 'rounded squares' proto-stereometry, or solid geometry, in the same spirit. They are a profound balance of understanding and expression between the measurable and immeasurable, that which is in time and the timeless, the changing and the changeless.

Whatever various interpretations are possible at every level of the larger monuments of the megalithic era, what is unavoidable in these small stone objects is their total clarity of 'language.' They are as clear and concise a statement in their own terms as any that could be made in either verbal or written form. And as such their challenge remains.

158.

This Neolithic sphere demonstrates that whatever the makers may have called this form they were aware of the *principle* of dodecahedral symmetry which Plato ascribed to the universal whole.

Who am I, who
Speaks from the dust,
Who looks from the clay?

Who hears
For the mute stone,
......?

(From the poem 'Self'
by Kathleen Raine,
Collected Poems, 1972)

Night comes, an angel stands
Measuring out the time of stars,
Still are the winds,
And still the hours.

(From the poem 'Nocturne'
by Kathleen Raine,
Collected Poems, 1972)

8. The Planets as Time Keepers: Patterns in Space and Time

Allah hath created seven heavens in harmony.

Quran LXXI.15

Each thing a certain course and law obeys,
Striving to turn back to his proper place;
Nor any settled order can be found,
But that which doth within itself embrace
The births and ends of all things in a round.

Boethius (AD 480–524?) *Consolatio Philosophiae* III.iii.[1]

The Pythagoreans said, that an Harmonic sound is produced
from the motion of the celestial bodies; and they scientifically
collected this from the analogy of their intervals; since
not only the ratios of the intervals of the Sun and Moon,
and Venus and Mercury, but also of the other stars, were
discovered by them.

Simplicus[2]

Where every where *and every* when *is focussed ...*

Dante, *Paradiso* XXIX.12

It is one thing to conclude from reasonable evidence that the Neolithic builders worked star polygons into the layouts of their circles, it is quite another to understand what practical meaning this may have held for them.

Sacred space, in the form of a temple, represents, in this world, a paradigmatic prototype which pre-exists in archetypal space, 'in the beginning' and therefore originates outside existent space; in a similar way sacred time is 'controlled' by the correct — 'timely' — exercise of rites within these boundaries. Sacred time is traditionally cyclic, implying therefore a recurrence of intervals,

159.
The cyclic totality of the 28 phase lunar cycle

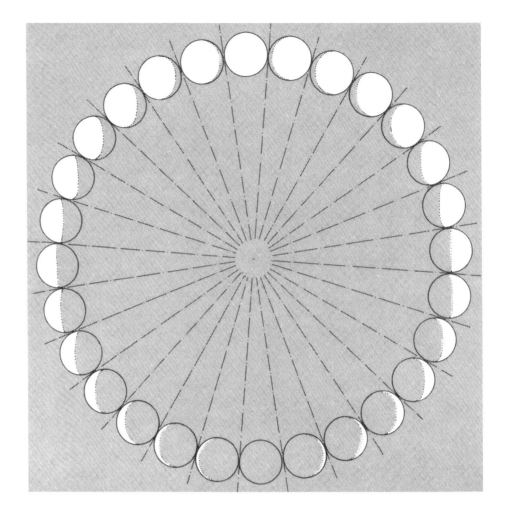

events and even exact circumstances. The circle is the most appropriate form to express undifferentiated space and a totality of time — the full unending cycle (Fig. 159). These two aspects or conditions of existence can be analogously related to properties of the circle in the following way: firstly 'qualified' space can be created by intervals along the circumference of a circle which, by joining with straight lines within the perimeter, create polygons; whereas secondly, sequential time can be considered as the 'cutting off' of similar intervals around the circumference (this is related to the image of Father Time — Chronos — whose moon-like sickle cuts off time, a sectioning which is etymologically related to seconds of time). The centre however is the controlling point, and represents, by a projection into the third dimension, the ontological axis and is thereby symbolically outside time and space. The centre is simultaneously the non-directional point and the non-measurable moment. Because the centre is indivisible (a-tomic) it symbolically represents the primal unity which is both source and goal of the existent.

The awareness of sacred time, or the harmonious concordance between heaven and earth, is by definition the responsibility of all traditional societies. This concordance is the basis of planting, tending, reaping and storing of crops, as it is also the basis of the timing of social events from marriages to initiations, investitures and sacrifices. Plato is a classical spokesman for this traditional view:

> The sight of day and night, the months and the
> returning years, the equinoxes and solstices, has
> caused the invention of number, given us notion of
> time, and made us enquire into the nature of the
> universe; thence we have derived philosophy ...
> we should see the revolutions of intelligence in the
> heavens and use their untroubled courses to guide
> the troubled revolutions in our own understanding,
> which is akin to them ... all audible musical sound is
> given us for the sake of harmony, which has motions
> akin to the orbits in our soul and which, as anyone
> who makes intelligent use of the arts knows, is not to
> be used, as is commonly thought, to give irrational
> pleasure, but as a heaven-sent ally, in reducing to
> order and harmony any disharmony in the revolutions
> within us.[3]

We have been brought up, generally speaking, to consider the revolutions of the planets as turning around the Sun. However our experience is that all the heavenly lights and bodies move around us. These two views are known respectively as the heliocentric or 'sun-centred' system and the geocentric or 'earth-centred' system. It is this latter view which is the common experience of all people who have studied the motions of the heavens, and it is this view that requires study if one is to understand the observational starting point of the ancients (Fig. 160, next page).

160.
The geocentric ('Earth centred') and
heliocentric ('Sun centred') planetary
schemas combined

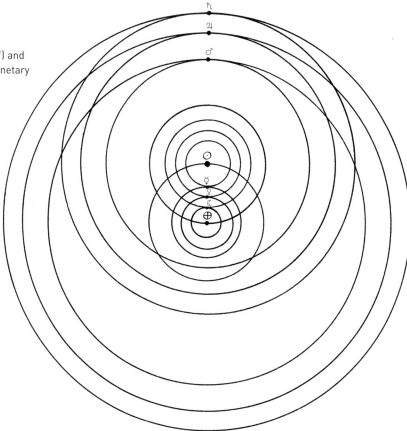

161.
A diagram of the annual path of Mercury
round the Earth using the cycle for 1945 as
an example. The triangle which emerges
from this visible pattern represents the
underlying archetype which is 'outside'
time whilst Mercury's path represents
moving time. The 'hidden' geometry and
the 'trace' represent the two poles of
Islamic pattern. The centre symbol is the
planet Earth, ⊕, the dashed circle is the
orbit of the Sun, ☉, and the heavier dotted
path is the trace of the planet Mercury, ☿,
around the Earth.

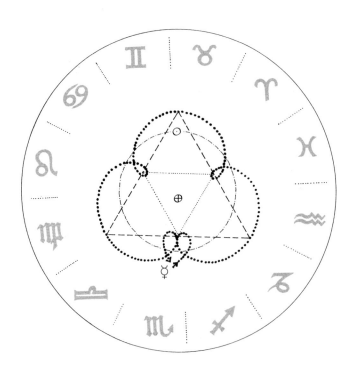

The planets are so named because of their characteristic 'wandering' across the sky and the retrograde loops that they weave on their way. Each planet was considered to be a 'sign of' an archetypal Intelligence both as an individual and unique 'luminary' and as the total pattern that each planetary body traces around the Earth, which is known as its 'sphere.'

Although we know of the sun-centred mechanics of our solar system, the earth-centred view of the ancients must not be dismissed as inaccurate or naïve. Perceptually it is perfectly correct. From our point of view all the 'lights' in the sky move around us. The patterns traced by each of the planets were considered an essential part of the significance of the archetypal intelligence symbolically reflected in that planet, signs for the wise.

The planets as observed from Earth follow looped paths, their retrograde motions, across the ecliptic of the sky. These loops, or epicycles as Ptolemy explained them, form significant symmetric patterns as each planet completes its circuit and returns to its same place in the sky. Mercury, for example, completes three such loops in its annual path (Fig. 161). These retrograde loops or paths have mechanical explanations which in no way alter the observed fact — we experience the universe from our own centre and this collectively is the geocentric view.

The crucial thing about the seven planetary time patterns is that their paths are humanly observed and to dismiss traditional astronomy as mechanically inaccurate misses the point that we are the *centre of the experience*. Similarly, the *literal* interpretation of many ancient texts which talk of the termination of the world in fire or water or the origination of the world in these elements also misses the point, and only serves to reinforce the misguided modern belief in the naïvety of the ancients.

G.H. Mees has pointed out that this prevalent modern view makes the mistake of solidifying the outer meaning of 'revealed words,' thereby blocking access to inner psychological meaning.[4] Earth, air, fire and water were traditionally taught to be the perceptible bases of our physical experience, but their origination in the metaphysical reality essentially unifies them as much with our psyche and spirituality as with our physical body. Hence the discontinuous energy levels between earth, water, air and fire — the solid, liquid, gaseous and radiation states as we would call them today — were to the ancients symbolic of discontinuous but related psychic and spiritual functions or levels of consciousness.

These integral functions can be categorized as the physical, sensorial earth; the animistic, emotive water; the mental or intellectual realm of air and the inspirational fire of the spirit. The ontological element of pure reality is the ether, the only element which truly *is,* since it is the subtle source and ground of all the others.

In the light of this interpretation, of levels of consciousness corresponding symbolically with the elements, the origin and termination of the world in either 'water' or 'fire,' refer to metaphysical realities not physical catastrophes. This can be understood, for example, in the fragments of Heraclitus where he says: 'the division of the Kosmos and all things in it comes into being by means of fire ...'; and further he states 'this fire is (spiritual) intelligence and the cause of the ordering of the whole.' And as if to reinforce the awareness aspect of the symbolism he says 'for those who are awake there is one common Kosmos, but to those who sleep each turns aside into his own world.'[5] This may be seen in several ways. Each psychological 'world,' or sphere, is interpenetrated by the next, more subtle, yet all are ultimately dependent on pure being as their source and are united in the One.

162.

The geocentric paths of Jupiter and Saturn

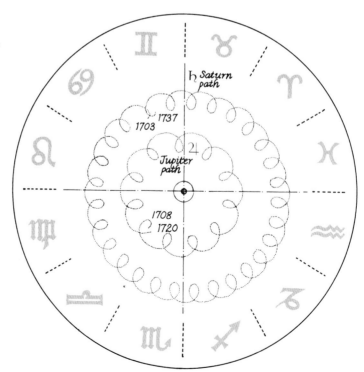

163.
Nine Stones, Dorset

According to tradition the planets are not in themselves arche-types, that would only repeat the error of ascribing a physical origin to a governing principle, but they are 'heavenly' expressions of archetypes. The ancient Greeks ascribed 'Gods' to each of the five planets, Hermes, Aphrodite, Ares, Zeus and Chronos, which became through latinization, Mercury, Venus, Mars, Jupiter and Saturn, thereby establishing the principle of reflection between the parts of the solar system and the inner psychological parts of an individual. This was the basis of the doctrine of analogia or the reflection of the macrocosm in the microcosm.

Saturn or Kronos (Chronos), the 'Father of the blessed gods as well as of man you changeful counsel' as the Orphic hymn puts it, '... strong titan who devours all and begets it anew,'[6] immediately touches on the archetype of 'moving' time, the devourer and re-creator of a continuous cycle. Saturn or Kronos was considered to hold an indestructible bond between heavenly eternity and earthly time: between changeless principle and acts of change. Proclus cites another significant Orphic fragment in his commentary on Plato's *Cratylus:*

> The greatest Kronos is giving from above the
> principles of intelligibility to the Demiurge
> (Zeus), and he presides over the whole 'Creation'
> *(demiourgia).* That is why Zeus calls him 'Daemon'
> according to Orpheus, saying: 'Set in motion our
> genus, excellent Daemon!' And Kronos seems
> to have with him the highest causes of junctions
> and separations ... he has become the cause of the
> continuation of begetting and propagation and the
> head of the whole genus of Titans from which
> originates the division of beings and gives him all the
> measures of the whole creation.[7]

On this point of Saturn having been granted the 'measures of the whole of creation,' Macrobius, the late classical commentator on Cicero and interpreter of classical mythology, says:

> Time is a fixed measure derived from the revolutions
> of the sky. Time begins there; and of this is believed
> to have been born Kronos who is Chronos.[8]

Again, the phrase 'derived from the revolutions of the sky' must not be taken literally but rather as the expression of 'moving time,' or the 'image of eternity,' as Plato put it, as it 'breaks through' from the archetypal world into our world of generation and cyclic duration.

There is evidence that the ancients knew of the heliocentric mechanics of our cosmos but had the wisdom to keep this knowledge esoteric, whilst teaching an exoteric doctrine which maintained a unified experience. There are two particular relationships between the Earth, Sun and planets which are called conjunctions and oppositions: these occur when two or more planets are either opposite each other or exactly in the same area of the sky as seen from the Earth. The geometry of the relationships between Earth and the planets was considered of paramount importance to the quality of the whole cosmos at the time of occurrence, both in passing time and as a point in a recurrent cycle.

164.
Harthill winter, Derbyshire

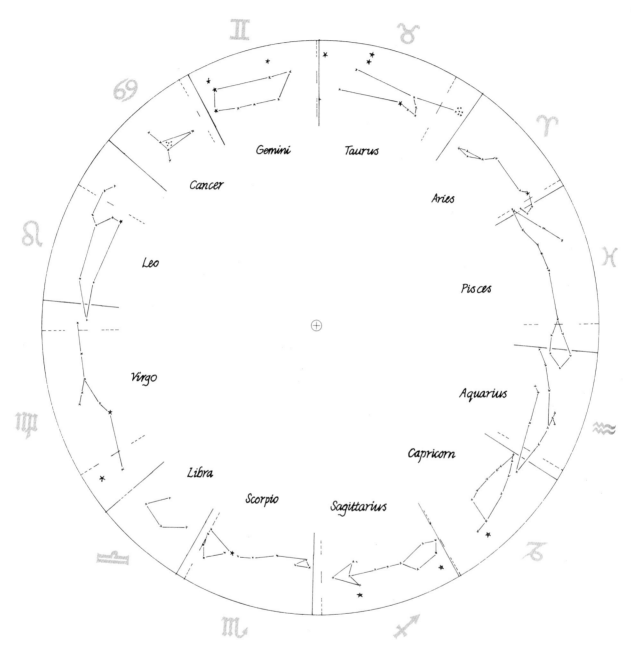

165.
The background constellations against which
the 'loops' of the planets are measured

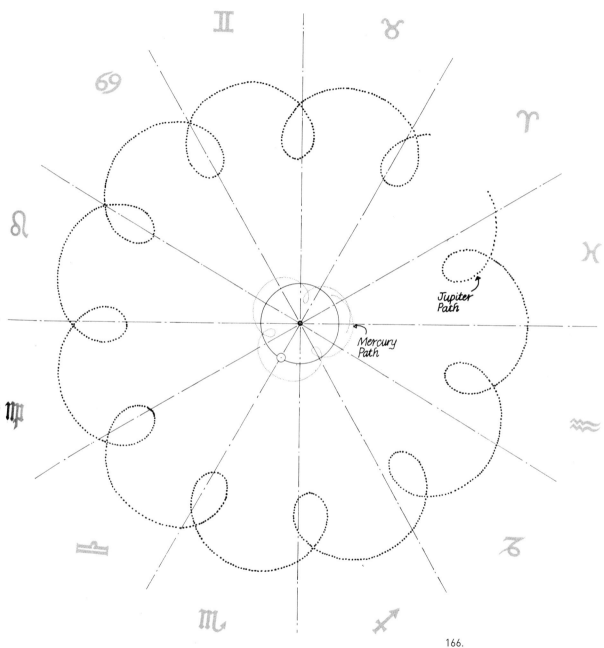

166.
The geocentric planetary loops of
Jupiter and Mercury

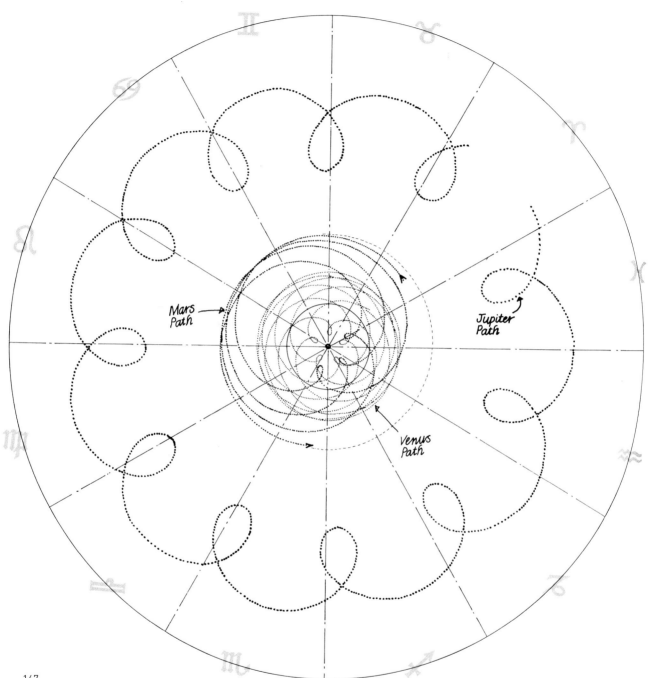

167.
The geocentric planetary loops
of Venus and three loops of Mars
plus the eleven loops of Jupiter

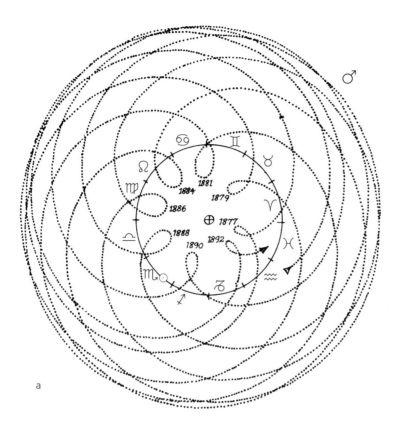

a

168a–b.

a.
The set of eight loops of the planet Mars from the geocentric viewpoint which are completed by returning to the same position in the sky. The cycle is shown from 1877–92.

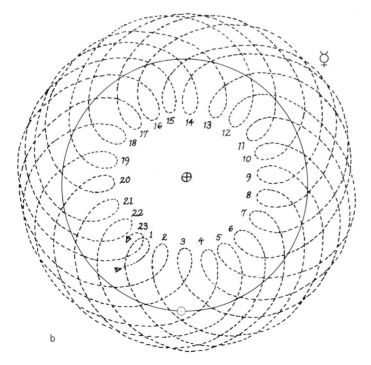

b

b.
The similar set of loops travelled by the planet Mercury from the geocentric view. The cycle of twenty-two is covered before returning to the same point in the sky. The God Mercury was Thoth for the ancient Egyptians — the bringer of writing. Three loops occur each year.

169.

The Grand Trine of Saturn and
Jupiter 1901–61 as it occurs in
the sixty-year cycle

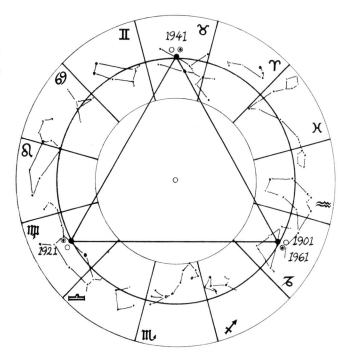

Saturn, being the outermost of the planets in the perceived cosmos, is considered the initiator of the primary conjunctions. The
cycle of conjunctions between Saturn and Jupiter is twenty years,
and altogether they make up a total cycle of sixty years (59.6 precisely), and during this cycle certain archetypal relationships are
established in space and time. These overall patterns have been
aptly described by Marcel Hinze as 'gestalt astronomy' and when
traced through time take the form of certain significant polygons,
either frozen as archetypes or in moving time precessing around
the zodiac. The great trigon was one such pattern. This triangular
pattern was created by drawing an imaginary line between three
successive conjunctions plotted on a circle representing the zodiacal belt (Fig. 169).

A substantial part of Kepler's work in the early seventeenth
century was devoted to this large trigonal relationship between
Saturn ($\hbar$) and Jupiter ($\mathcal{4}$) during the 60 year, 800 year and 2,400
year cycles (that is 59.6, 794 $^3/_4$ and 2,383 respectively). He was
particularly concerned with the traditional time-defining role of
Saturn. It is as if Kepler had been inspired by the Platonic directive

to look to the intelligence of the heavens which made him devote so much time to relating the orbits of the planets to the so-called Platonic solids: the cube, tetrahedron, octahedron, icosahedron and dodecahedron, and their inspheres. He also investigated the larger patterns formed by the trigon: the time, for instance, that the great conjunction took to move through the sets of 'elements' or triple grouping of zodiacal houses, the threesomes of earth, air, fire and water, and he was particularly interested in the 'fiery triplicity' of Aries (Υ), Leo (Ω) and Sagittarius ($\nearrow$). The great trigon conjunction takes about 200 years to move through one such triplicity or 'element' (194 $^3/_4$ years precisely in 'moving' time). On the basis of the 'fiery trigon' Kepler made a speculative reconstruction of the important events throughout historical times. As each of the zodiacal mansions or constellations are associated with an element it would therefore take 4×200 years for the trigonal conjunction to traverse the zodiacal circuit.

The Arab and Persian centres of learning also inherited the Platonic succession or teachings. The Sasanian astronomical handbook, *Zij-i Shah,* contains, according to E.S. Kennedy's translation, a version of the doctrine of 'transit' *(Mamarr)* based on this trigonal relationship.[9] The 'great' conjunction of Kepler is described in the *Zij-i Shah* as a 'small' conjunction, and after approximately twelve of these 'small' conjunctions the trigon moves into the next triplicity. This movement, the transit *(intigâl al-mamarr)* was called the 'middle' conjunction. Four of these 'middle' conjunctions or triplicities will obviously take the whole trigon through the twelve zodiacal houses. This phenomenon was called a 'big' conjunction. A complete return to the starting point of any calculation of these trigons requires three 'big' conjunctions. Thus the cycle of conjunctions is complete.

This mighty conjunction of 2,400 years based on a sixty-year interval is to be considered the archetypal pattern, whereas in the relative world of 'moving time' it will be 2,383 and 59.6 years respectively. This mighty conjunction is also related to the Platonic month, popularly called 'age': for example the age of Pisces began, by this timing, in 6 BC. Although this is in fact only one method of calculating the Platonic months. The sixty-year cycle is also evident in the traditions of China, India, West Sudan and Iran. Tycho Brahe looked forward for many years to the event of 1603 of the great conjunction moving into the fiery triangle in Sagittarius, but it was his disciple, Kepler, who observed it for him as Brahe had died two years earlier.

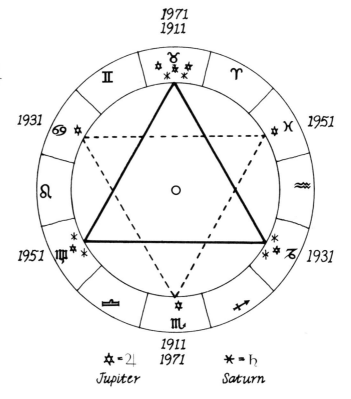

170.
Conjunctive patterns of Saturn and Jupiter 1911–71 that occur during the sixty-year cycle

To return to the qualitative values in the geometry of these conjunctions: there is the possibility that members of the megalithic community manipulated this same geometry which can be represented in a cyclic manner by the ninefold division of a circle. The Bush Barrow template with its 40° angle has been shown capable of setting up an enneagon within a circle which would facilitate this manipulation. As if to reinforce this there is also the pattern of nine triangles 'decorating' each side of the four sides of this rhombic plate. It cannot be avoided that the planets and their apparent retrograde motions are the most challenging and enigmatic patterns in the heavens, whatever we may believe about the astro-mentality of megalithic mankind.

As an instance of the way in which polygonal patterns are traced through time on the 'circle' of the heavens (Fig. 170), we begin in 1911 when Saturn (♄) was in Taurus (♉) and Jupiter (♃) was in Scorpio (♏), an 'opposite' relationship from our Earth view in the zodiacal circle. In 1931 Jupiter was in Cancer (♋) while Saturn was opposite in Capricorn (♑). Both planets, though in opposition to each other, lay at 120° to their previous opposition in 1911. Next time these two were in opposition was in 1951, Jupiter in Pisces and Saturn in Virgo. By 1971 the original opposition was regained and so the 60-year cycle contains three sets of opposites which describe 120° to each other. Jupiter's positions describe a (20-year sided) large equilateral triangle (dashed in the diagram) with point downwards to Scorpio, while Saturn's positions describe another of these triangles with the apex uppermost in Taurus. The whole gives the natural hexagonal division of a circle with the star hexagram as an inner constituent.

Further examples of these patterns will now be examined (Fig. 171), using recent conjunctions for convenience and ease of checking. Firstly we will take the zodiacal ecliptic band around which the twelve constellations appear to be travelling as a background to the seven wanderers because of the Earth's movement: Sun, Moon, Mercury, Venus, Mars, Jupiter and Saturn. This pattern has Taurus (♉) uppermost and proceeds clockwise with Aries (♈) at one o'clock, Pisces (♓) at two o'clock, etc. By taking the conjunction of 1901 in Capricorn (♑) as the first corner conjunction to our first

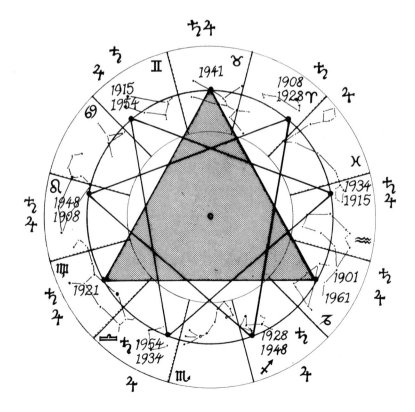

171.
Further patterns between Saturn and Jupiter 1901–61. The dates show the positions of the two planets making up a nine-pointed star over sixty years. 1901, 1921, 1941 and 1961 represent the Grand Trine when both planets are together in the sky.

trigon, we find that the next time that these two planets are in the same part of the sky is 1921, in Virgo (♍), which makes up the second corner of the trigon. Finally, twenty years later, in 1941, the third period of the sixty-year cycle, both the major planets are in Taurus (♉). When the cycle was viewed in totality, this, the great conjunction of Kepler's, made a great equilateral triangle within the circle of the heavens.

There are also lesser triangulations which, occurring during the sixty-year cycle, create a triplicity of trigons in a most interesting way. Triangular relationships, or relationships in which two planets were 120° from each other with Earth as the centre of the angle, were considered harmonious. However this may be, in this study we shall stick to the demarcations of time between Saturn and Jupiter, as the resulting figures have particular bearing on the intrinsic geometry of the Borrowstone Rig stone circle, and the geometry of the Bush Barrow breastplate.

Saturn was in Aries in 1908 while Jupiter was 120° away in Leo, making two corners of a trigon. In 1928 Saturn was in Sagittarius, 120° from Jupiter in Aries. Finally, in 1948 Saturn was in Leo, 120° away from Jupiter who was passing through the position in Sagittarius occupied by Saturn in 1928. Thus by triangulation in 20 year intervals both Saturn and Jupiter had set up another large equilateral triangle in the sky. Now, by the same 120° relationships starting in 1915 when Saturn was in Gemini (♊), Jupiter was in Aquarius (♒) and, by 1934, when Saturn had reached this latter position in the belt, Jupiter had moved 120° away to Libra (♎). When Saturn reached Libra in 1954 Jupiter was back in Saturn's first position of 1915, and this gives the third large triangle. Significantly, when the positions of these conjunctions and triangulations are put together as features of the same 60 year cycle they describe a nine-pointed star.

This enneagon is made up of one grand trigon, the first major equilateral triangle made when the planets appear in the same area of the sky at the same time (in our case the Earth trigon), and two others which, described by delayed action as it were, are secondary in effect: the fire triangle of Aries, Sagittarius and Leo and the air triangle of Aquarius, Libra and Gemini. None of the water signs would occur in this cycle (Pisces, Scorpio and Cancer).

The three overlapping equilateral triangles making up this version of the nine-pointed star are a static and discontinuous version. In other words, each triangle is self-contained within its own lines

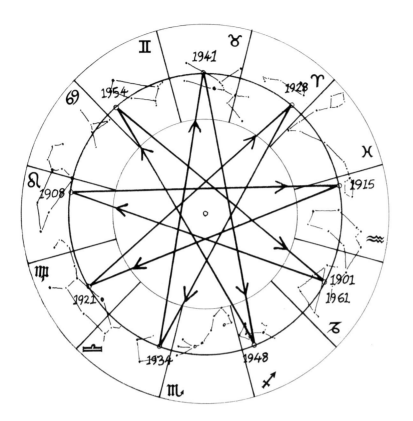

172.
The sequential pattern of Jupiter during the sixty-year conjunctive cycle with Saturn, 1901–61, demonstrating the most dynamic nine-pointed star

and cannot 'move' into another. There is another version of this star that it is possible to inscribe within nine regularly distributed points (Fig. 172), making a continuous line which does not come back to its origin until it has traversed all other eight points. The particular quality of Figure 172 is not only that it makes a beautifully symmetrical pattern in space but that it follows exactly the sequential pattern of Jupiter throughout our cycle from conjunction point to conjunction point.

Starting the sequence and following the clockwise route, missing three points at a step, from 1901 the next point is in Leo seven years later, 1908 (from an earth point to a fire). The next leg is to Aquarius in 1915 relating to Saturn in Gemini at 120°. The continuation comes to its next significant conjunction with Saturn in 1921 (in Virgo) when both major planets are in the same sky position. From here the next point is in Aries, coinciding with the next Saturn conjunction in the Jupiter cycle. This is a corner of the fire trigon in Aries in 1928. At the end of the next seven years, in 1934,

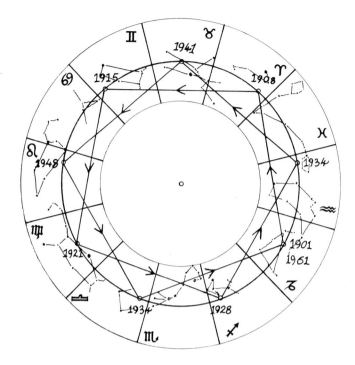

173.

The sequential pattern of Saturn during the sixty-year conjunctive cycle. with Jupiter, 1901–61, demonstrating the 'slower' nine-pointed star

Jupiter makes a triangular relation with Saturn in Aquarius, and this lower point of the enneagon star now traces a seven-year path up to the apex in Taurus, arriving simultaneously with Saturn to make the top angle of the great trigon. This is 1941. In 1948 Jupiter is in Sagittarius and in 1954 back up in Gemini, making special relationships with Saturn in both Leo and Aquarius in turn. From here, Gemini in 1954, the next seven years complete the sixty-year cycle and both the planets and the star pattern return to their origin in Capricorn in 1961.

The whole figure demonstrates what would be considered traditionally a ninefold archetype in the underlying pattern of the relationships of Jupiter and Saturn. We can also see that Saturn's path follows a logical sequence through the nine places of triangular conjunction but in an *anti-clockwise* direction. Could this be another facet of meaning to the symbol of Saturn consuming his progeny?

There is one more way of traversing this sixty-year cycle. This is as a polygonal path through the nine points which represents a stepping stone sequence, whereby one 'steps over' each adjacent point to land on the second away each time (Fig. 173). This creates a particular kind of nine-pointed star, at the same time giving a significant pattern relating to Saturn's position in the whole enneagon. Starting at Capricorn in 1901 we move over one point up to Aries in 1908, the next significant position, and then to Gemini in 1915, the next Saturnine date in the cycle. From Gemini we move to Virgo for 1921, the second corner of the grand trigon. From here Saturn travels on to a conjunction with Jupiter in 1928 in Sagittarius, then to Aquarius in 1934. Next there is a hop into the apex of the grand trigon in Taurus in 1941. Two more stops, Leo in 1948 and Libra in 1954, and the path comes back to Capricorn in 1961. This is a nine-pointed star in 'frozen' time which is described with 'lines' seven years long.

If we choose to study and plot carefully the positions of our planetary neighbours from our earth-centred position we find that they set up very particular patterns in the sky by their retrograde motions. These patterns or loops are bound to have been observed and most likely noted by the first astronomer of megalithic Britain. Beginning with Mercury, which from our view on Earth makes a beautiful loop towards us and three large loops away each year, the diagram gives the pattern for 1945 and demonstrates its triangular nature in relation to its transit of the zodiacal belt (Fig. 174); at the same time it

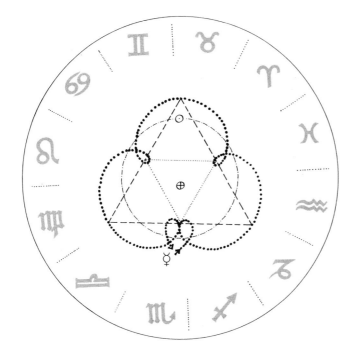

174.
The annual path of Mercury round the Earth. The relationship between the path and its extreme positions is characterized by two equilateral triangles, the lesser inside the greater. This in turn relates the pattern to the $\sqrt{3}:1$ proportion over the year. The four equilateral triangles happen to be the 'net' of the tetrahedron when taken into the third dimension.

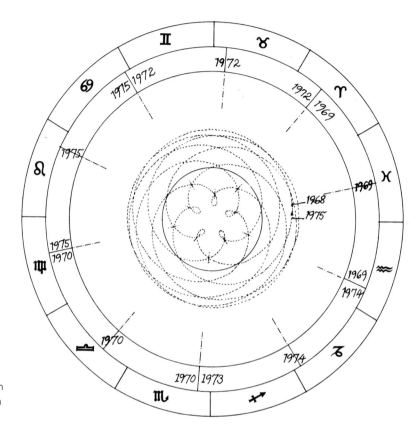

175.
The pentagonal nature of the path
of Venus through an eight-year
cycle, 1968–75

176.
The retrograde loops of Mars as seen from
Earth, 1955–59 (top). The set of loops from
1950–63 (below).

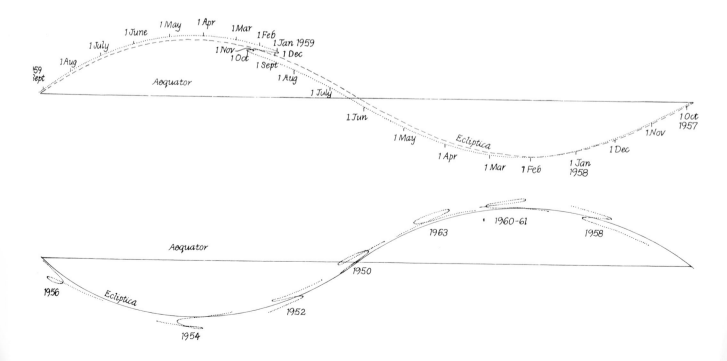

shows how the fourth loop does not exactly cover the first but continues around the orbit of the Sun until it completes a returning cycle twenty-two loops later, the precessional principle of 'moving' time.

Venus, as seen from Earth, moves around us, looping in close five times in eight years before repeating the cycle (Fig. 175). The diagram emphasizes the pentagonal nature of the pattern. The path we have illustrated begins in 1968 and moves from Pisces round the twelve houses until it loops in towards the Earth in the same sign ()-(). The path continues, the swing in toward the Earth and out again, due to the mechanics of the solar system, repeated five equally spaced times before coming back virtually to the same position at the end of the eight-year period. To bring out the symmetrical beauty, the 'gestalt' of Venus, one can connect the crossover points of the path to obtain related pentagons and star pentagons.

It was on the basis of this pentagonal archetype that we proposed Moel Ty Uchaf may have been dedicated to the goddess 'Venus' or by whatever name the building community called this planetary archetype. We are not proposing that the ancient builders of Britain 'saw' these loops in exactly the same form as our illustrations describe, but that they were acutely aware of the retrograde patterns and found them of as great significance as all the ancient philosophers did, and there is no reason to believe they did not record the pentagonal nature of the pattern in time. It is important to remember the metaphysical and symbolic meaning both the planetary archetypes (as represented by the heavenly body) and the areas of the sky known as the zodiacal mansion hold for the integral mind of traditional mankind. As the Cosmos 'is one to he who is awake'[10] all primary events in the heavens are significant of the essential structure of this totality. For a planet to be delayed, or pause, in a particular zodiacal mansion for a certain period (its retrograde motion) would carry all the symbolic importance that the particular combination signified.* It is notable for instance from our 'modern' scientific viewpoint that Nelson concluded from his studies that the positions of the planets across the solar system could be characterized as *'causing'* the Sun spots — demonstrating in modern

---

* For example in our illustration (Fig. 174) Mercury (the messenger of the gods) 'chooses' to delay his journey in the houses of Scorpio, Pisces and Cancer, which happen also to be the three 'water' signs of the year.

terms a total interdependence of the solar system.[11] Rather than suggest unexplained mysteries as the basis of the knowledge of the Neolithic sages, we suggest a knowledge based on observation, a heightened sensitivity to the environment, and sense of wholeness: a sensibility grounded in an understanding of the role of humanity in the scheme of things and an acute empirical observation of the total environmental interdependence. To be 'awake' does not necessitate complicated machinery.

Conclusions

For nothing comes into being nor yet does anything perish, but there is mixture and separation of things that are.

    Anaxagoras

Heraclitus says that for those who are awake there is one common Kosmos, but to those who sleep each turns aside into his own world.

    Heraclitus, Fragment 23

Those who speak with understanding must hold fast to the common in all things.

    Heraclitus, Fragment 21

The beginning and the end of a circle are common.

    Heraclitus, Fragment 26

It can be argued that one role humanity has to play on this planet is to harness the dynamic interactions of contending ecological forces and synthesize them into a form of peaceful co-existence, a stewardship which holds a responsible balance between the needs of 'our kind' and the rest of the created order. The stages in the realization of this role from the historical perspective can be seen at certain critical periods in time. One such was in establishing domesticity with certain animals, most importantly mankind's partnership with the dog; this in itself is far more of an unexplainable mystery than it is usually given credit for. Many observers have pointed out that the dog does not require breaking in at each generation, and has such a special relationship with mankind that a sense of guilt can be transferred from man to dog only too easily. The team of hunter-man and hunter-dog represented not only an ecological revolution but a harnessing and division of labour which had the desired effect of giving mankind greater contemplative and recreational time, in the intrinsic meaning of these terms. Another major step in this process of husbanding the planet was the Neolithic agricultural revolution. This represents the time when people — most likely the womenfolk — began to take on the responsibility of organizing and tending to grain crops. This agricultural revolution during the Neolithic period also gives definition to the term Neolithic, which 'simply implies food production based on crops and domesticated stock, without metals.'[1]

It is not easy to imagine the immense implications to a community, who had spent so much of its time moving to new hunting-grounds, often in a limited area, suddenly becoming aware that corn-gathering would give rich supply with far less effort.

J.R. Harlan conducted experiments in Turkey attempting to assess the values gained by a grain-harvesting Neolithic community.[2] By using a flick-bladed sickle he gathered enough wild wheat in one hour to produce 1 kilogramme of grain. Most important, however, was the fact that this wild variety of wheat turned out to be twice as rich in protein as our modern cultivated wheats — a necessary requirement for a meat replacement diet. He therefore calculated that a family working for three weeks when the wild wheat was ripe could harvest more grain than they would need as a single group throughout the whole year. This grain surplus was the basis of a complete new relationship between mankind and his environment.

Wheat and barley were the foundations of the European grain economies, as were later rice and millet, characterized in the Far Eastern civilizations of India, Indonesia, China and Japan. Maize became the fundamental grain of settled American Indian economies.

Because we live in times of great disruption and major world-wide human conflict, we tend to lose sight of the intrinsic meaning of civilization. As 'moderns' we have alienated ourselves from metaphysical realities — even our own highly individual genetic pattern is weightless, metaphysical, but nevertheless dictates our total physical shape — as our massive industrialization has alienated us from our vital roots in the land and the grain harvests that it yields. Man's worst enemy will always be his own greed which is the outcome of a lack of personal discipline and a diminishing of concern for the overall needs, not only of others but the whole system of which he is merely a part. As Mahatma Gandhi said: 'There is always enough to feed mankind's needs. But never enough to feed his greeds.'

Great social ills have emerged in modern competitive industrial society due to the violent interpretation of Darwin's wolf, who hunts better than the rest of the pack. Apart from this, there lies the obvious fallacy that should the wolf breed further superhunters his stock would hunt themselves right out of prey, and thereby destroy their own food supply and ecological niche. This may well be the fate of industrial man if he continues blindly adhering to the subconscious philosophy of an environmentally exploitive industrial system.

There have been some remarkable and encouraging developments recently in Britain where archaeological research has turned towards the experimental and the living. Butser Ancient Farm in Hampshire near Portsmouth, under the direction of Peter Reynolds, has taken a prehistoric site and reconstructed the whole economy, as far as is practicable. The domestic stock, the grain crops, buildings and tools are all living experiments designed to reconstruct the exact patterns, genetic and geographic, that were believed to have been in operation on Butser Hill during the early Iron Age.

Reynolds explained to us the principal differences in performance of his farm, where the yields were less in bulk than modern wheat but the differences in stem and protein value were significant. Modern short stand wheat yielded more grain per area but produced only about 8.7% dry protein whereas the long stalk of the ancient farmer's crop was a vital economic resource for building, bedding, storage and many other uses. The protein count has shown a 19% dry weight value, more than twice the food value of modern grain. This presents a challenge to the quantitative assumptions of modern industrial farming, which have created some of the most fragile ecological balances in the history of agriculture. It also reminds us of the fractured thinking that has arisen from specialization. Straw is a valuable building material today, in insulation terms, as are differing degrees of pulp or building-block making. There is no need to think of a modern romantic return to thatched cottages, (although this is not necessarily out of the question either), but rather to consider the conversion of straw into many and various types of insulation board, needing only a small percentage of adhesive to bond them. The most important fact for ourselves, eventually, will be the energy costs to the planet as a whole. The use of recurrent cellular natural materials to replace the energy-expensive plastic varieties is as sensible to our modern economy as was their original use for early farming communities, six or seven thousand years ago.

However it would be a common but serious mistake to overstress the material criteria of archaic economy and life. It seems obvious to us that any really valuable account of an ancient people must take into account the totality — not just the physical and convenient.

Archaic man, from all reliable evidence, placed himself in a metaphysical context: the 'Gods,' as principles of the created order, were more *real* than the actual daily events — be they food-gathering or building. Without recourse to the study of comparative religion, our view of megalithic man can only be less than fully human.

Mircea Eliade, after forty years of published findings in the field of comparative religion, concluded that his task would have been incomplete had he not discovered the function of symbolism from all his research.[3] He concludes that symbols for the traditional and archaic societies, because they 'reveal' underlying realities and con-ditions of the world which are not normally evident to immediate experience, are *always religious* since they point to the *real* (as in contradistinction to the actual or relative), and to a *world-pattern*. This he qualifies by saying that at the archaic levels of culture the *real* — the powerful, the living, the significant — is equivalent to the *sacred.* This also means that as a symbol it has *several simul-taneous meanings* and therefore through *paradox* the symbol has the capability of expressing *patterns of ultimate reality* that can be expressed in no other way. Because of this, the value of religious symbolism as a universal phenomenon is that it *always points toward a reality concerning human existence;* in other words, the person who *understands* or is the proper recipient of a symbol is thereby *'opened' to a comprehension of the universal.* Thereby *one emerges from one's personal situation* at such a moment.

The symbol, then, whether a temple, a ritual or a natural event, is capable of revealing a *perspective of integration* in which appar-ently diverse realities can be fitted together.

Eliade cites an archetypal instance of direct relevance to our study — the Moon — which he concludes reveals a connatural unity as a symbol between lunar rhythms (the physical facts), tem-poral becoming, the 'Waters,' the growth of plants, women, death and resurrection, the human destiny, the weaver's craft and so on. In sum the Moon as a total symbol reveals a correspondence between all the levels of cosmic reality as expressed in human conscious-ness and experience. He adds, as if in warning to our perpetual searching for immediate empirical causes for all symbolism, that to understand the 'lunar destiny' of human existence requires quite another order of cognition than an act of critical reason.

It is totally unwarranted to deny megalithic communities their human-ness by attempting to approach their works without taking into account these findings and all the studies so far made in the field of human societies of a primary, traditional and archaic nature. To them the ultimate reality was of a symbolic and religious nature. As Eliade points out, the religious symbol reveals a pattern of existence which brings *a meaning to human existence,* translating any human existence into cosmological terms; in other words it reveals the unity of human and cosmic structure. At moments of such revelatory experience, differences between the individual and the rest of the cosmos become illusory — thus giving rise to the doctrine of illusion. It is not that the sensorial world is non-existent, but that ultimately separation between the different levels of actuality and reality are illusory from the viewpoint of 'revealed' Unity.

The explanation of the world, our modern obsession, by a series of reductions has, Eliade believes, one aim in view: to rid the world of any extramundane values. This systematic banalization of the world, as he calls it, is pursued with one purpose: that of conquering and mastering it. Despite the massive damage such an attitude can cause, its aim is obviously an impossibility, yet Eliade is at pains to point out this conquest of the world is not the purpose of all human societies (at least not until half a century ago), but an idiosyncrasy of modern Western man. Traditional societies, he finds, pursue the aim of understanding the mystery of the World in order to live as the World 'lives,' that is to say, by perpetual renewal. It is the meaning of human and therefore cosmic existence that matters, and this meaning is of a spiritual order.

'If there is mystification,' he continues, 'it is not among the primitives ... but among modern materialists who believe that the cosmic rhythms can ultimately be reduced to the periodicity of the crops.' Nourishment reduced to a merely physiological or economic activity is a banalization and an abstraction — notwithstanding that through forced starvation people can be reduced to tragic subhuman behaviour. For traditional man, food represents his active participation *in* and part of his total behaviour *toward* the Cosmos — an act of reciprocal renewal. It is in this sense of responsibility toward the renewal of the World that Eliade believes lie the origins of all forms of politics, both 'classical' and 'millennarist.' We need nourishment, shelter, kinship, occupation, purpose, respect and accomplishment as much today as ever. In the same way we desire peace, friendship and affection more than conflict, disruption and discord. We also need to know something of our origin and destiny and it is in this final area that we have most to learn from the ancient traditions.

Technological wizardry, the current pervading preoccupation, may not be the only criterion of a civilization. To be wise may be more valuable than to be clever. To have less knowledge, but in more depth, may be wiser than accumulating vast amounts of data in breadth which no individual can synthesize.

Possibly the ancients ran the economy of the British Isles so well, leaving themselves time to build permanent guides in the form of their temples, for this reason: they placed so much emphasis on wisdom and the ultimate relationships between mankind and the Cosmos that they found little value in technological distractions which made water flow upwards and fire burn downwards.

The abstract concepts of calculation, the calendar, time and space all relate to the immediate present, but the great sagas and creation myths of mankind embody the recurring theme that the gift of 'knowledge' comes from the Gods. So we may expect that not only the 'ground rules' of the stone circles originate with the 'Gods,' but that the main purpose of the temple circle was to maintain contact with the transcendental. That is, truths of a universal nature that transcend the individual ego or sectional interest.

In their own mute way these proto-temples point heavenward, symbolically directing mankind's attention to a metaphysical source of existence. The energy of the Sun, the unceasing rhythm of the planets, repeat without words Plato's plea to look to 'the revolutions of intelligence in the heavens and use their untroubled courses, to guide the troubled revolutions in our own understanding.'[4] Not least these 'timeless' stones should cause us to question the real nature of permanence and the real nature of what it means to be human.

Appendix

Astrology, modern statistics and cosmic sensitivity

*We tend to think of the Stars as mere bodies or items arranged
in order, quite without soul or Life. We ought rather to regard
them as possessed of Life and activity, for the consequences of
this will not seem unreasonable.*

    Aristotle, *De Caelo* II xii.292a

*For everything there is a season and a time for every matter
under heaven: a time to be born and a time to die. That which
is, already has been; that which is to be already has been ...*

    Ecclesiastes

*The marvellous and incredible regularity of the stars in their
eternal and unvarying courses, shows that they have divine
power and intelligence, in fact anyone who cannot see that
they possess the power of the Gods would seem to be quite
incapable of understanding anything.*

    Cicero

Astrology, for so long a Cinderella amongst the human activities, is
beginning to find her foot actually does fit in some tentative places
the shoe of modern scientific statistical data — quite beyond the
realms of pure chance. Not that this matters in any way to the tradition of genuine astrologers and those old masters who believed, as
did Plato, Aristotle and Sir Isaac Newton, that the planets influenced
the destinies of states and of peoples. For them, as for Al-Biruni, the
great Persian scientist/philosopher of Islam, the objective of astrology was firstly understanding and secondly to put the information
indicated to wise use.

    Let us first look at the tradition itself. Albert Rehm has discov-
ered and described a stone pegboard which was used as a zodiacal
calendar, and was assumed to be a regular feature in the public
place *(agora)* of any ancient Greek town.[1] Its invention has been

credited variously to Democritus, Meton and Euktemon, and the date is given as at least as far back as 400 BC. The knowledge represented is no doubt older still. Rupert Gleadow describes this parapegma stone as:

> A tablet with 300 holes arranged in rows of thirty, corresponding to the sun's longitude in the Tropical Zodiac, and thus forming a zodiacal calendar. It was presumably put up like a public notice board ... and every day the responsible official would put a stick in the proper hole, which might be marked on the head with the date in the civil calendar ... The Zodiac at this stage was a division of the ecliptic circle into twelve equal divisions of 30 each ...[2]

Another such pegged calendar was found at Caligny near the Franco-Swiss border and is illustrated in Kendrick's *The Druids*.[3]

Although Plato calls the planets the 'visible gods' as well as assigning living powers to the zodiac in the form of 'animals,' they are of the archetypal world, not to be taken literally as actual animals, and are to be considered the twelve principal manifestations of the Creative Force which motivates the universe: the *Dodeka Theoi*. A beautiful symbol of an earth-centred place of the Gods is the central milestone of Athens, from which all distances were measured, and on which, as if reminders of their centrality and immeasurability, were carved the twelve *Theoi*.

In the *Laws* Plato specifically discusses the arrangement of both city and landscape into appropriate divisions of twelve. From the city around the central circular acropolis radiate twelve portions. Around these:

> There are to be twelve hamlets in the twelve country districts, each with a temple to the proper use of the twelve gods, but Zeus and Hestia have temples everywhere.[4]

Here again we see the universal tradition of attempting to establish the heavenly prototypic image of the archetypes of the gods into 'our' world, to guarantee its correct adornment *(kosmos)* and sustain the cosmos from chaos.

In Hinduism, one of the oldest continuous religions, when the building of a temple is contemplated, the very first ritual preliminaries are:

> astronomical and astrological calculations, these are
> followed, if propitious, by long sequences of essential
> rituals for the resultant temple to become effective.
> These range over tests for auspiciousness of site,
> ploughing by bulls and the sowing and germination
> of seed, offerings to Gods and masons, laying of
> pegs and demarcation by threads or by sutras. These
> are followed by four types of foundation ceremony,
> digging of the foundation pit and implanting of
> articles, and so on, until the time that the physical
> foundations are laid.[5]

Without reference to the position of the heavenly bodies nothing may begin.

From Islam, Suhrawardi, speaking for the philosophers of the illuminationist school, said 'our master is Plato, especially in his works *Timaeus* and *Phaedo*'[6] thereby establishing unequivocally the influence on the Islamic philosophical tradition by Greek philosophy. This influence dates from as early in Islam as Al-Kindi, who still held a position of the very highest esteem for the scholars of the European Renaissance. During this period he was categorized as one of the world's most influential and important intellectual figures. He can also be considered a father to some other great names of Islamic science and philosophy, including Avicenna and Al-Biruni. All these men were jointly masters of many sciences and arts, in particular those of astrology and astronomy.

There are important differences however between genethliac astrology, judicial astrology and the popular divinatory sort. As to the latter, Al-Biruni spoke of the transition away from the proper use of astrological information as 'when this boundary is passed, where the astrologer is on one side and the sorcerer on the other, you enter a field of omens and divinations which has nothing to do with astrology.'[7] Judicial astrology traditionally deals with the relation of the cosmos to the whole of an institution, a society, a dynasty or rule; whilst genethliac astrology is concerned with casting of horoscopes ('indications of the hour') for an individual: Al-Biruni was known to have had knowledge of and practised both these branches of astrology throughout his life. His position is likely to have been similar to that of Cicero, who called popular astrology 'incredible, mad folly'[8] while also saying:

> The marvellous and incredible regularity of the
> stars in their eternal and unvarying courses, shows
> that they have divine power and intelligence, in
> fact anyone who cannot see that they possess the
> power of gods would seem to be quite incapable of
> understanding anything.[9]

It is also salutary to consider those minds throughout European history who made no fundamental division between astronomy (the placing) and astrology (the logic or interactions of the heavenly bodies). In Chartres library there are some comments by the twelfth-century Adelard of Bath on a tract of judicial astrology by John of Seville, pointing to a connection at intellectual level between medieval Christianity and scholars of both Judaism and Islam, in Spain. Robert Grosseteste, Bishop and leader of Oxford University, recommended the use of astrology for agriculture, medicine and weather prediction (all aspects of modern astrology that have had a measure of scientific verification). Paracelsus, the great sixteenth-century physician, used it for his understanding of the health and treatment of his patients. Cornelius Agrippa, (friend of Erasmus), Zollett, Ramon Lull, John Dee, who was court astrologer to Elizabeth I: all are individuals who committed themselves openly to astrology, disregarding the dangers of being associated with the 'incredible, mad folly,' or worse, heresy.

For the great philosophers of medieval Islam the Quran is the primary and unifying source and Plato a secondary support:

> We shall show them our portents upon the horizons
> and within themselves, until it be manifest unto them
> that it is the Truth. *Quran XLI*; 53.

> Nowise did God create this but in Truth and
> Righteousness (Thus) doth He explain His signs in
> detail, for those who understand. *Quran X;* 6.

On the subject of the assimilation of astrology into the Muslim perspective, S.H. Nasr sees it as due to:

> the unitive point of view of this very ancient form
> of wisdom. This perspective is based on the idea of
> the polarization of Pure Being into the qualities of
> the signs of the zodiac which as the archetypes are
> transmitted by the intermediate planetary spheres
> whose last sphere, that of the Moon, synthesizes all
> the cosmic qualities and as the 'cosmic memory'
> transmits these qualities to the terrestrial domain.
> The qualities found here on Earth are themselves the
> reflections of the heavenly archetypes which are the
> causes of all the diverse phenomena of Nature.[10]

Dante was a vehement supporter of astrology in his *Il Convito:*

> The science (of astrology) more than any (other)
> is high and noble on account of its high and noble
> subject (the measurement), and high and noble by
> its certainty, which is without any defect, as coming
> from a most perfect and most regular principle. And
> if any conceive it to have a defect, it does not belong
> to it, but, as Ptolemy says, comes of our negligence
> and to that should be imputed.[11]

There is another complete study for those who deem it worthwhile, and that is to trace the progressive disgrace that Dante's 'noble subject' fell into. It appears to mark the parting of the ways in Europe between empiricism and insight, traditionally the role of the human soul, the process finally crystallizing in the 'dismissal' of the soul by Descartes. This dismissal would have been a shock to Aristotle, who, as father of modern empiricism, said, 'we should always be respectful in the presence of the Gods; and surely this is never more true than when we are discussing the planets.'

The contemporary rift between Art, Science and Religion can be directly linked to the intellectual neglect of the traditional uniting function of the human soul.

Recent scientific work on astrology

The recent emergence and demonstrative evidence that there is an active interrelation between the bodies of the solar system was due to the work of John Nelson.[12] In 1951 he was engaged by RCA broadcasting to investigate the factors which affect radio reception. It was known that sunspots were a direct source of interference with our ionosphere and thereby radio reception, but greater accuracy was required as to precise cause, tuning and intensity. Nelson, under contract from the radio company, discovered that there was another and quite unexpected factor. The sunspots and the radio interference both occurred when two or more of the planets were in line, that is, at right angles or arranged at 180° to the Sun. He managed a sunspot prediction of 93 percent accuracy by refining this observation!

Concrete and useful scientific data therefore demonstrated not only that the planets' positions appeared to be responsible for the sunspots, but that the angles between them and the Sun coincided with just those angles which the astrologers called 'opposition' and 'square.' Both these relationships were given negative values in traditional astrology. This 'negativity' affects the Earth in quite surprising ways. In the Soviet Union workers on terminal heart disorders found a direct relationship with 'z' radiation reaching the Earth from an emission on the surface of the Sun from the sunspots.[13] In other words, a number of deaths from heart disease occurred after the event of sunspots. These magnetic disturbances were enough to make possible the discovery of the magnetic fields of Saturn, Venus and Jupiter in 1955, and the great length of the magnetic 'tails' that each planet leaves behind it as it weaves its sinuous path around the long trail of the Sun. The whole solar system, bathed in the solar wind, has taken on the aspect of a magnificent and delicately coloured spindle shape with the whirling 'white' ball of the Sun leading the direction of the whole body. In 1964, H.S. Burr demonstrated a connection between biopotential in trees and sunspots using highly sensitive instruments. Even as early as 1942 he had demonstrated an electrical reading to the timing of human ovulation using the same biopotential field for the readings.[14]

Michel Gauquelin of the psychophysiological laboratory in Strasbourg spent many years on painstaking and voluminous statistical research to establish what connections there are between the positions of the heavenly bodies and the behaviour and occupations of humans. It is as well to remember that the delicate membrane of life that adheres to the surface of our planet is due to its position in the solar system. This unique harmonic placing, fourth from the centre of the solar system, is a dual phenomenon counterbalanced by the largest passenger any member of the system has to carry, the Moon.

This delicately balanced totality has settled into a series of helically elliptical orbits over the untold billions of years of its life and represents a remarkably precise set of interwoven sheaths. The sheen of life on Earth flushes gently from green to brown and back again during one orbit of the planet around the Sun according to the distance and angle. The molten metal core of the Earth has apparently formed a toroid, a doughnut shape, which acts like a huge magnetic ring and sends massive radiating and returning vortices of magnetic fields that interpenetrate the solid, liquid, gaseous envelopes of the planets' system. This delicate filter system of radiant particles is seen by us as the blue of the sky.

These fields are the Van Allen belts and without their filtering action no life would be possible. The radiations and cosmic waves that arrive each second at the surface of the world are precisely monitored and those that are least harmful to life are let through. A great many of these, at very long wavelengths, arriving from the furthermost depths of the universe, move straight through the planet; we have yet to fully understand the effects of them.[15]

Michel Gauquelin was looking for correlations between the planetary rhythms and possible responses on Earth. His work was made possible because of the particular moment in French medical history: the exact time of birth of at least three generations of French people were on record. Gauquelin selected 576 members of the French Academy of Medicine and found, to his great surprise, that far more were born with Mars and Saturn rising or in mid-heaven than could be attributed to chance. On checking a further 508 birth times of famous physicians, the same results occurred. The two sets taken together represent ten million to one odds against this being a chance occurrence.

Here then, after two senior professors of statistics had approved his findings (Tornier of Berlin and Faverge of the Sorbonne), was a vital link between the ancient premise of astrology and those of modern statistical methods. Yet we must proceed with caution to say that *one* of the major premises has been demonstrated statistically: that is, that the positions of certain planets relate to the occupation of the individual when they are present above the horizon.

Gauquelin's statistical work, by the time of his death in 1991, covered four nations and thousands of records.[16]

The relevance of these findings to the present work is that for both the extensive studies of Stonehenge and the proposals of Thom for many other stone circles, it is the reading of Sun and Moon risings that support the theories of alignments. Again the question is bound to arise: what kind of knowledge, instinctive, inspirational, intuitive or empirical, were the megalithic builders employing? Once again we can only conjecture. What we do know is that the solar and lunar rhythms and the different radiant particles that come into the earth all affect life in very subtle but positive ways. Quite apart from the symbolic correspondences, did the megalithic Britons utilize this knowledge, however they arrived at it, for the reciprocal benefit of their community? If the answer is positive then it becomes more reasonable that they should spend so much of their effort, almost superhuman in the case of Stonehenge, on the erection of their cosmic templates, the stone circles.

At a lecture when Professor Thom was asked why he thought so much emphasis was put into computing the occurrence of eclipses by megalithic Britons, he replied tangentially, though not unwisely, by reminding the questioner of the ancient Chinese astronomers who were put to death for miscalculating an eclipse.[17]

New knowledge, using eclipses, has emerged from Japan in the form of the 'Takata reaction,' which is a measure of the amount of albumen in blood serum, named after its discoverer, Maki Takata of Toho University, Japan. After twenty years of tests it was demonstrated conclusively that there was a direct connection between the behaviour of the sunspots affecting the Earth's magnetic field and the body chemistry of humans in terms of their blood serum's albumen content, which amongst other functions affects blood coagulation. During the eclipses of 1941, '43 and '48, Takata's tests revealed a marked inhibition in the reaction, equivalent to the levels that were obtained in the tests he took 600 feet underground in normal Sun conditions. This prompts us to suppose we may be on the threshold of discovering new biological responses that made eclipse prediction so important to the ancients, apart from the awe-inspiring psychological effect of daytime darkness during a solar eclipse.

Another important addition to the statistical approach has been made by the British philosopher, John Addey. I was introduced to his harmonic theory of related human birth times when we were both contributing to a conference in Cambridge in 1972. Fascinated by the ideas of traditional astrology, Addey decided to apply the statistical method to such concepts as the longevity of Capricornians and short-lived fate of Pisceans. Although he found no significant connection at all, rather more interesting facts did emerge. Having looked at polio victims for the short-lived, he discovered that there was a wave pattern to the birth-dates flowing through the year. This rhythmic phenomenon peaked 120 times during the year.[18] Addey concluded that this phenomenon could be considered a vibration running through the year at the 120th harmonic. Further data yielded a 7th harmonic corresponding to 2,593 clergymen's birth times and a 5th harmonic fitting 7,302 doctors' birth times. Whatever the ultimate conclusions that may be drawn from this material, it does reinforce the basic assumption already demonstrated by Gauquelin that there are patterns in the cosmic environment that link birth times with eventual occupation.

Addey, himself a student of Plato, pointed out at this same conference that there were oblique references in the Platonic works to a date-planned birth system. This last idea has had a quite dramatic new lease of life in one sense — and that is the choice of sex of a child. Slovak psychiatrist Eugene Jonas's great interest in lunar rhythms led him to explore the accepted conclusion that female ovulation in humans is directly related to the Moon. Previously statistical evidence had demonstrated a slight predominance of the female menstrual cycle to follow the actual phases of the Moon — it was accepted that the 27-day cycle of all women had a lunar rhythm.[19] But Jonas's investigations showed that the actual ability of a mature woman to conceive coincides with the phase of the Moon which prevailed on the day she was born. The contraceptive charts set up by Jonas, which apparently operate in several countries, have been given a 97 per cent effectiveness rating. An added aspect of these charts is that they can be used in the Platonic sense of establishing the likelihood of fertilization.

The persistent Jonas further discovered that the prediction of the sex of a child could be made with a high degree of accuracy.[20] This method is also based on lunar correlations, in this case on the position of the Moon in the sky at the time of conception. The clue to his discovery lay in the male and female categorizations of the twelve divisions of the zodiacal belt. Jonas observed and later confirmed that if conception took place when the Moon was in a 'female' zone the child would almost certainly be female. The Bratislava maternity clinic has given a 95 percent confirmation of 'correct' sex-predicted births from 8,000 women. Although Jonas has his critics, when his findings were tested by a team of gynaecologists, giving him intercourse time only, he managed a 98 percent accuracy in predicting the outcome of the sex of the child concerned.

Although we are still far from relating this kind of research to the knowledge used by the megalithic builders, what we can say is that by the time the British circles were being erected it was quite likely that Moon phase recording was already twelve thousand years old. This is based on the interpretation of markings on an ivory shaft of mammoth tusk found in the Ukraine at Gontzi. According to Gerald Hawkins, these markings are precise and appear to be based on scientific observation.[21] If the interpretation is correct, four complete months are recorded in carefully engraved, small and large lines punctuated with U and V shapes which are based, accurately, on the phases of the Moon. Twelve thousand years seems ample time to build up a store of 'wisdom,' however the knowledge was arrived at — with or without a written language. The oral tradition is the oldest and most universal in traditional societies.

Those who would care to investigate the, reputedly, most scientific and rigorous tests made so far on the current art of astrology, may like to check the results of Vernon Clark, an American psychologist.[22] His tests and the conclusions we found most interesting, and his guarded verdict was that 'astrologers, working with material which can be derived from birth data alone, can successfully distinguish between individuals.'

Finally, let us return to the 'scientifically' acceptable work of Gauquelin and Nelson. If it has been shown that there is a relationship between the planets rising or recently risen at the time of birth, to the predisposition of an individual's future life, the harmonious and discordant geometrical angles between the planets which cause Sun eruptions, the least we can do is to acknowledge that similar observational knowledge appears to have been found embodied in the layouts of the stone circles. The rising Sun, Moon, certain stars and possibly planets together with particular occurrence of the angles 30°, 45°, 60° and 135°, these latter connecting both traditional astrological values and representing the equilateral triangle, the square, the hexagon and finally the octagon,* all have been demonstrated to be a part of what we will call megalithic science.

---

* The station stone rectangle at Stonehenge is the central rectangle of an octagon — as demonstrated in the British Arts Council 1978 film *Reflections.*

Afterword to the New Edition

Whatever we do, we must avoid approaching the study with the idea that megalithic man was our inferior in ability to think.

Alexander Thom

This final paragraph of Alexander Thom's *Megalithic Sites in Britain,* states his conclusions that however we may differ from our ancestors in technical desires and achievement, to be *human* is unchanged and not subject to Darwinian evolution. In short to *be* human is constant; what we do with our humanity is then our responsible choice.

What the Neolithic mind does exhibit to the authentic seeker is a faith in geometrical reasoning — prior, it is evident, to numeracy and literacy. This is what contemporary orthodoxy finds so difficult. Traditional science, that of wisdom as distinct from knowledge, is based on the archetypal or intelligible principles available to the mind above and beyond the senses — yet residing within the physical world and recognizable by the human mind.

The Neolithic genius seems to rest in their wise understanding of the balance between the two. And, like Plato, they were most likely to have held their focus on the nature of the soul rather than the mortal body. What we see is a remarkable understanding of pure archetypal geometry being used in these monuments and stone spheres to measure the actual world by. As Plato says in his *Epinomis* dialogue:

> ... to the person who pursues their studies in
> the proper way, all geometric constructions, all
> systems of numbers, all duly constituted melodic
> progressions, the single ordered scheme of all
> celestial revolutions, should disclose themselves .... if
> pursued with the mind's eye fixed on their single end.
> That person will receive the revelation of a single
> bond of natural interconnection between them all ...
> (*Epinomis* 991.e.)

In addressing this issue, I would like to draw attention a few books that have been published since the first edition of this volume: *The Book of Coincidences* by John Martineau; *The Golden Section* by Dr Scott Olsen (both authors I have had the privilege of being tutor to); *Sun, Moon and Stonehenge* by Robin Heath; and also *The Need for a Sacred Science* by S.H. Nasr. In addition there are two important books by John Michell, *The View over Atlantis* and *Dimensions of Paradise.*

John Martineau studied for his Masters Degree with me at the Prince's Institute of Architecture in the Visual Islamic and Traditional Arts Department. His findings were so outstanding that we had to recommend he entitled his thesis 'The Book of Coincidences' as it was bound to be confrontational to contemporary astronomers, the great majority of whom subscribe to the theory of a Big Bang and, therefore, an 'accidental' universe. Robin Heath's work is equally challenging. Both these writers not only indicate the exceptional intellectual capacity of Neolithic science (we use this word in its original sense of the study of objective truths), but also arrive at the proposition that the Golden Section (see below) permeates the natural world and the cosmic time cycles, thus indicating that we live in a true cosmos based on intelligible principles. The work of Scott

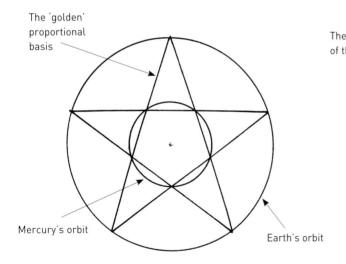

The 'golden' proportional basis

Mercury's orbit

Earth's orbit

177.
The mean orbits and the mean physical bodies of the Earth and the planet Mercury are in the same golden ratio to each other. The relationships are 99% accurate. (After John Martineau)

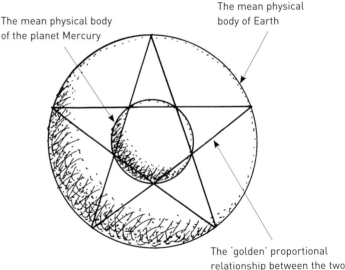

The mean physical body of the planet Mercury

The mean physical body of Earth

The 'golden' proportional relationship between the two

178.
These are the mean bodies of the Earth and the planet Mercury: that is each in its archetypal form. The accuracy of this relationship is 99%. (After John Martineau)

Olsen gives breadth and insight regarding the persistent recurrence of the Golden Section throughout our created world.

Martineau realized that by adjusting the actual form of both physical body and orbit of each planet to their 'mean' size — that is, by not changing the mass or distance, only bringing them to their archetypal sphere or circle — he could reveal the extraordinary inner order underlying the outer facts (see Figs. 177–78). This conforms to the Platonic/Pythagorean philosophical position that the pure principles were of the order of 'being' whilst the actual physical expression was aptly described as the domain of 'becoming.' This last is what we would probably call the 'relative' or changing world rather than the en-forming principles, or what we might call the 'laws' today.

Robin Heath has followed Professor Alexander Thom by focussing on the geometry of the Pythagorean right triangles (also known as Pythagorean triplets, or triads), which can be constructed with three whole numbers together making up a right-angled triangle. Thom demonstrated through his meticulous surveys of the stone monuments that these Pythagorean triangles constantly recurred in the constructional geometry of Neolithic builders. The best known of these triangles is the 3, 4, 5 right triangle, as used even today when setting out building foundations on site more than any other method. The remaining five mentioned by Thom are:

5, 12, 13   (the subject of much research by Robin Heath)
8, 15, 17
7, 24, 25
20, 21, 29
12, 35, 37   (this last was the most exploited by the Neolithic builders according to Thom.)

In his remarkable book *Sun, Moon and Stonehenge,* Robin Heath also picks up the important difference between 'being' — the absolute values — and 'becoming' — the values of the physical world which only ever approach the absolute world. This is well expressed in the Vedic word *Upanishad* which means 'close approach' and is used for sacred texts which lead *towards* the absolute truth, but cannot reveal it directly. Robin Heath's discoveries are in relation to the Moon and Sun time-making rhythms and their 'unlikely' relationship to mathematical properties of Pythagorean right triangles; and in one case the containing circle of a regular pentagon and its 'star' diagonal in relation to the lunar cycles. Such correspondences have nothing to do with empirical (modern) science or the measurements of the physical world, which empirical science represents, but rather indicate another order of reality where cosmic principles correspond to geometrical and mathematical principles. We recommend the reading of all three books to gain further insights into this traditional (sacred) science.

The Golden Mean within the cosmic scheme

This extraordinary proportional relationship has been called by many names: Golden Cut, Golden Proportion, Golden Ratio, Golden Section, Golden Mean, and so on. It is based on the remarkable principle of being virtually self-generating once the first ratio is established. The Golden Number is $(\sqrt{5}+1)/2$ or $(\sqrt{5}-1)/2$, the first giving 1.6180339, the second, called the lesser Golden Number, being 0.618033988..., both of which are unresolvable in whole numbers. Thus 0.6180 represents this special number adequately.

Drawn geometrically, the relationship can be 'seen' to be a property of fivefold symmetry — or, put more directly, a property of a five-pointed star. This is best seen graphically (see Fig. 179). It is clear from the survey of Professor Alexander Thom that this ratio was embodied in the Moel ty Uchaf circle in North Wales.

The reverence for numbers held by such as the Pythagoreans is necessary to begin to understand the cardinal mysteries of our world. When deriving numerical values from the finally inexpressible Golden Number — which approaches closer and closer to a conclusion rather than ever reaching it — we have our sense of reasoning stretched to the limit, that is, whilst we still cling on to the accidental and chaotic model of our cosmos. Once we concede the fact that number is our unique entrance to understanding the order of our world (cosmos, universe, what you will), then we should not be surprised that such unresolvable values as the Golden Number — so clearly expressed in a five-pointed star yet not expressible in whole numbers — should hold such a key position in our world's inner structure.

Robin Heath in the late 1990s uncovered a remarkable series of coincidences similar in character to the golden proportional relationships of the mean bodies and orbits of the Earth and Mercury (see Figures 1 and 2) as discovered by John Martineau.

The numbers 18 and 19 relate respectively to the number of years in the Ecliptic cycle (or Saros cycle) and the Metonic cycle (when

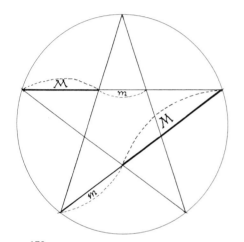

179.
The 'golden' proportion, intrinsic to the pentacle or regular five-pointed star. The larger **M** is to the smaller **m** in the ratio of the Golden Section. Thus the five-pointed star exhibits at least twenty possibilities of demonstrating this ratio.

Sun and Moon become in exact alignment again). When Heath put the Golden Number together with these two cosmic rhythms, he found the most remarkable coincidences. The Moon's nodes or the crossing points of the solar and lunar orbits as viewed from Earth, take 18.618 years to rotate once around the whole sky. This is 18 plus the lesser Golden Number. This same number multiplied by itself is 346.6299 or 346.63, which is a highly accurate value for the eclipse year in days. If we then add 18.618 to this number, we get 365.25 or 365.2479, which is close enough to the number of days in a solar year! Also if we multiply 18.618 by 19.618, we get 365.2479 or virtually 365.25 again.

Biological aspects of the Golden Mean

The ratio is clearly seen, as well, in biological growth patterns, usually in the form of the Fibonacci series. The series progresses as follows: 1, 1, 2, 3, 5, 8, 13, 21, 34, 55 and so on indefinitely.

In the progression of the Fibonacci series, we arrive at the next in the series by adding the previous digit. Starting with 1, to find the next number we add 0 thus $1+0=1$, so we start the series with 1, 1, then $1+1=2$, $1+2=3$, $2+3=5$, $3+5=8$, $5+8=13$, $8+13=21$, and so on. The relationship between two members of the sequence gets closer and closer to the Golden Mean proportion, that is:

$$8 \div 5 = 1.6 \quad 34 \div 21 = 1.6190... \quad 55 \div 34 = 1.617647... \text{ and so on}$$

Lunar-Moon and Solar-Sun facts

The numerical data given here are with acknowledgments to Robin Heath.

What is a lunation?

A lunation is the period from one new Moon to the next. We call this a lunar month or the period of the Moon's revolution. This is calculated to be 29 days, 12 hours and 44 minutes.

What is a lunar or Moon year?

This is known as twelve synodic lunar months, which is 354.367 days. The word synodic comes from the Greek roughly meaning 'assembled way,' but astronomically it means one full revolution measured against the Sun from the Earth. A sidereal lunar year will be 355.18158 days (that is, 12 lunar orbits). Sidereal means a revolution or orbit measured from a fixed star.

What is a solar tropical year?
It is what we call a Sun year of 365.242199 days. A sidereal solar year measured against the fixed stars becomes 365.256360 days.

What is a precessional year?
This is assuming the solar system precesses at 50.2 minutes of arc per year, so to achieve a complete return it takes 25,800 years.

The difference between Moon/lunar years and Sun/solar years is calculated at 10.875119 days.

A Saros (Ecliptic) Cycle is 223 lunations or 18.03081293 years.

A Metonic Cycle (attributed to the Greek astronomer/philosopher Meton) is 233 lunations or 19.00023784 years, that is, approximately only 2 hours off exactly 19 years.

All these figures represent *actualities* in our experienced world. The principles underlying these will be (a) hidden and (b) archetypal by nature in the Platonic sense of 'being' rather than 'becoming'. It is also clear how hard it is to be precise with calendars with these actualities. Yet the evidence increases with each new investigation as to how accomplished the Neolithic science had become, with their evident use of both actualities and 'pure' archetypal forms.

180.
If a pentacle or five-pointed star is constructed within a circle measuring 13 units in diameter (dashed line) then the arms of that pentacle will all be 12.364 in length. This is a good near approach to the 12.368 lunations in a single year. If the five arms of the pentacle are added together their sum becomes 61.8200 — another near approach to the 'golden' number of 6.18033 or ten times this. (Acknowledgments to Robin Heath)

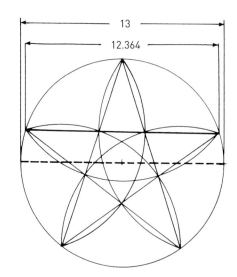

References

Chapter 1

1. Schuon, 'On the Margins of Liturgical Improvisation.'
2. Nasr, 'Sufism and the Perenniality of the Mystical Quest.'
3. Quoted in Guénon, *Yoga: Science de l'Homme Intégral*.
4. See Renfrew, *Before Civilization*.
5. Renfrew, *Before Civilization*, p.20.
6. Renfrew, *Before Civilization*, p.142.
7. Renfrew, *Before Civilization*, pp.6.
8. Renfrew, *Before Civilization*, pp.251.
9. Renfrew, *Before Civilization*, pp.253.
10. Thom, *Megalithic Sites in Britain;* Hawkins, *Stonehenge Decoded*.
11. Evans, *Earlier Religion of Greece*.
12. Isikowitz, *Primitive Views of the World*.
13. Fürer-Haimendorf, 'Megalithic Ritual among the Gadaba and Bondos of Orissa,' p.157.
14. See Isikowitz, *Primitive Views of the World*.
15. See Isikowitz, *Primitive Views of the World*.
16. See Isikowitz, *Primitive Views of the World*.
17. See Isikowitz, *Primitive Views of the World*.
18. Renfrew, *Before Civilization*, p.160; Scoresby, *The Mystery of Easter Island*.
19. Metraux, *Easter Island: A Stone Age Civilization of the Pacific*.

Chapter 2

1. Black Elk, *The Sacred Pipe*, p.49.
2. Peet, *Rough Stone Monuments*.
3. Milarepa, quoted in Wentz, *Tibet's Great Yogi*.
4. Pausanius on the early Greeks.
5. Kerenyi & Jung, *An Introduction to the Science of Mythology*.
6. Corbin, *Mundus Imaginalis or The Imaginary and the Imaginal*.
7. Nasr, *An Introduction to Islamic Cosmological Doctrines*.
8. Eliade, *The Sacred and the Profane*, p.30.
9. Eliade, *The Sacred and the Profane*, p.40.
10. Chan, *The Way of Lao Tzu (Tao-te Ching)*, p.176.
11. Erkes, *Ho-Shang-Kung's Commentary on Lao Tzu*, p.80.
12. Chan, *A Source Book in Chinese Philosophy*, p.588.
13. Chan, *A Source Book in Chinese Philosophy*, see Chapter 34.
14. Thom, *Megalithic Sites*.
15. Plato, *Timaeus*, 47, c-d.
16. Burkhardt, *The Mystical Astrology of Ibn 'Arabi*.
17. Thom, *Megalithic Sites*, p.96.
18. Govinda, *Foundations of Tibetan Mysticism*, p.75.
19. Govinda, *Foundations of Tibetan Mysticism*, p.75.
20. Thom, *Megalithic Sites*, see chapter 4.
21. Mackie, *Science and Society in Prehistoric Britain*, pp.60f.
22. Thom, *Megalithic Sites*, p.69.

Chapter 3

1. Black Elk, *The Sacred Pipe*.
2. Nichomachus of Gerasa (between AD 50–150) *Introduction to Arithmetic 1*, Chapter 3 (5).
3. Plato, *Epinomis*, 991E1–4.
4. Zolla, *Language and Cosmogony*.
5. Eliade, *Shamanism: Archaic Techniques of Ecstasy*.
6. Rhys, *Lectures on the Origin and Growth of Religion*, pp.360–64.
7. *Skirmismol*, Stanza 21 from Axol Olrik, *Viking Civilization*, p.31.
8. MacCulloch, *Mythology of All Races* Vol. II, pp.88–9, Stanza 7.
9. MacCulloch, *Mythology of All Races* Vol. II, p.249.
10. *Voluspa*, Stanza 2.
11. MacCulloch, *Mythology of All Races*, p.115.

12. *Skirmismol,* Stanza 40 from Olrik, *Viking Civilization.*
    See also MacCulloch, *Mythology of All Races,*
    pp.153–4.
13. Joyce & Weston, *A Social History of Ancient Ireland,*
    pp.391f.
14. *Vita Merlini,* lines 629f.
15. MacCulloch, *Mythology of All Races,* p.191.
16. *Vita Merlini II,* lines 916–26.
17. Rhys, *Lectures,* p.256.
18. Chambers, *Arthur of Britain,* p.61.
19. Julius Caesar, *De Bello Gallico* as quoted by A.R.
    Burn, 'Holy Men on Islands.'
20. Dillon & Chadwick, *The Celtic Realms.*
21. Giles, *San Tsu Ching.*
22. Zolla, *Spiritual Perspectives,* p.172.
23. Black Elk, *The Sacred Pipe,* p.80.
24. Nasr, *Introduction to Islamic Cosmological
    Doctrines,* see section on *Ikhwān al-Safā.*
25. Wilhelm Pelikan, *The Secrets of the Metals.*

Chapter 4

1. Black Elk, *The Sacred Pipe.*
2. Burkhardt, *Sacred Art East and West,* p.42.
3. Radin, 'Die Religiöse Erfahrung der Naturvölker.'
4. Burkhardt, *Sacred Art East and West,* pp.41f.
5. Burkhardt, *Sacred Art East and West,* see Chapter 1.
6. Volwahsen, *Living Architecture, Indian,* p.44.
7. Thom, *Megalithic Sites,* pp.164f.
8. Volwahsen, *Living Architecture, Indian,* p.53.

Chapter 5

1. Nichomachus of Gerasa, *Introduction to Arithmetic,*
   Chapter 6 (1).
2. Moses de León was a thirteenth-century Spanish
   Kabbalist who introduced the Zohar into Spain. In G.
   Sholem, *Major Trends in Jewish Mysticism,* p.223.
3. Chan, *The Way of Lao Tzu,* p.238.
4. Eliade, *The Two and the One,* p.171.
5. Eliade, *The Two and the One,* see Chapter IV.
6. Eliade, *The Two and the One,* see Chapter IV.
7. Thom, *Megalithic Sites,* p.69.

8. Critchlow, Carroll, Vaughn-Lee, *Chartres Maze,
   A Model of the Universe.*
9. Shankaracharya, *Vedic Mathematics.*

Chapter 6

1. Black Elk, *The Sacred Pipe*, p.71.
2. *Shekel Hakodesh,* a metrical Hebrew work of a
   medieval Spanish Jewish scholar, Joseph Kimchi of
   Narbonne, 1105–70, based on maxims in Arabic by
   Nestorian Christian Honeia (d. 873) translated into
   Hebrew by Yehuda Alcharisi. In Perry, *A Treasury of
   Traditional Wisdom,* p.1131.
3. Moessel, *Die Proportion in Antike und Mittelalter.*
4. Hentze, *Tod, Auferstehung, Weltordnung,* pp.15–19.
5. Wieger, *Chinese Characters.*
6. Matthews, *Chinese-English Dictionary,* p.311.
7. Keith Critchlow, *Britain, a Study in Patterns,* p.42.
8. B. Karlgren, *Grammata Serica.*
9. J. Needham, *Science & Civilization of China.*
10. E. A. Wallis-Budge, *Amulets and Talismans,* p.395.
11. *Josephus, The Works of Flavius.*

Chapter 7

1. Hughes, *Chinese Philosophy,* p.287.
2. Horten, *Die Philosophie der Erleuchtung nach
   Suhrawardi,* p.264.
3. Plato, *The Timaeus and the Critias,* pp.173–175.
4. Plato, *The Timaeus and the Critias,* pp.173–175.
5. Plato, *The Timaeus and the Critias,* pp.173–175.
6. Plato, *The Timaeus and the Critias,* pp.173–175.
7. Plato, *The Timaeus and the Critias,* pp.173–175.
8. Plato, *The Timaeus and the Critias,* pp.173–175.
9. Microbius, *Commentary on the Dream of Scipio,*
   p.175.
10. Critchlow, *Order in Space,* p.47, illus. 5.

Chapter 8

1. Boethius, a Roman philosopher, called first of
   the scholastics. In Stewart & Rand, *Boethius, The
   Theological Tractates.*

2. Taylor, *The Mystical Hymns of Orpheus.*
3. Plato, *Timaeus and Critias,* pp.164f.
4. Mees, *The Revelation in the Wilderness.*
5. Heraclitus, *Fragment 9.*
6. Grandt, *Orphei Hymni.*
7. Kern, Fragment 155, *Orphicorum Fragmenta.*
8. Macrobius, sat. 1.8.6–7 or *Conviviorum Saturnaliorum Septem Libri.*
9. E.S. Kennedy (trans.), 'The Sasanian Astronomical Handbook *Ziji-i Shah* and the Astrological Doctrine of "Transit" *(Mamarr).*'
10. Heraclitus, *Fragment 9.*
11. J.H. Nelson, 'Shortwave Radio Propagation Correlation with Planetary Positions.'

Conclusions

1. Sonia Cole, *The Neolithic Revolution,* p.viii.

2. J.R. Harlan, *Crops and Man.*
3. Eliade, *The Two and The One,* Chapter V.
4. Plato, *Timaeus I,* 14.47. or Plato, *Timaeus and Critias.*

Appendix

1. Albert Rehm, 'Parapegmastudien,' Illustrations from Diels and Rehm, 'Parapegmafragmente aus Milet,' pp.92, 752. As illustrated in Gleadow, *The Origin of the Zodiac,* p.7, illus. 5.
2. Gleadow, *The Origin of the Zodiac,* p.76.
3. Kendrick, *The Druids,* p.116.

4. Plato, *Laws VIII,* 848.
5. Trans. Acharya, *Mānasāra Shilpa Shāstra.*
6. Nasr, *Three Muslim Sages,* see chapter on Suhrawardi.
7. Al-Biruni, *Elements of Astrology,* pp.317–19. Quoted in Nasr, *An Introduction to Islamic Cosmological Doctrines,* p.165.
8. Gleadow, *The Origin of the Zodiac,* pp.66f, see Chapter 5: Cicero.
9. Gleadow, *The Origin of the Zodiac,* pp.66f.
10. Nasr, *An Introduction to Islamic Cosmological Doctrines,* see Chapter 3, p.75 and Chapter 9, p.151.
11. Dante, *II Convito* II. xiv 13.
12. Nelson, 'Shortwave Radio Propagation Correlation with Planetary Positions.'
13. Schulz, 'Les globules blancs des sujets bien portants et les tâches solaires.'
14. Burr, 'Tree Potential and Sunspots;' and with Langham, 'Electrical Timing of Human Ovulation.'
15. König & Ankermüller, 'Über den Einfluss besonders niederfrequenter elektrischer Vorgänge.'
16. Gauquelin, *The Cosmic Clocks.*
17. A lecture by Professor A. Thom to RILKO Trust, 1973.
18. West & Toonder, *The Case for Astrology.*
19. Huff, *Cycles in Your Life.* See the work of Dr Andrews for the relation of bleeding to phases of the Moon.
20. E. Jonas, 'Predetermining the sex of a child,' in Ostrander and Schoeder, *Psychic Discoveries Behind the Iron Curtain.*
21. Hawkins, *Beyond Stonehenge,* p.237.
22. V. Clark in West & Toonder, *The Case for Astrology.*

Bibliography

Acharya, P.K. (trans.), *Mānasāra Shilpa Shāstra.* Oxford University Press, 1934.

Black Elk, *The Sacred Pipe.* Recorded by Joseph Epes Brown. New York: Penguin, 1971.

Burkhardt, Titus, *The Mystical Astrology of Ibn 'Arabi.* London: Beshara Publications, 1977.

—, *Sacred Art East and West.* London: Perennial Books, 1967.

Burn, A.R. 'Holy Men on Islands, in Pre-Christian Britain,' *Glasgow Archaeological Journal,* Vol.1, 1969.

Burr, H.S. 'Tree Potential and Sunspots,' *Cycles* 243, October 1964.

Chambers, Edmund Kerchever, *Arthur of Britain.* London: Sidgwick & Jackson, 1927.

Chan, W.T. *A Source Book in Chinese Philosophy.* Princeton, 1969.

—, *The Way of Lao Tzu Tao-te Ching.* Library of Liberal Arts, 1965.

Cole, Sonia, *The Neolithic Revolution.* London: British Museum, 1970.

Corbin, Henri, *Mundus Imaginalis or The Imaginary and the Imaginal.* Golgonooza, 1975.

Critchlow, Keith, *Britain, a Study in Patterns.* London: RILKO, 1971.

—, *Order in Space.* London: Thames & Hudson, 1969.

Critchlow, Carroll & Vaughn-Lee, *Chartres Maze, A Model of the Universe.* London: RILKO, 1976.

Dante, *Il Convito,* trans. K. Hillard in *The Banquet of Dante Alighieri.* London: Kegan Paul Trench, 1889.

Diels, H. & Rehm, A. 'Parapegmafragmente aus Milet,' *Sitzungsberichte Akad. Berlin,* 1904.

Dillon, Myles & Chadwick, Nora, *The Celtic Realms.* London: Weidenfeld & Nicolson, 1972.

Eliade, Mircea, *The Sacred and the Profane,* trans. William R. Trask. Harvest, 1959.

—, *Shamanism: Archaic Techniques of Ecstasy.* London: Routledge and Kegan Paul, 1970.

—, *The Two and the One.* London: Harvill, 1965.

Erkes, E. *Ho-Shang-Kung's Commentary on Lao Tzu,* trans. Artibus Asiae. Switzerland, 1950.

Evans, Sir Arthur, *The Earlier Religion of Greece in the Light of Recent Cretan Discoveries.* London: Macmillan, 1931.

Fürer-Haimendorf, C. von, 'Megalithic Ritual among the Gadaba and Bondos of Orissa,' *Journal of the Asiatic Society of Bengal,* 9, 1943.

Gauquelin, M. *The Cosmic Clocks*. London: Peter Owen, 1969.

Giles, H.A. *San Tsu Ching*. New York: Ungar, 1963.

Gleadow, R. *The Origin of the Zodiac*. London: Cape, 1968.

Govinda, Lama, *Foundations of Tibetan Mysticism*. London: Rider, 1969.

Grandt, W. (ed.), *Orphei Hymni*. Berlin, 1962.

Guénon, R. *Yoga: Science de l'Homme Intégral*. Paris: Cahiers du Sud, 1953.

Halevi, Z'ev Ben Shimon, *Kabbalistic Universe*, New York: SPI Books, 2007.

Harlan, J.R. *Crops and Man*. American Society of Agronomy, 1992.

Hawkins, G.S. *Beyond Stonehenge*. London: Hutchinson, 1973.

—, *Stonehenge Decoded*. New York: Doubleday, 1965.

Heath, Robin, *Sun, Moon and Stonehenge,* Bluestone Press, 1998.

Hentze, Carl, *Tod, Auferstehung, Weltordnung*. Zurich, 1955.

Horten, M. *Die Philosophie der Erleuchtung nach Suhrawardi,* Halle, 1912.

Huff, Darrell, *Cycles in Your Life*. London: Gollancz, 1965.

Hughes, E.R. *Chinese Philosophy*. London, 1954.

Isikowitz, Karl, *Primitive Views of the World*. New York: University of Columbia Press, 1964.

Josephus, The Works of Flavius. Oxford, 1839.

Joyce, W. & Weston, Patrick, *A Social History of Ancient Ireland*. London & Dublin, 1913.

Karlgren, B. *Grammata Serica*. Stockholm, 1940. Reprint, *Bull. Mus. Far Eastern Antiq.* No.12.

Kendrick, T.D. *The Druids*. London: Methuen, 1927.

Kennedy, E.S. (trans.), 'The Sasanian Astronomical Handbook *Ziji-i Shah* and the Astrological Doctrine of "Transit" *Mamarr,' Journal of the American Oriental Society,* vol. 78, 1958.

Kerenyi, Carl & Jung, C.G. *An Introduction to the Science of Mythology,* trans. R.F.C. Hull. London: Routledge and Kegan Paul, 1970.

Kern, O. *Orphicorum Fragmenta* Berlin, 1963.

König, H. & Ankermüller, F. 'Über den Einfluss besonders niederfrequenter elektrischer Vorgänge in der Atmosphäre auf den Menschen,' *Naturwiss,* 21:483, 1960.

Langham, L. 'Electrical Timing of Human Ovulation,' *American Journal of Obstetrics & Gynaecology,* 44:223, 1942.

MacCulloch, John Arnorth, *Mythology of All Races*. Boston, 1918.

Mackie, E.W. *Science and Society in Prehistoric Britain*. London: Elek, 1977.

Macrobius, *Conviviorum Saturnaliorum Septem Libri* (Latin & French). Paris: Bornecque & Richard, n.d.

Martineau, John Southcliffe, *A Little Book of Coincidence*. Wooden Books, 2000.

Mees, G.H. *The Revelation in the Wilderness: An Exposition in Traditional Psychology,* 3 vols. Deventer: Kluwer, 1951.

Metraux, A. *Easter Island: A Stone Age Civilization of the Pacific.* London: André Deutsch, 1957.

Michell, John, *The View over Atlantis,* Ballantine Books, 1977.

—, *Dimensions of Paradise,* Harpercollins, 1988.

Microbius, *Commentary on the Dream of Scipio,* trans. William Harris Stahl. New York: Columbia University Press, 1966.

Moessel, Ernst, *Die Proportion in Antike und Mittelalter.* Munich: C.H. Beck, 1926.

Nasr, S.H. *The Need for a Sacred Science,* RoutledgeCurzon, 1993.

—, *An Introduction to Islamic Cosmological Doctrines.* Harvard University Press, 1964.

—, 'Sufism and the Perenniality of the Mystical Quest,' *Studies in Comparative Religion,* Autumn 1970.

—, *Three Muslim Sages* Harvard University Press, 1964.

Needham, J. *Science & Civilization of China.* Cambridge University Press.

Nelson, J.H. 'Shortwave Radio Propagation Correlation with Planetary Positions,' *R.C.A. Review* 12:26, 1951.

Nichomachus of Gerasa, *Introduction to Arithmetic,* trans. M.L. D'Ooge. New York, 1972.

Olrik, Axol, *Viking Civilization,* trans. Jacob Wittmer Hartman & Hanaa Astrup Larsen. New York, 1930.

Olsen, Scott, *The Golden Section.* Wooden Books, 2006.

Ostrander, S. and Schoeder, L. *Psychic Discoveries Behind the Iron Curtain.* Prentice Hall, 1971.

Peet, T. Eric *Rough Stone Monuments.* London, 1912.

Pelikan, Wilhelm, *The Secrets of the Metals.* New York: Anthroposophic Press, 1973.

Perry, W.N. *A Treasury of Traditional Wisdom.* New York, 1971.

Plato, *The Timaeus and the Critias,* trans. Thomas Taylor Bollingen. Pantheon Books, 1952.

—, *Timaeus and Critias,* trans. H.D. Lee. Harmondsworth: Penguin Classics, 1971.

Radin, Paul, 'Die Religiöse Erfahrung der Naturvölker,' *Albae Vigiliae Neue Folge,* 11. Zurich: Rhein, 1951.

Rehm, Albert 'Parapegmastudien,' *Bayerische Akademie der Wissenschaften. Phil-hist. K1, neue Folge,* vol.19, 1941.

Renfrew, Colin, *Before Civilization.* London: Jonathan Cape, 1973.

Rhys, John, *Lectures on the Origin and Growth of Religion.* Edinburgh, 1892.

Schulz, N. 'Les globules blancs des sujets bien portants et les tâches solaires,' *Toulouse Medical* 10:741, 1960.

Schuon, Frithjof, 'On the Margins of Liturgical Improvization,' *Studies in Comparative Religion,* Autumn 1970.

Scoresby, Mrs Routledge, *The Mystery of Easter Island.* London: Sifton Praed, n.d.

Shankaracharya, Jagadguru (Sri Bharati Krisna Tirthaji) *Vedic Mathematics.* Delhi: Motilal Banarsidass, 1965.

Sholem, G. *Major Trends in Jewish Mysticism.* New York: Schocken Books, 1954.

Stewart, H.F. & Rand, E.K. *Boethius, The Theological Tractates.* Harvard University Press, 1946.

Taylor, Thomas, *The Mystical Hymns of Orpheus.* London, 1896.

Thom, Professor Alexander, *Megalithic Sites in Britain.* Oxford University Press, 1967.

Volwahsen, Andreas, *Living Architecture, Indian.* London: Macdonald, 1969.

Wallis-Budge, E.A. *Amulets and Talismans.* Collier Books, 1970.

Wentz, Evans ed., *Tibet's Great Yogi.* Oxford University Press, 1928.

West, J.A. & Toonder, J.G. *The Case for Astrology.* London: Macdonald, 1970.

Wieger, Dr L. *Chinese Characters.* Dover, 1965.

Zolla, Elémire, *Language and Cosmogony.* Golgonooza Press, 1976.

—, *Spiritual Perspectives.* London: Heinemann, 1975.

Image Credits

Photographs by Rod Bull: Figs. 1, 3, 4, 5, 11, 14, 18, 25, 43, 48, 64, 69, 76, 91, 111, 125, 149, 156, 163, 164.

All line drawings are hand-drawn by Keith Critchlow. Figs. 142–44 and 146 were first published in Keith Critchlow, *Order in Space,* Thames and Hudson, 1969. Photographs by Keith Critchlow: Figs. 2, 38, 57, 70a–d, 129b, 148.

Photographs by Graham Challifour: Figs. 87, 126, 127, 128, 129a, 133a–b, 134a–b, 145, 155, 158.

Ankara Museum, Turkey, Photographs: Josephine Powell: 117–21
Bibliothèque Nationale, Paris: 45
British Museum: 157
Cambridge Air Survey, Cambridge University: 23, 30
Devizes Museum, Wiltshire: 109
Dorset County Museum, Photo: Christine Knight: 110
Mansell Collection: 85
Public domain: 7, 10
Victoria and Albert Museum, London: 99

Michael Bezzina: 6
John Glover: 17
Thomas A. Goskar: 12
Tony Jenkins: 142a–b, 143a–b
Johan Mattson: 17
Jason Morley: 33
David Powell: 8
Alun Salt: 9
Worthington G. Smith: 71

Index

Addey, John 220f
Adelard of Bath 216
Agrippa, Cornelius 216
Al-Biruni 215f
Alaca Huyuk 155–58
al-Kindi (Alkindus) 179, 215
Allan Water 76–78
Aristotle 213, 217
Atkinson, R.J.C. 15
Atreus 32
Avicenna 215

Bacon, Francis 129
Biruni, Al- 215f
Bond, Frederick Bligh 152–55
Borrowstone Rig 71–75
Brahe, Tycho 197
Brotherhood of Purity (Ikhwān al-
        Safā) 91f
Bull, Rod 22
Burkhardt, Titus 102f
Burr, H.S. 218
Bush Barrow breastplate 141–43,
        146f, 150
Butser Ancient Farm 209

Castle Rigg 57, 59, 61f, 64–67
Chadwick, Nora 90
Chartres 125
Chu Hsi 43
circle, squaring the 103–8
circumpolar sighting template 146
Clandon breastplate 141f, 146, 149
Clark, Vernon 222
Coomeraswamy, Ananda 48, 123
Corbin, Henri 41
cube 169, 171, 177
cuboctahedron 176f

Dante, Alighieri 217
Dee, John 216

Democritus 214
Descartes, René 217
Dillon, Myles 90
dodecahedron 170f
Duc de Berry 133
Dunstable Down 114

Easter 136
Easter Island 28, 32
eclipses 220
Elémire Zolla 82
Eliade, Mircea 41f, 81, 86, 210f
Eliot, T.S. 129
Euktemon 214
Evans, Sir Arthur 32f, 35
evolution 11

Fibonacci series 227
five 113
Furer-Haimendorf, C. von 33

Gadaba 32f, 35
Gandhi, Mahatma 208
Gauquelin, Michel 218–20, 222
geocentric system 185f
geometrical progression (G.P.) 132
Gleadow, Rupert 214
Glob, P.V. 64
Golden Mean 108, 128, 224, 226
Golden Section 224
Gotr ceremony 34
Govinda, Lama 61
Grosseteste, Robert 216

Harlan, J.R. 208
Hawkes, Jaquetta 155
Heath, Robin 224–26
Heisenberg's uncertainty
        principle 18
heliocentric system 185
Hentze, Carl 145

Heraclitus 188
Hinze, Marcel 97, 196
Ho Shang Kung 43

icosahedron 169, 171
icosidodecahedron 176
Ikhwãn al-Safã 91f
Isikowitz, Karl 33–35

Jagadguru 130, 132f, 136f
Jantar Mantar 48
John of Seville 216
Jonas, Eugene 221
Jung, C.G. 40, 41
Jupiter 193f, 198, 200–3

Karlgren, Bernhard 146f
Kepler, Johannes 179, 196f
Kerenyi, Carl 40f
Kindi, al- 179, 215
Koya 35
Kreitner, John 20f

Lao Tsu 42f, 122
Lloyd, Seton 156, 158
Long Meg 67–70
Lull, Ramon 216

Macaulay, Anne 22
Macrobius 190
Maes Howe 32
Mars 194f, 204
Martineau, John 224f
Mees, G.H. 129, 187
megalithic yard (MY) 63
Mercury 186f, 193, 195, 203
Meton of Athens 135, 214
Metonic cycle 135, 155
Metraux, Alfred 36
Michell, John 224
Minoan civilization 32
Moel Ty Uchaf 109–11, 116–19, 205
musical scales 10

Nasr, S.H. 18, 41, 217, 224
Nelson, J.H. 205, 218, 222
Neugebauer, Otto 135

New Grange 32
Newton, Sir Isaac 213
nine 84, 89, 91, 176

octahedron 169, 171, 177
Olsen, Scott 224
Omphalos 33

Paracelsus 216
pebbles 9, 126f
Pelikan, Wilhelm 99
pentagon 115
pi 146, 180
Plato 9, 11f, 163–65, 167, 173f, 179,
     212–14, 223
Platonic solids 163, 166, 169
Plutarch 47
Proclus 190
Ptolemy 179
Pythagorean triplet 19f

Rehm, Albert 213
Renfrew, Colin 26–28, 30, 36
Reynolds, Peter 209
Rhys, John 86
Rome 47

Safã, Ikhwãn al- 91f
Salisbury Cathedral 40
Saturn 189f, 198, 200–3
Schuon, Frithjof 40, 94
seven 84, 91f, 94f, 97f, 102, 137, 176
shamanism 81f, 84
six 151
Smith, W.G. 114
squaring the circle 103–8
Suhrawardi 215

Takata, Maki 220
tetrahedral symmetry 162, 165
tetrahedron 169, 171
thirteen 125

Thom, Alexander 19, 21, 31, 49, 52,
     56, 59, 61–72, 75–77, 220,
     223, 226
triads 45

Underhill, Ruth M. 82

Van Allen belts 219
Vãstu-Purusha-Mandala 106
Vaughn-Lee, Llewelyn 76
Venus 194, 204f
vesica pisces 54, 115
Vitruvian man 104f

Wang Ying-Lin 90
Wieger, Leon 145

Yin and Yang 43
Yorke, Dr M. 33

Zij-i Shah 197
Zollett, Mr 216